William Francis Tiemann

The 159th Regiment Infantry, New York State Volunteers

In the War of the Rebellion, 1862-1865

William Francis Tiemann

The 159th Regiment Infantry, New York State Volunteers
In the War of the Rebellion, 1862-1865

ISBN/EAN: 9783337116002

Printed in Europe, USA, Canada, Australia, Japan

Cover: Foto ©ninafisch / pixelio.de

More available books at **www.hansebooks.com**

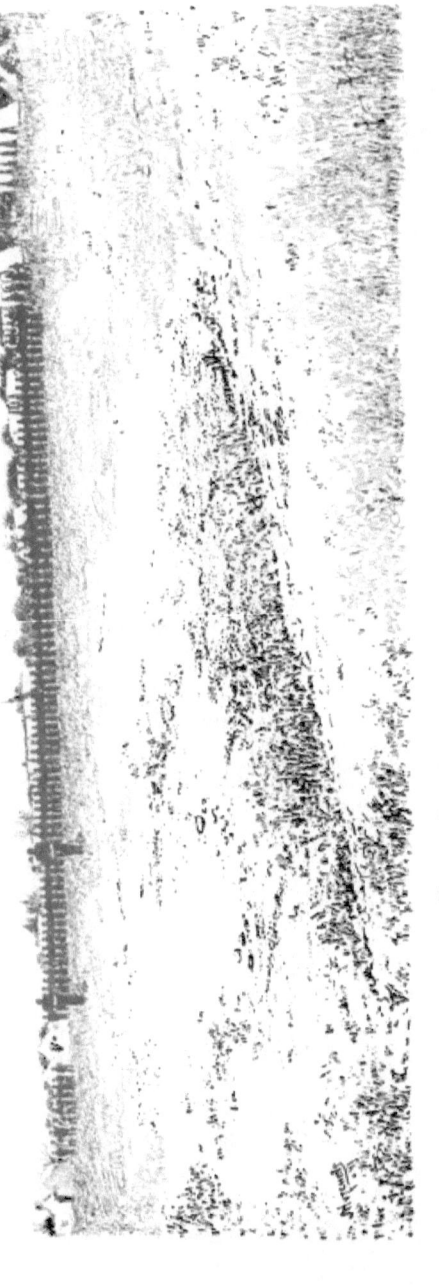

Dress Parade, 159th N. Y., Thibodeaux, La.

Captain R. McD. Hart, commanding; Lieutenant H. M. Howard, Acting Adjutant.

THE
159th REGIMENT INFANTRY,
NEW-YORK STATE VOLUNTEERS,

SEMPER PARATUS   SEMPER FIDELIS

IN THE

WAR OF THE REBELLION,
1862–1865.

COMPILED AND PUBLISHED BY
WILLIAM F. TIEMANN, CAPTAIN AND COMMISSIONED MAJOR.
BROOKLYN, N. Y.
1891.

COPYRIGHT, 1891,
BY WILLIAM F. TIEMANN.

PREFACE.

INTRUSTED by the survivors of the regiment with the writing of its history during the War of the Rebellion, I submit herewith the result of my labors. The work has been mainly compiled from letters sent home while serving with the regiment; but much valuable aid and information have been obtained from other sources. I am greatly indebted to the Adjutant-General U. S. A., though the information from this source has been very limited owing to the dilapidated condition of the rolls preventing any but necessary reference to them by the department. To the Adjutant-General S. N. Y. I owe my thanks for the uniform courtesy extended, the full information given as far as in possession of the State, and for the permission to copy and verify the muster-out rolls of the regiment.

My sincere thanks are also due to General Molineux, Sergeant Berridge, and Musician Dunham for the use of their war diaries, by which I have been enabled to verify dates and obtain much valuable information. To Colonel Gaul, Lieutenant-Colonel Burt, and Lieutenant-Colonel Waltermire I am also under obligations for information furnished. Lieutenant Day, Lieutenant Brown, Mrs. E. Spencer Elmer, Captain Reynolds, and Captain Stayley all kindly loaned me the bi-monthly muster and pay rolls of the companies as far as they had them, and from these very much otherwise unobtainable information was derived. Many others of the regiment aided me, and to one and all my sincere thanks are due.

My work is not claimed to be perfect. That would be impossible, even with the fullest information at my command; but I have endeavored to give a succinct and true account of our regimental life and doings, claiming no glory not our own, and making no boastful allusions to the conduct of the command, preferring that the history should show for itself the credit to which the regiment is entitled. That many errors will be found, even with all the care exercised to prevent them, I am well aware, and I ask of each comrade perceiving such that he will notify me, stating the facts, that I may make proper corrections.

With this request I submit my work.

Respectfully,

WILLIAM F. TIEMANN,

Historian.

BROOKLYN, N. Y., March, 1891.

CONTENTS.

CHAPTER I.
Organization — Recruiting — Muster-in 7

CHAPTER II.
Camp Nelson, New Dorp, S. I. — Departure with the Banks Expedition — Arrival at New Orleans and landing at Baton Rouge, La. 14

CHAPTER III.
Baton Rouge, La. — The first march to Port Hudson, La 20

CHAPTER IV.
Leave Baton Rouge — Irish Bend, La. — Our losses 26

CHAPTER V.
The first march to Alexandria, La. — Port Hudson, La 36

CHAPTER VI.
Port Hudson, La. — Assault, May 27, 1863..................... 40

CHAPTER VII.
Port Hudson, La. — Assault, June 14, 1863 — The surrender — Our losses during the siege.. 46

CHAPTER VIII.
Leave Port Hudson, La. — Donaldsonville, La. — Camp Kearny, Carrollton, La. — Thibodeaux, La............................ 55

CHAPTER IX.
Leave Thibodeaux, La. — Alexandria, La. — Red River campaign . 68

CHAPTER X.
Leave Alexandria, La. — Marksville, La. — Mansura Plains, La. — Arrival at Morganza, La.. 74

CONTENTS.

CHAPTER XI.

Leave Morganza, La.—Presentation of colors—Leave Louisiana for Virginia—Arrival at Bermuda Hundreds, Va., and Washington. D. C.—Our bear 82

CHAPTER XII.

We join Sheridan's command—Halltown, Va.—Berryville, Va.. 91

CHAPTER XIII.

Winchester, Va.—Our losses—Fisher's Hill, Va 98

CHAPTER XIV.

Cedar Creek, Va.—Our losses 107

CHAPTER XV.

Leave the Valley for Baltimore, Md.—Savannah, Ga.—Morehead City, N. C.—Augusta, Ga.—Madison, Ga. 115

CHAPTER XVI.

Muster-out—Death of our bear—Leave for home—Final discharge—Recapitulation 126

Muster-out Rolls 137

CHAPTER I.

Organization — Recruiting — Muster-in.

UNDER the call of Abraham Lincoln, President of the United States, July 1, 1862, for three hundred thousand troops to aid in the suppression of the Rebellion, and the proclamation in accordance therewith of Edwin D. Morgan, Governor of the State of New York, July 2, 1862, authority was given from Albany, N. Y., August 28, 1862, by S. O. 485, to Edward L. Molineux, as Lieutenant-Colonel, to recruit and organize a regiment, in conformity with G. O. 52, Albany, N. Y., from the first three Senatorial districts of the State, embracing Long Island and Staten Island, with headquarters at Brooklyn, N. Y., and which, until officially numbered, was designated the " THIRD SENATORIAL."

Lieutenant-Colonel Molineux had for many years made military matters a study, having been much interested in the State Militia, and also at one time in correspondence with the Governors of States and the heads of numerous educational institutions in regard to the giving to the youth of our land a thorough, practical military instruction. He had been connected as an officer (Lieutenant-Colonel) with the "Brooklyn Twenty-third" State Militia, and served as a volunteer in the Second Company "New York Seventh" State Militia, when that regiment was sent to Washington, D. C., at the outbreak of the war, and was, by his studies and experience, eminently fitted to organize and command. Energetic and active, under his supervision and direction recruiting was pushed vigorously. Recruiting stations were established in the City Hall park and other places in the city, and at several of the towns and villages of Long Island, the headquarters of the regiment being in Marble Hall, No. 14 Court Street, corner Joralemon Street, Brooklyn, where recruits were taken as soon as enlisted, examined by the surgeon, sworn in the service by the Adjutant, Lieutenant Edward Sherer, and then sent to the depot on the Clove road, where clothing was issued and rations regularly distributed.

The clothing comprised a dark blue cloth fatigue cap, dark blue woolen blouse with brass buttons emblazoned with the coat-of-arms of the State, light blue woolen trousers, two canton flannel undershirts, two pairs canton flannel drawers, two pairs thick woolen socks, and one pair shoes, all of good quality. The eating utensils comprised a tin pint cup, tin platter, knife, fork, spoon, and a canteen (as the tin water-bottle with cloth cover was called), while the rations were coffee and fresh bread for breakfast, soup, meat, potatoes, and fresh bread for dinner, and tea or coffee with fresh bread for supper; and, though at times not as nicely cooked or served as at home, the diet was plentiful and wholesome. Later there was issued to each man a knapsack for his clothing and a haversack for his rations. The first depot for recruits was on the Clove road, south of Fulton Street, in an old oil-cloth factory, and the ground adjoining where large tents were pitched; but as the accommodations were limited and several of the men deserted, though guards were placed around to prevent any passing out without authority, the depot was moved and established in the barracks at East New York, which were entirely inclosed, having been constructed especially for the purpose. A high board fence had been erected around a piece of ground several acres in extent, and a close wooden shed, in which were bunks for sleeping, constructed against the fence inside, forming a square and leaving a large open space in the center for exercise and drill. The entrance was a large double gate which was guarded by sentries; and guards were also placed around on the outside of the inclosure to prevent any recruits from scaling the fence. The men already enlisted were marched there October 6, 1862. While at East New York a recruit in a drunken frenzy attempted to shoot Lieutenant-Colonel Molineux but was overpowered and afterward punished.

Men did not come forward as at the commencement of the war, and though liberal bounties in money were offered and paid, the regiment progressed but slowly. October 29th the recruits were marched to the Park Barracks, New York City, where they were joined the same day by those of the ONE HUNDRED AND SIXTY-SEVENTH REGIMENT which had been recruited during September and October in Columbia and Dutchess counties by virtue of S. O. 15, Albany, N. Y., September 3, 1862, giving Homer A. Nelson (as Colonel) authority to recruit and organize an additional regiment of volunteers in the Eleventh Senatorial district of the State in conformity with the provisions of G. O. 52, Albany, N. Y., with headquarters at the city of Hudson. Colonel Nelson was prominent and popular in the district, and though not a military man, imbued with that spirit of patriotism which filled so many, determined to do all he could to aid his country in her hour of trial; and troops being needed, he saw no better way than to organize a regiment to aid in upholding the laws which had been violated. Men were enlisted in the various towns and villages in the two counties, with headquarters and the depot for recruits in the "fair grounds" at Hudson, N. Y., where they were sworn in the service by Lieutenant James A. Farrell, Adjutant, after passing examination as to physical ability by the Surgeon.

During October an expedition, to be commanded by Major-General Nathaniel P. Banks, was organized at Washington to comprise all the troops not yet in the field, and as the regiment had not enlisted its full complement of men, October 28th, it left Hudson, N. Y., by boat, proceeding to the Park Barracks, New York City, where it joined the "Third Senatorial," and November 1, 1862, the two regiments were consolidated by authority of S. O. 750, Albany, N. Y., October 28, 1862, and officially numbered the

ONE HUNDRED AND FIFTY-NINTH REGIMENT,

NEW YORK STATE VOLUNTEER INFANTRY;

the letters A, C, E, G, I being given to the Hudson companies, and B, D, F, H, K to those from Brooklyn, with the following

FIELD AND LINE OFFICERS.

Lieutenant-Colonel	EDWARD L. MOLINEUX	Brooklyn
Colonel	HOMER A. NELSON	Hudson
Major	GILBERT A. DRAPER	Brooklyn
Surgeon	CHARLES A. ROBERTSON	Hudson
Assistant-Surgeon	WILLIAM Y. PROVOST	Brooklyn
Second Asst.-Surgeon	CALEB C. BRIGGS	Hudson
Chaplain		
Adjutant	ROBERT D. LATHROP	Hudson
Quartermaster	MARK D. WILBER	Hudson

Company A.

Captain	EDWARD L. GAUL	Hudson
First-Lieutenant	FRANCIS E. ATWOOD	Hudson
Second-Lieutenant	WESLEY BRADLEY	Hudson

Company B.

Captain	AUGUSTUS J. DAYTON	Brooklyn
First-Lieutenant	JULIUS H. TIEMANN	Brooklyn
Second-Lieutenant	ALFRED GREENLEAF, JR.	Brooklyn

Company C.

Captain	Ariel M. Gamwell	Hudson
First-Lieutenant	Crawford Williams	Hudson
Second-Lieutenant	Edgar G. Hubbell	Hudson

Company D.

Captain	Joseph A. Hatry	Brooklyn
First-Lieutenant	Charles A. Loretz	Brooklyn
Second-Lieutenant	John W. Manley, Jr.	Brooklyn

Company E.

Captain	William Waltermire	Hudson
First-Lieutenant	Nathan S. Post	Hudson
Second-Lieutenant	Robert H. Traver	Hudson

Company F.

Captain	Robert McD. Hart	Brooklyn
First-Lieutenant	William Burtis	Brooklyn
Second-Lieutenant	George W. Hussey	Brooklyn

Company G.

Captain	William H. Sliter	Hudson
First-Lieutenant	Charles Lewis	Hudson
Second-Lieutenant	Byron Lockwood	Hudson

Company H.

Captain	Wells O. Pettit	Brooklyn
First-Lieutenant	Charles C. Baker	Brooklyn
Second-Lieutenant	George R. Herbert	Brooklyn

Company I.

Captain	Edward Wardle	Hudson
First-Lieutenant	John W. Shields	Hudson
Second-Lieutenant	Jacob Fingar	Hudson

Company K.

Captain . .	. Joe B. Ramsden	. Brooklyn
First-Lieutenant .	. Edward Sherer . . .	Brooklyn
Second-Lieutenant .	. William R. Plunkett	. Brooklyn

Of these officers several were with experience in military matters. Lieutenant-Colonel Molineux, as already mentioned, was Second-Sergeant Company C, and an officer in the Twenty-third Militia, and a volunteer in the Second Company, Seventh Militia. Major Draper had seen service in the field during 1861–62 as Captain Sixty-fifth New York Volunteers. Adjutant Lathrop had served as First-Corporal Company K, Fourteenth New York Volunteers. Captain Gaul, Company A, was Paymaster's Clerk in the Navy. First-Lieutenant Julius H. Tiemann, Company B, was a member Second Company, Seventh Militia. He was a student in Göttingen and Wiesbaden, Germany, when the war broke out, but returned home to give his services to his country. Second-Lieutenant Manley, Company D, was Sergeant-Major Thirteenth Militia. Captain Hart, Company F, was a member Third Company, Seventh Militia, and went with his regiment to Washington in 1861. Second-Lieutenant Hussey, Company F, was a member of the Fourteenth Militia. First-Lieutenant Lewis, Company G, had served as a private in Company K, Fourteenth New York Volunteers. First-Lieutenant Sherer, Company K, had served in the Sixty-seventh New York Volunteers as First-Lieutenant in 1861–62.

On the same day (November 1, 1862) the regiment was mustered into the service of the United States "for three years, or during the war," by Lieutenant R. B. Smith, U. S. A. Mustering Officer. Colonel Nelson, Surgeon Robertson, and Second-Assistant Surgeon Briggs, were not mustered with the regiment. November 2d the Non-Commissioned Staff was appointed: William F. Tiemann, Sergeant Company B, Sergeant-Major; John H. Charlotte, private Company C, Quartermaster-Sergeant; William F. French, Sergeant Company G, Commissary-Sergeant; Alfred H. S. Moore, private Company H, Hospital Steward; John W. Mambert, private Company G, First Principal Musician; George D. Dayton, First-Sergeant Company B, Second Principal Musician. November 2d, leaving the Park Barracks late in the afternoon, the regiment marched to Castle Garden, at the Battery, embarked on a steamboat in waiting, and was transported to Staten Island; there it landed and marched nine miles to New Dorp, near the center of the island on the eastern side, about eleven miles from New York, where it arrived late at night and went into quarters which was called "Camp Nelson" in honor of our Colonel. November 3d, First-Lieutenant Edward Sherer, Company K, resigned, as his remaining would have thrown out Duncan Richmond, one of the officers who had recruited the company; Second-Lieutenant William R. Plunkett was promoted to First-Lieutenant, and Duncan Richmond appointed Second-Lieutenant Company K. Lieutenant Sherer afterward served as a volunteer in the Twenty-third Militia during the three months' service of that regiment in Pennsylvania in 1863 when Lee with his forces invaded that State.

CHAPTER II.

Camp Nelson, New Dorp, S. I.— Departure with the Banks Expedition — Arrival at New Orleans and landing at Baton Rouge, La.

THE One Hundred and Fifty-ninth Regiment was now in the service of "Uncle Sam"; tents, arms, and accoutrements were issued, and under the practical supervision of Lieutenant-Colonel Molineux full and complete military discipline was at once instituted, the camp being regularly laid out, tents pitched, guards detailed and posted, hours for reveille, roll-call, meals, drills, tattoo, and taps fixed, and under the direction and instruction of the officers the men were drilled in company formation and movements, the manual of arms, and other requirements to fit them to take the field. We had here a specimen of the material furnished by contractors, there being issued to the regiment a lot of Austrian muskets which had been condemned by that government and had been bought by some speculator and sold to the United States. For drill they were as good as the best, but for war purposes were absolutely worthless, as the majority of them could not be discharged; the nipples not having been bored, no powder, consequently, could get through. They were inspected just before we broke camp, and condemned, and Enfield rifles were substituted, much to the satisfaction of the men.

The regiment remained at New Dorp three weeks, during which time it attained considerable proficiency and became familiar with the daily routine of military life, while the officers became acquainted with each other and with their men and attained more confidence in themselves as they became better posted in their practical duties, making of the regiment a harmonious body, which was not always done even where all the men were enlisted in one locality.

During the first week the regiment lost a number by desertion, though guards were given strict instructions to pass no one without authority — in some instances the guards themselves deserting while on duty; but after that the number was small, those remaining being perfectly contented. They became well indurated to the exposure and rigors of camp life, as the weather was very cold and there were several severe storms, while the tents furnished but little protection; but being warmly clothed and well fed, the men were well satisfied, though all were anxious to start for the seat of war. While at New Dorp Surgeon Robertson and Second-Assistant Surgeon Briggs joined the regiment. November 10th Isaac L. Kipp was appointed Chaplain and reported for duty. November 13th Second-Lieutenant George R. Herbert, Company H, was detached to the Signal Corps, with which he served until his final discharge from service. First-Lieutenant Crawford Williams, Company C, was detached as Acting Assistant Commissary Subsistence, taking charge of stores on transport steamers from New York to New Orleans.

November 24th the regiment broke camp, and marched to the wharf, where it was taken on a steamboat and transported to New York City; there it was embarked on the United States steam transport *Northern Light*, which was lying at pier 3, North River. November 25th Colonel Homer A. Nelson resigned to accept office as Member of Congress, to which he had been elected. Lieutenant-Colonel Edward L. Molineux was promoted Colonel, Major Gilbert A. Draper was promoted Lieutenant-Colonel, and Charles A. Burt,

Captain Ninety-first Regiment New York Volunteers, with which he had been serving since October, 1861, at Pensacola, Fla., was promoted Major One Hundred and Fifty-ninth Regiment. December 3d the steamer hauled into the stream, and the same night the One Hundred and Sixty-first Regiment New York State Volunteers was also put on board. December 4th, at 4 o'clock a. m., the steamer sailed, bound for some unknown destination so far as the regiment was concerned, no intimation having been given as to where we were going. During the day a death occurred, Corporal James Bennett, Company D; December 5th the impressive funeral service was read by Chaplain Kipp, and the body was committed to the deep with the usual military honors, a volley being fired as the remains sank from sight in the closing waters. December 12th the steamer was brought to by a gun fired by the sloop of war *Ohio*, which spoke us, the officer commanding the boat which was sent to investigate us stating they had been engaged in destroying the Confederate salt works at Saint Andrews, Fla. December 13th the steamer stopped at Ship Island, Miss., nineteen hundred and sixty-seven miles from New York, for orders. Here was gathered a large fleet of transports all loaded with troops. The island is long and narrow, flat and sandy, with a partially constructed fort at one end. It is located in the Gulf of Mexico seventy-two miles west of New Orleans in a direct line, ninety-five miles north from the mouth of the Mississippi River, and one hundred and ninety-five miles from New Orleans by water. December 14th, taking a pilot, we passed Balize, the small pilot town at the mouth of the river, at 9 a. m. Sailing up the Mississippi we passed Forts Saint Philippe and Jackson, one on each side of the river, seventy-eight miles below New Orleans, at 12.30 p. m., and saw the wrecks of several rebel gunboats destroyed at the time of Farragut's gallant passage up the river. These, with the

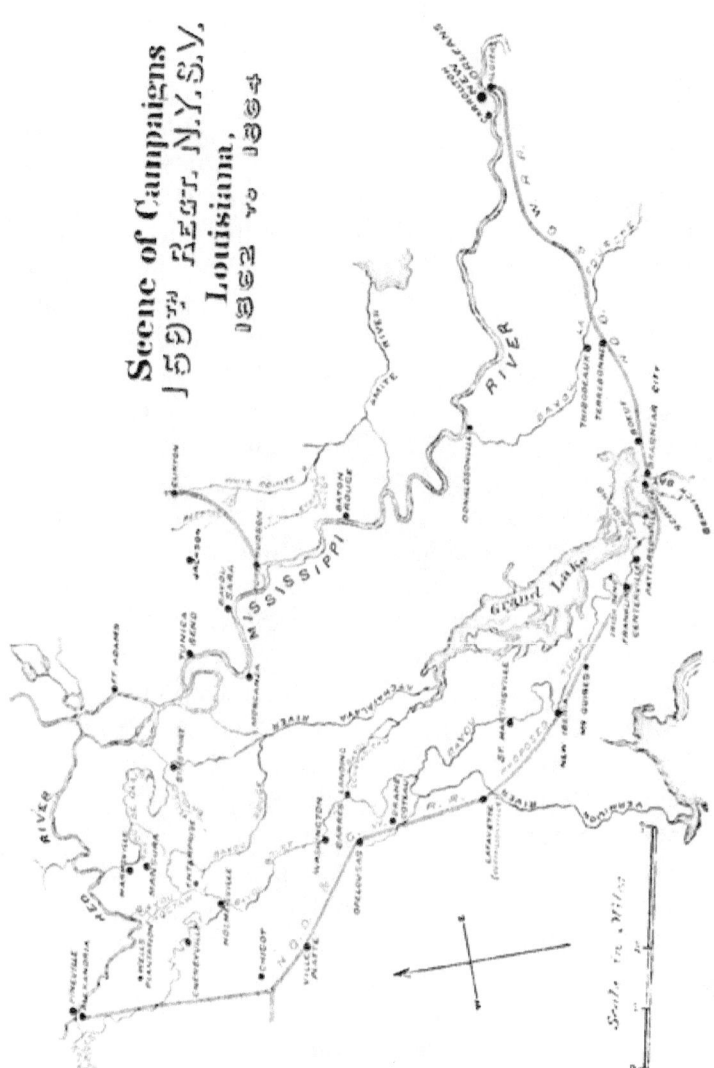

bristling armaments of the forts and the troops on guard, showed us we were in an enemy's country, and we saw for the first time something of what "war" meant. Apart from this the scene was peaceful, and it seemed strange to us who had so lately left bare, bleak-looking trees, and ground covered with snow, to see on either bank large groves of orange trees laden with the golden fruit, and everything as bright and fresh as in our mildest weather. Another curious sight was numbers of tall dead cypress trees, their long skeleton-looking branches covered with a heavy gray moss which hung from them like great streamers, presenting a weird aspect to us to whom all the surroundings were such a novelty. As we sailed by the plantations the negroes waved their hats and aprons, while the whites stood by in sullen silence and with scowling looks, evidently not having the best of feelings toward their "country's invaders."

At 7.30 p. m. we came in sight of the lights of New Orleans, and at 7.45 p. m. we anchored off the "Crescent City," one hundred miles from the mouth of the river.

December 16th, with five other transports, convoyed by six gunboats and "ironclads," as the gunboats which were cased with railroad iron or thick iron plates were called, we sailed up the river and arrived off Baton Rouge, one hundred and thirty miles above New Orleans on the east bank of the river, on the morning of December 17th. The "ironclad" *Essex* went up the river half a mile and fired a number of shells at a rebel battery posted there, which drove it off. The city is situated on a bluff twenty-five feet above the river at high water. Our steamer hauled alongside the hulk of an old river steamboat, the *Natchez*, once famous for the number of races won but now lying against the bank and used as a landing stage, and we landed in the afternoon after being twenty-three days on board and making a voyage of two thousand two hundred and ninety-two miles. During the voyage the men were closely packed, there being about twelve hundred on the transport; sleeping accommodations were very poor, as there were not sufficient berths, and the men had to sleep on deck or wherever they could find room to lie down, and at first it was almost impossible to get anything to eat owing to the inefficient and miserable arrangements for cooking for so many, but this was partly remedied before the steamer reached its destination. Fortunately the weather had been very fine, there having been but two days of rain. The health of all on board was generally good. The troops were all vaccinated just after we left New York, and in some cases severe erysipelas set in, caused by the impure blood of the subjects; but at our arrival there were few if any seriously ill, the plain food and fresh sea air having made all on board feel well and hearty. After landing line was formed near the levee and we were then marched a mile and camped on the United States Arsenal grounds just opposite the barracks which had been occupied by the "Regulars" until the outbreak of the Rebellion when the property had been seized by the rebels. The troops from the other transports were landed and assigned various positions best adapted to cover the approaches to and guard the city. Company, regimental, and brigade drills were the order of the day, and the men were also thoroughly drilled in the manual of arms, a partial instruction in which had been given while in Camp Nelson, New Dorp. The enemy being in close proximity,— Port Hudson, which was garrisoned by a rebel force of fifteen thousand men, being only twenty-two miles distant,— the utmost vigilance was exercised. Standing under arms from early daybreak until sunrise was a daily routine, while being roused from sleep just after midnight by the "long roll" was of constant occurrence. Formed in line, we stood waiting a possible onslaught by the enemy, unable to see more than a few yards in our front owing to the heavy, thick mist which usually prevailed from midnight to sunrise, chilled through by the damp, cold night air and heavy dew which fell like light rain, and when dismissed to our quarters we felt far from comfortable. We took it cheerfully, however, as a part of a soldier's duty, and were soon as used to it as to the daily routine of drills. Assistant Surgeon William Y. Provost was detached to Classon's and Nims' batteries and in charge of the sick and wounded at Baton Rouge. December 28th the State House was destroyed by fire, caused by a defective flue, though the troops used every exertion to quell the flames, our own Company K (which had been a fire company at home) and Lieutenant-Colonel Draper of our regiment rendering valuable assistance. December 29th heavy rain fell.

Major Charles A. Burt reported for duty and joined the regiment while we were stationed at Baton Rouge.

CHAPTER III.

Baton Rouge, Louisiana — The First March to Port Hudson, Louisiana.

DECEMBER 30th, by S. O. 599, the regiment was, with the Thirty-first Massachusetts, Twenty-fifth Connecticut, and Twenty-sixth Maine regiments, organized into the THIRD BRIGADE, the other regiments being likewise assigned to brigades, and the whole constituted a DIVISION commanded by Brigadier-General Cuvier Grover. January 1, 1863, our regiment was moved outside the city to the ground on which had been fought August 5, 1862, the battle of Baton Rouge.

January 5th, by G. O. No. 5, A. G. O., War Department, the troops in the "Department of the Gulf" were constituted the NINETEENTH ARMY CORPS, to date from December 14, 1862, and Major-General Nathaniel P. Banks was assigned to the command. General Banks had assumed command of the department on December 17th, relieving Major-General Benjamin F. Butler, who had been in command since the capture of New Orleans.

January 11th, it being reported the enemy were approaching in force from Vicksburg, where, it was rumored, they had received a serious reverse, all the troops were moved in to cover the city and gain the protection of the gunboats, the regiment camping just north of the State Penitentiary, about one-half mile from the battle-ground where we had been stationed. January 14th First-Lieutenant Nathan S. Post, Company E, was discharged, Second-Lieutenant Wesley Bradley, Company A, was promoted to succeed him, Sergeant-Major William F. Tiemann was promoted Second-

Lieutenant Company A, and Alfred H. Bruce, First-Sergeant Company G, was promoted Sergeant-Major.

Grover's division was numbered the FOURTH, and the brigade was reorganized January 14th, the Thirty-first Massachusetts being transferred and replaced by the Thirteenth Connecticut, Colonel Henry W. Birge, who by virtue of seniority assumed command of the brigade.

The troops stood under arms from early daybreak to 6.30 a. m. daily for a week, when, the report of attack having proved false, we resumed the usual routine. January 19th First-Lieutenant Francis E. Atwood, Company A, was discharged. January 22d we were again moved out on the Port Hudson road about a mile from the battle-ground, our brigade being the advance of the division as it had been from the first. The regiment was camped with the rest of the brigade on a small hill surrounded partly by Cypress Bayou (the Louisiana term for creeks and streams is *bayou*), the water in which was from six to eight feet deep, across which bridges of rough logs and dirt were constructed to reach the city. The location was almost impregnable, being protected at the rear and sides by the bayou which was impassable except by bridge, and the front of the camp defended by a dense woods through which no enemy in force could move.

At this time affairs seemed to be much mismanaged, as it was impossible to get shoes, socks, or other clothing for the men, and for two weeks the regiment was on short rations. For three days the men had neither bread nor flour. We had previously received regular and full rations of coffee, salt pork, salt beef, beans, fresh beef, and flour, or "*soft bread*," so-called in contradistinction to the flat crackers, or "*hard tack*," afterwards issued and which was carried on all campaigns. We learned later what it was to go hungry of necessity, but that was on the march through the enemy's country when other regiments had "foraged" in advance of us. January 24th First-Lieutenant Julius H. Tiemann, Company B, was detached as acting Aide on the brigade staff. First-Lieutenant Crawford Williams, Company C, who had been relieved and rejoined his company, was again detached as A. A. C. S. on the brigade staff. January 26th all the troops in Baton Rouge were reviewed by Major-General C. C. Augur, commanding the First Division. Shortly after this a general inspection was held, and the regiment, through Colonel Molineux, was complimented as having the cleanest camp in the division. January 26th Captain Edward Wardle, Company I, and Second-Lieutenant Jacob Fingar, Company I, were discharged. January 27th First-Lieutenant Charles C. Baker, Company H, was promoted Captain Company I; Second-Lieutenant Duncan Richmond, Company K, was promoted First-Lieutenant Company H; Second-Lieutenant John W. Manley, Jr., Company D, was promoted First-Lieutenant Company A; Sergeant Henry M. Howard, Company D, was promoted Second-Lieutenant Company D; Sergeant Lambert Dingman, Company G, was promoted Second-Lieutenant Company I; Sergeant Charles P. Price, Company H, was promoted Second-Lieutenant Company K. Major Charles A. Burt was detached to the division staff as Judge Advocate and A. A. D. C. While on the staff he was appointed Commissioner of Exchange to receive from the rebels and receipt for the prisoners of war basely surrendered by Major-General Twiggs to the rebels at the outbreak of the war.

February 11th Captain Ariel M. Gamwell, Company C, resigned. February 22d at noon a salute of thirty-two guns was fired by two of the batteries and one of the gunboats, and at 2 p. m. the brigade was marched to headquarters, where an address was delivered by one of the Chaplains. The 22d falling on Sunday, the troops were given a holiday

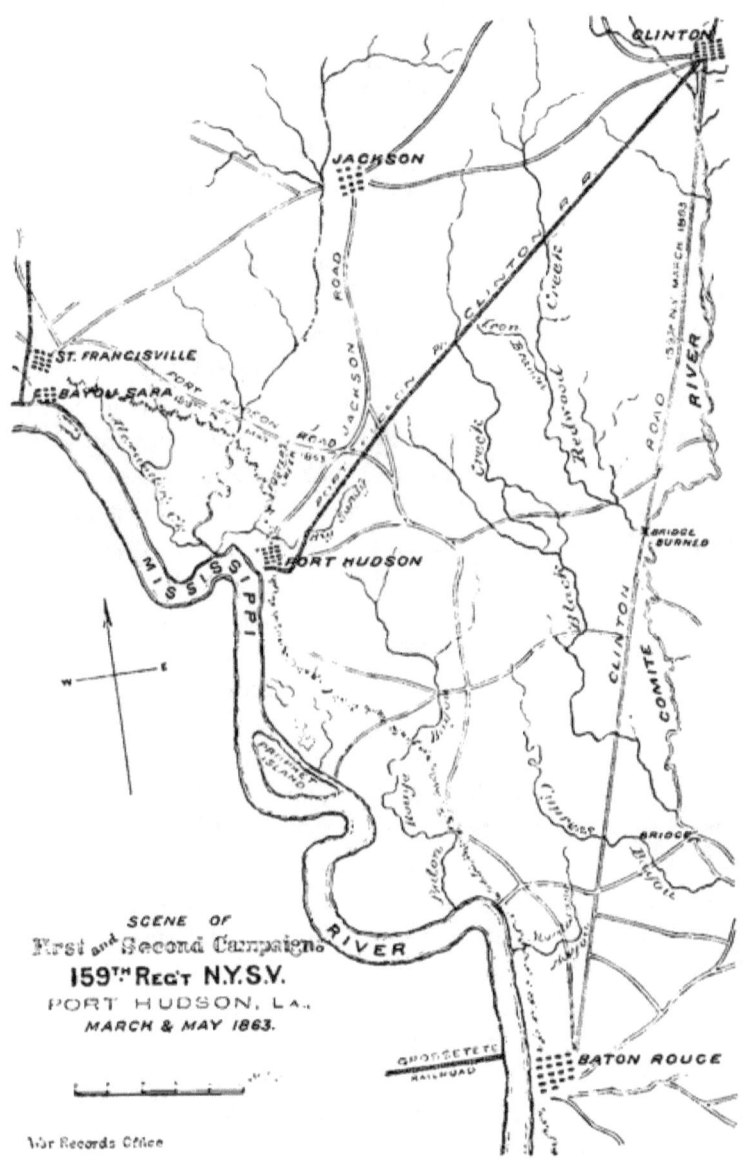

February 23d, all drills being suspended, and as much freedom allowed as was compatible with the necessary military duties of the camp. February 26th Major-General C. C. Augur was assigned to the command of all the troops at Baton Rouge. February 28th Captain Augustus J. Dayton, Company B, was discharged. March 6th First-Lieutenant Charles Lewis, Company G, was promoted Captain Company C; Second-Lieutenant George W. Hussey, Company F, was promoted First-Lieutenant Company G; Sergeant-Major Alfred H. Bruce was promoted Second-Lieutenant Company F, and Herman Smith, First-Sergeant Company H, was promoted Sergeant-Major. Captain Edward L. Gaul, Company A, who had for some time been ill with typhoid fever, went home on furlough.

March 7th orders were received for a move, tents were struck, and rations issued. It was more than six months before we were again under canvas. For many days troops had been gradually concentrating at Baton Rouge, making it evident that an important move was in contemplation. March 12th the entire force was reviewed by Major-General N. P. Banks. March 13th the One Hundred and Fifty-ninth New York, three companies of the Twenty-sixth Maine, Company E, First Louisiana Cavalry, and a section of Nims' Second Massachusetts Battery were detached as a provisional brigade under command of Colonel E. L. Molineux and marched up the Clinton road to the rear of Port Hudson, the main army moving up the Bayou Sara, or river road, which ran parallel to the one we were on. The cavalry was in advance, followed by the infantry with skirmishers deployed on either flank pressing through the dense brush which was almost impenetrable. We started quite late in the afternoon, and just after dark heard several shots fired in front. They were fired at a negro who had attempted to signal our advance with a torch and endeavored to escape when he saw he was discovered. We marched nine miles that day. March 14th we started at 7 a. m. and had marched two miles when our advance encountered a rebel picket which was fired at by one piece of our artillery. Just after starting again our skirmishers discovered a queer looking obstruction in the road which was fired at by our artillery and, no response being evoked, was approached cautiously by our skirmishers, who found it to be a "Quaker gun"—an old boiler mounted and at a short distance presenting the appearance of a large cannon. Removing the obstruction by rolling it to one side, the march was resumed. We marched in all twelve miles, reaching Redwood River bridge, seven miles east of Port Hudson, just after noon, where a strong picket of rebel cavalry and artillery was encountered which was opened on by the artillery and fell back with a reported loss of six, after first destroying the bridge by fire. The brigade was then marched back six miles and camped in a dry swamp. About 1 a. m., March 15th, the rain began to fall in torrents, the ground was soon saturated, and the men were forced to seek shelter on the knolls under the trees. The whole place was ankle deep in mud and water. We were moved to a drier spot when the rain ceased just after daybreak. There was no lack of food here, as chickens, ducks, and turkeys were plentiful, and fresh beef and mutton also. March 16th the camp was startled by a negro, badly wounded, coming in with the report that Colonel Molineux had been captured, and the regiment was at once formed by Lieutenant-Colonel Draper and marched up the road, but was met just after starting by Colonel Molineux himself, who was greeted with cheers, so we were marched back to camp. The Colonel stated that while riding up the road in company with the Captain of Cavalry (Yeaton), followed by an orderly and negro servant, they heard several shots fired in their rear and at once rode into the woods at the side of the road, just after which ten rebel cavalrymen dashed by at full gallop. The orderly was not found and it was presumed he was captured, while the negro was shot in three places. March 20th we rejoined the main body and marched back to Baton Rouge to our old camp. The movement had been made to cover an attempt by Admiral Farragut to take the gunboats above Port Hudson, which was only partly successful, as but two passed, the *Hartford* and *Albatross*, while the *Mississippi*, having grounded, was destroyed by her commander.

CHAPTER IV.

Leave Baton Rouge—Irish Bend, Louisiana—Our Losses.

FOR the next eight days the regiment was held in readiness to move at a moment's notice. March 28th it was embarked on the transport *Laurel Hill* and taken to Donaldsonville, fifty miles south of Baton Rouge on the west bank of the river at the junction of the Bayou La Fourche, where it landed at 9 p. m. during a heavy rain. March 31st the regiment was detailed to guard the division supplies and property on board the transport *Empire Parish*, on which it sailed up the bayou, arriving at Thibodeaux, fifty-five miles west of New Orleans, thirty-five miles southeast of Donaldsonville, at 2 p. m., where the regiment was landed and marched just back of the levee. April 3d First-Lieutenant Charles A. Loretz was discharged. Captain Edward L. Gaul, Company A, who had gone home on sick leave in February, was detailed to command the barracks, Albany, N. Y., by S. O.—A. G. O., War Department. We remained at Thibodeaux three days, when (April 3d) we marched to Terrebonne, a small station on the New Orleans and Opelousas Railroad, three miles south of Thibodeaux, and April 4th we took the cars, arriving at Bayou Bœuf, seventy-three miles west of New Orleans and seven miles east of Brashear City, where we went into camp with the rest of our division. Weitzel's division was in advance at Brashear City, the terminus of the railroad eighty miles west of New Orleans on the east bank of Berwick Bay (a widening of the Atchafalaya River), and twenty miles from the Gulf of

Mexico. The transports and gunboats came around through the gulf and up the river to this point. Berwick City was directly across the bay one mile distant.

April 6th orders were issued (G. O. 68) to store all superfluous baggage, and restricting officers to a small valise or carpet-bag, a small roll of blankets, and mess utensils absolutely necessary. As during the following June the place was captured by the enemy, and the sugar-house, in which the goods were stored, was entirely destroyed with all its contents, we lost everything left there. April 8th we left for Brashear City, a march of seven miles, which we reached in the afternoon and remained there two days while Emory's and Weitzel's forces were moved across Berwick Bay. April 11th we were marched on board the transport *Laurel Hill*, the rest of our division being embarked on other transports, and April 12th we sailed up Berwick Bay and the Atchafalaya River, the fleet being preceded by two gunboats. That night we anchored. April 13th at 4 a. m. we started again and at 8 a. m. a stop was made at Hudgin's Point, Indian Bend, thirty-five miles northwest of Brashear City on the west bank of Grand Lake (another widening of the Atchafalaya), at the McWilliams plantation. Two companies of the First Louisiana (loyal) Infantry which had been landed were deployed as skirmishers and advanced across the field, when a heavy fire was opened on them by two guns and the skirmishers of the enemy, a body of cavalry dismounted. Our regiment, which was the second to land, and other troops were landed on flat-boats under a scattering fire, and we, rapidly forming line of battle, were marched up to the woods which skirted the field, closely supporting our skirmish line, and the rebels retreated. During the afternoon the division crossed the Bayou Teche about five miles from Grand Lake, and in the evening our regiment was thrown forward, two companies deployed as skirmishers, our right extending to the woods, and with the Thirteenth Connecticut on our left, their line extending to the bayou, were kept in the front all night. The night, which was quite cold, the rain falling heavily at intervals, passed without event, and in the early morning of April 14th our regiment was drawn in and resumed its position in the column which was marching down the road, our brigade in advance, the Twenty-fifth Connecticut deployed as skirmishers a short distance in front. The place was called IRISH BEND, the bayou making a turn forming a horse-shoe, and we were marching to the eastward towards Franklin, about three miles distant, for the purpose of intercepting the rebels whose main force was supposed to be at Fort Bisland, a short distance from Berwick City, where they were to be attacked by our main army comprising Emory's and Weitzel's divisions under command of Major-General Banks. Shortly after the march commenced we heard firing from our skirmishers, who had discovered the enemy in a wood to our right. The front of our skirmish line was at once changed and the Twenty-sixth Maine ordered forward to their support. Soon was heard the rolling fire of musketry as the Twenty-sixth Maine became engaged. From our position we could see it advance in line; then the men lay down, but continued the firing, which was replied to by the rebels in volleys. We were about two miles west of Franklin, which is one hundred miles west of New Orleans and thirty miles northwest of Brashear City, marching along the levee road when the attack was begun. Just off the road was a large sugar-house, "McKerall's," which was used as a hospital during and after the engagement. The field, which was intersected with deep ditches, was planted with sugar-cane, now about a foot high, in furrows some four feet apart with a depression between them of about a foot. Having been recently plowed, the ground was soft and heavy. The enemy was posted in a

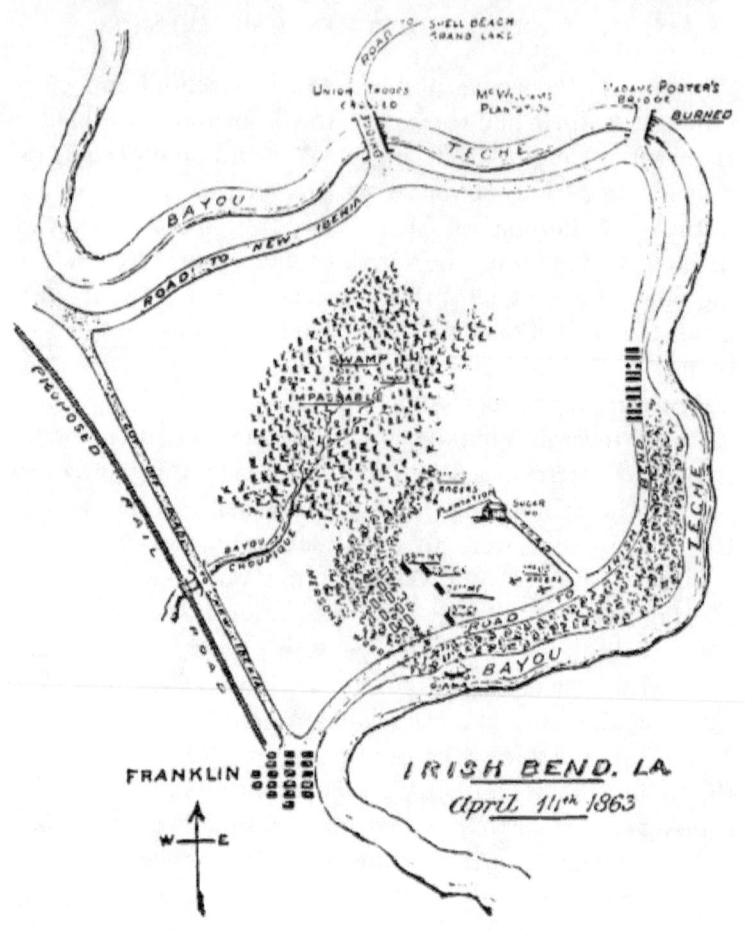

From Confederate Sketch in possession of Colonel R. B. Irwin.

dense wood, their right resting on the bayou up which they had come in transports from Fort Bisland when warned of our landing at Indian Bend, covered by the gunboat *Diana*, and were further protected by a strong fence in their front. Upon our right was a transverse ditch, and towards the woods, extending from them for some distance, thick heavy bushes. Just after the Twenty-sixth Maine lay down, Lieutenant Bradley's section of Battery C, Second United States Artillery, was taken across the field towards the right and just outside the bushes. Our regiment was then ordered in. Marching forward in line of battle at the double-quick, the right of the regiment passed over the left of the Twenty-sixth Maine, then over and past the skirmishers of the Twenty-fifth Connecticut, being met as it advanced by a heavy fire from the rebels who were entirely concealed from view by the fence and woods. Their forces comprised the Twenty-eighth Louisiana, Colonel Gray; Fourth Texas Mounted Volunteers, dismounted, Colonel Reilly; Major Clack's Confederate Guards Response Battalion, and Second Louisiana Cavalry dismounted, over twelve hundred men in all, Major-General Richard Taylor in command, and the gunboat before mentioned. The regiment struggled on until within fifty yards of the position held by the rebels, when, finding the men utterly exhausted by the weight of the blankets and overcoats they carried and the heavy marching they had undergone, as well as suffering severely from the fire of the enemy, the regiment was ordered to "halt," "lie down," and "commence firing," and was soon pouring a heavy, well-directed fire into the enemy. The fire in our front slackened materially and Colonel Molineux had just given the order "Forward, New York," when he was struck in the mouth by a ball and fell, and at the same moment the rebels, who had taken advantage of the bushes and ditch, charged in on the right and rear of our regiment, which was wholly unprotected except by the battery which was some distance to the right, at the same time delivering their fire. Our ammunition almost expended, and the rebels in our rear, the order was given to fall back, which was obeyed and the regiment retired to the edge of the road. The charge on our right was the last effort of the enemy and their retreat was at once commenced. The First Brigade coming in was met with no opposition, the enemy having abandoned their position and being in full retreat towards Franklin, where was a cut-off road to New Iberia, up which the enemy from Fort Bisland (where had been fought a severe engagement resulting in the total defeat of the enemy) had already passed. No report of the loss of the enemy in killed and wounded has been made, but Colonel Reilly was killed and Colonel Vincent and several other rebel officers wounded, and when the battle was over the fence in our front was found almost cut to pieces with bullets, showing how effective and well-delivered had been the fire of our regiment. The Thirteenth Connecticut, which had gone in at the same time on our left over more favorable ground, was more fortunate, as it drove the rebels and captured a piece of artillery with the battle-flag inscribed "From the Ladies of Franklin to the St. Mary's Cannoneers," as well as some prisoners.

The fight lasted until noon. The rebels destroyed the gunboat *Diana* to prevent its falling into our hands. The victory was ours, but the regiment paid dearly for it in this its maiden fight. Lieutenant-Colonel Gilbert A. Draper, Adjutant Robert D. Lathrop, First-Lieutenant John W. Manley, Jr., Company A, and Second-Lieutenant Byron Lockwood, Company G, were killed; First-Lieutenant William R. Plunkett, and Second-Lieutenant Charles P. Price, both of Company K, were mortally wounded and both died April 17th; Colonel Edward L. Molineux was severely wounded, being shot through the mouth and jaw, and Captain Wells O. Pettit, Company H, and Second-Lieutentant William F. Tiemann, Company A, were wounded. Of the officers who fell no fitter words can be written than those of the official report made by Colonel H. W. Birge commanding the brigade:

"A complete list of casualties has already been forwarded to you. It records the name of Lieutenant-Colonel Draper, who fell with three wounds either of which would have been fatal. A good soldier, a gallant officer, an estimable gentleman, his death is mourned by his friends, and is a loss to his country. Adjutant Lathrop and Lieutenants Manley and Lockwood . . . . all instantly killed on the field. Lieutenants Plunkett and Price mortally wounded and since dead. Their names are added to the list of patriots who have illustrated their devotion to their country by the sacrifice of their lives."

The regiment lost 115 in all: killed, 4 officers, 23 men; wounded, 5 officers (2 mortally), 70 men (9 mortally); missing, 13 men. Number engaged, about 375. The following list is as nearly perfect as can be made:

KILLED.

Lieutenant-Colonel	. . . .	GILBERT A. DRAPER
Adjutant		ROBERT D. LATHROP
	Company A.	
First-Lieutenant	. . . .	JOHN W. MANLEY, JR.
	Company G.	
Second-Lieutenant	. . . .	BYRON LOCKWOOD

WOUNDED.

Colonel	. . . .	EDWARD L. MOLINEUX
	Company A.	
Second-Lieutenant	. . .	WILLIAM F. TIEMANN

Company H.
Captain . . . . WELLS O. PETTIT

Company K.
First-Lieutenant . . . . WILLIAM R. PLUNKETT, mortally.

Second-Lieutenant . . . . CHARLES P. PRICE, mortally.

Quartermaster-Sergeant . . . . JOHN H. CHARLOTTE

KILLED.

Company A.
Private, CONNERY, PATRICK   *Private*, REYNOLDS, JAMES
" KELLY, JOHN   " SNYDER, JOSEPH
" KIPP, ROBERT L.

Company C.
Private, HOUGHTALING, JAMES   *Private*, RILEY, DANIEL
" MORRISON, JAMES

Company D.
Private, HULFAS, CHARLES

Company E.
Private, BOICE, RICHARD   *Private*, WOLF, HENRY D.
" SILVERNAIL, PETER

Company F.
Private, EATON, HENRY   *Corporal*, LAWS, JOHN G.
" FLOWERS, ZEBULON V.

Company G.
Private, MURPHY, JOHN   *Private*, SHARON, JAMES W.

Company I.
1st-Sergt. BAKER, MARK   *Corporal*, HAWS, WILLIAM H.
Sergeant, BOHRER, THEODORE

Company K.

Corporal, ASBELL, ANDREW
Private, MILLER, DAVID

Private, CARR, GEORGE

WOUNDED.

Company A.

Private, AKINS, THOMAS
" BRENZEL, WILLIAM
" DALEY, THOMAS
" DENNIS, JOHN
" FINNEY, GEORGE
" HOLLENBECK, WM. H.
Corporal, HIGGINS, JOHN, mortally.
Private, KEEGAN, PATRICK

Private, MAURER, SOLOMON
" MOSIER, RICHARD
" TATOR, JOHN G.
1st-Sergt. TYNAN, EDWARD
Private, WINSLOW, WARREN, mortally.
" WARD, THOMAS
" WINANS, CHARLES I.

Company B.

Private, CORSON, THOMAS
" FRENCH, STEPHEN
1st-Sergt. GAVAN, FRANK P.
Private, KERON, JOHN

Private, LEWIS, SMITH H.
" SIEGLER, FREDERICK
" WURTZ, BALTHAZAR

Company C.

Private, COONS, AMBROSE, mortally.
" CALKINS, WILLIAM, mortally.
" ROCKFELLER, MORTIMER

Private, RILSING, JOHN, mortally.
" SHUFELDT, WM. J.
" SCHNACK, CHRISTIAN

Company D.

Private, KISTERS, FRANK W.
" MESSONSOLE, LEWIS

Sergeant, ROSE, ISAAC L.
Private, SCHUCK, ADAM

Company E.

Private, BURNS, JAMES, mortally
" DECKER, JAMES
" DORAN, JAMES, mortally.
" HART, WILLIAM H.

1st-Sergt. MACY, SAMUEL B.
Private, MILLER, JESSE
" PETERSON, CHAS. H.G.
" SYRE, FRANCIS R.

Company F.

Private, DOYLE, JOHN
" DOSER, BARTHOLOMEW
" KERON, RICHARD
" MILLER, AARON

Private, MACKEY, EDWARD J.
" MACKEY, TERENCE
" WHITE, THOMAS

Company G.

Corporal, DEVLIN, JOHN
Private, FORTIN, MICHAEL
" STICKLES, CORNELIUS

Private, SMITH, LEONARD
Sergeant, TANNER, WESLEY,
    mortally.

Company H.

Private, ADAMS, WASHINGTON
" BENNETT, JAMES
" HOPKINS, BRYAN
1st-Sergt. KENNEDY, WILLIAM J.

Private, MURTHA, MICHAEL
Corporal, NEEFUS, JOHN,
    mortally.
Private, RODAN, GEORGE

Company I.

Private, COON, ALVARUS
" COON, JACOB

Corporal, REED, JOSEPH O.

Company K.

Private, COUGHLAN, JOHN
" CORCORAN, JOSEPH
Sergeant, DAY, JOHN
Private, EMMONS, JOHN

Private, HAHN, HENRY
" KELLY, JAMES
" KEWAN, JOHN M.

MISSING.

Company A.

Private, FUNK, MORGAN
" FERRIS, JOSEPH
" JENNINGS, DANIEL

Private, JUNES, JUSTUS
" MAGUIRE, JOHN
" STEPHENS, GEORGE C.

Company D.

Private, VOLKINUR, PETER

Company F.

Private, CORBOY, DANIEL
" DURIE, JOHN

Private, McMAHON, MICHAEL
" NICHOLS, FLOYD C.

Company K.

Private, ASHTON, SAMUEL.   *Corporal*, MILLS, JAMES M.

Most of the "missing" returned to the regiment within a week, those captured having been paroled by the rebels. The wounded were taken by transport to New Orleans, there being no accommodations for them in the field, the army intending to move at once.

CHAPTER V.

The First March to Alexandria, Louisiana — Port Hudson, Louisiana.

MAJOR Burt, who had been detached as Acting Aide and Judge-Advocate on the staff of Brigadier-General Grover, immediately returned to the regiment and assumed command, being the only field-officer remaining for duty. The same day, April 14th, he was promoted Lieutenant-Colonel, and Captain Edward L. Gaul, Company A (absent detached), was promoted Major. April 15th our regiment started at 7 a. m., marched up the Bayou Teche 15 miles to McGuire's plantation, and camped at 5 p. m. On the 16th we started at 6 a. m. and marched ten miles to New Iberia (one hundred and twenty-five miles west of New Orleans), being joined on the road by several of our men who had been captured at Irish Bend and liberated on parole, and on the 17th, starting at 6 a. m., marched twenty miles to Vermilion Bayou. At this place Appleton W. Rackett, private, Company D, was killed, and William J. Brown, private, Company F, was wounded by the rebels, while drawing water. April 19th, after a day's rest, the regiment was detached to collect horses and cattle. The country was a vast prairie on which were feeding numerous herds, and we succeeded in collecting about five thousand head, as well as a number of horses and mules, which were driven by the regiment to Berwick City, sixty-five miles east from Vermilion Bayou, where we arrived April 29th, having stopped on the way at Fort Bisland where we leveled the earthworks to the ground. April 30th, Second Lieutenant William F. Tiemann, Company A, was promoted First-Lieutenant, Company A; Second-Lieutenant Henry M. Howard, Company D, to First-Lieutenant, Company F; Second-Lieutenant Alfred H. Bruce, Company F, to First-Lieutenant, Company K, and Sergeant-Major Herman Smith to Second-Lieutenant, Company G. Owing to the non-receipt of their commissions these officers were not mustered in the respective grades until June 10th. Immediately on our arrival at Berwick we were ordered to return with a wagon train. We started April 30th at daybreak, and marched to Opelousas, one hundred and sixty-six miles west of New Orleans, where we arrived May 3d, and having delivered the wagons, May 4th, marched to Barre's Landing at the junction of Bayou Cortableau and Bayou Teche, eight miles east from Opelousas, eighty miles west from Berwick City, where we rejoined our brigade. May 5th we started at 1 p. m. to join the main army, which was two days in advance, and, passing through Washington, Holmesville, and Cheneyville, marched seventy-seven miles in the four days ending May 8th, halting May 9th for a rest. May 10th we marched four miles to Wells' plantation (twelve miles from Alexandria) where we halted for another rest. First-Lieutenant Wesley Bradley, Company E, who had been absent sick, died in hospital, May 10th. May 14th we again started on the march, partially retracing our route, passing through Cheneyville and Enterprise, to the Bayou Rouge and along the Bayou de Glaise, reaching the west bank of the Atchafalaya River May 17th, a march of sixty miles in four days, and were transferred across the river on large flatboats rowed by negroes to Simmsport (sixty miles north-northwest from Baton Rouge) on the afternoon of May 18th.

Marching a short distance from the river we went into camp. May 21st we broke camp again, embarking on the transport *Empire Parish*, passing up the Atchafalaya to its junction with the Mississippi where we anchored, and at dark started again, arriving at the town of Bayou Sara on the east bank of the Mississippi (forty-six miles from Simmsport and fourteen miles above Port Hudson), where we landed at 11 p. m., and marched a mile and a half inland, camping overnight in a cemetery. May 22d we were advanced to the front in support of a section of artillery placed there on the road towards Port Hudson. There we remained until our brigade came up, when we rejoined it and marched on with the rest of the army in the direction of Port Hudson, which we understood was the objective point. May 23d a junction was made with the forces under Major-General Augur from Baton Rouge. We camped at the junction of the Jackson and Port Hudson roads. It rained heavily during the night. May 24th we rested, and May 25th the advance was resumed. At 11.30 a. m. we came to the outer rifle-pits of the fort and the action commenced, our skirmishers pressing forward in advance.

The works covered a point at a bend in the Mississippi (twenty-two miles above Baton Rouge) called Port Hudson, extending along the river for about three miles, where a number of heavy batteries were planted and encircling it, making a line inland about seven miles long. The following description from the *New Orleans Era* shows more plainly the nature of the works we were about to invest:

The principal defenses are on the river side. They comprise seventeen separate embrasures, mostly built in an arc of a circle. They are finely revetted, and command all the approaches by way of the river. In three of them pivot guns were mounted, which were used both for front and rear. The land breastworks are built in the ordinary manner on the outer side. They extend in a semicircular direction from river to river for a distance of nearly seven miles.

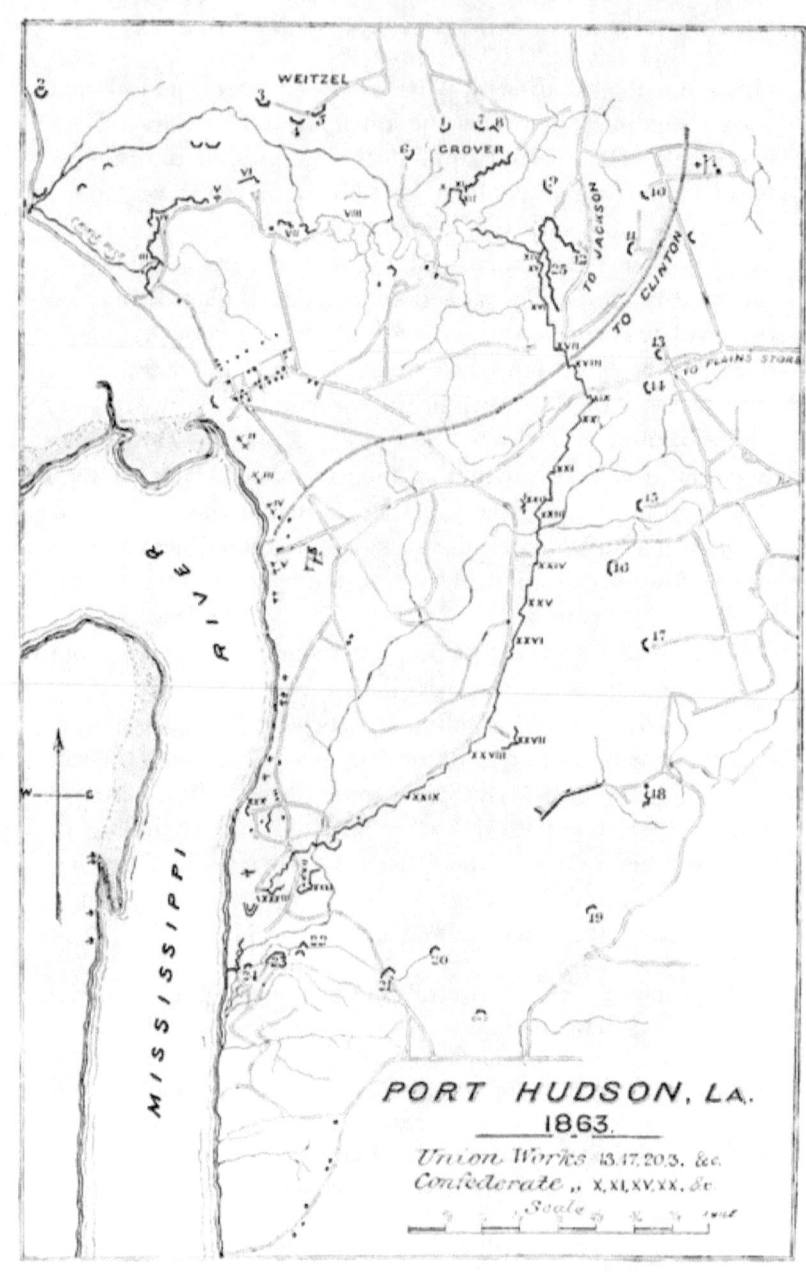

From Official Map in possession of Colonel R. B. Irwin.
See also page 23.

The river was occupied above and below the works by our mortar and gun boats. On the right of the land forces, to the north of the works, was the division of General Weitzel, next on his left Grover's (our) division, then General Dwight's division, while to his left were the divisions of Generals Augur and T. W. Sherman, the army entirely surrounding the works. The outer pits were only one-half mile from the works, and on our approach the enemy opened sharply. Our regiment, with the Thirteenth Connecticut and Twenty-fifth Connecticut, advanced through the woods on the right of the Bayou Sara road down which we had marched, the rebels vigorously opposing us, the shells bursting overhead tearing away great limbs of trees, and solid shot striking the trees and ricochetting over our heads as we pressed the enemy from their outer line. Their defense was stubborn and our advance was very slow. We lost one man killed and several wounded. We were under fire all day and thoroughly tired when night fell causing a temporary halt. May 26th our regiment was marched to the front in support of the skirmishers. The musketry was terrific, and the noise reverberating through the woods was deafening. The advance was made as rapidly as possible, but it was difficult work to dislodge the rebels, and only at nightfall we reached the edge of the woods where we remained in the extreme advance as pickets, the rebel sharp-shooters keeping up a constant fire from behind the felled trees which were lying in all directions between our position and their works.

CHAPTER VI.

Port Hudson, Louisiana — Assault, May 27, 1863.

WE remained on the line all night and until the afternoon of May 27th, when we were drawn in and, with the Twenty-fifth Connecticut under command of Lieutenant-Colonel Burt, were marched two miles towards the right of the line to the left of General Weitzel's division, where we came out on a road under a heavy artillery and musketry fire from the enemy. We then struck into a ravine which was filled with logs and fallen trees, through which we had to pass in single file, at times crawling under the logs and at others jumping over them. After a tedious march of half a mile, which it took us an hour to make, we reached the base of a hill up which we were to climb before we could arrive at our destination, a part of the main breastworks it was intended we should assault. Just before reaching the hill we captured a rebel captain and six sharp-shooters who were concealed in the ravine and had been unable to retreat to the fort. So tortuous and winding was the route that the officers had to stand and direct the men which way to turn; but at last all were got together, line was formed as well as could be done, and the order was given to charge. Making a gallant dash up the steep bank, the regiment was at once exposed and the rebels poured in a galling enfilading fire. We were not thirty yards from the works, but we got no farther, as we were met by a concentrated force of the rebels who had been fully apprised of our intention through seeing us as we came out in the road and along the ravine

PORT HUDSON, LA.   SCENE OF CHARGE, MAY 27, 1863.

and had prepared for our coming. The force in our front was a large one massed four deep and extending considerably beyond our flanks, as we saw very plainly when we reached the top of the hill. It was simply impossible to advance under the murderous fire, and the men sought such shelter and protection as they could secure. Color-Corporal Jonathan J. Race, Company A, was killed, and Color-Sergeant William H. Spanburg, Company C, while bravely advancing was shot in three places, severe and dangerous wounds. The color-staff was shot in two by one of the bullets which wounded the bearer, and one piece of the staff was left on the field, but the colors were seized by Lieutenant-Colonel Burt as the bearer fell and were by him given to Robert A. Smith, Company F, the State colors to Sergeant William E. Palmer, Company D, by whom they were carried until the formation of the Volunteer Stormers. The regiment was repulsed with a loss of 54: 14 men killed, 1 officer (Captain Charles Lewis, Company C) and 39 men wounded, 4 fatally. For several hours the regiment lay close up to the breastworks in the position it had gained, unable to move, exposed to a heavy fire on the least indication, though in comparative safety from the constant volleys poured in by the rebels, protected by the fallen trees and stumps behind which the men had sheltered themselves, returning the fire steadily and well. At this juncture what was supposed to be a flag of truce was raised, and the rebels, thinking it a signal for a cessation of hostilities, ceased firing along the line, during which the regiment sought and secured a safer position not quite so near the works. Our army supposed the fort had surrendered, but finding such was not the case, hostilities were quickly resumed, though the advantage was given to the rebels as our forces showed the positions they had gained thus enabling the enemy to drive them from their positions in many cases. The assault, which had been made by several other columns at the same time as ours, was not successful at any point though it served to bring our army closer to the works. Our regiment was withdrawn at 11 p. m., just after which we heard several volleys fired by the rebels who, we presumed, were attacking the position we had occupied supposing it to be still held by us, but we were then safely out of it though none too soon. A burial party was detailed next day, under Captain Hart and Lieutenant Howard, who met on the field an officer of an Arkansas regiment which had been one of those opposed to us the day before, and he spoke in the highest terms of the brave and gallant charge made by our regiment. The piece of the color-staff left on the field was not permitted to be removed. The dead lay very close together not far from the works and were interred where they fell. May 28th the regiment was temporarily consolidated into five companies, owing to there being so few officers present for duty.

May 29th the rain fell in torrents through the day and night, after a long spell of hot dry weather. We were held in reserve in the rear until June 4th, when at night we were sent to the front to man the entrenchments within two hundred yards of the rebel works. Our rifle pits were of earth thrown to the front from a ditch, dug parallel with the fort, and on top of which was a double line of logs, one over the other, separated sufficiently to admit a rifle to be passed between and fired. As the firing was constant, not one of the enemy dared show himself as he was certain to be fired at by one or more of our sharpshooters, who were constantly watching for such opportunities, but that there were numbers of them was evidenced by the return fire provoked by any exposure on our side.

Directly in our rear was a detachment of the First Indiana Battery, with one 32-pounder rifled cannon and several smaller pieces. That their practice was good, was shown one morning by their blowing out from the roots of an old tree, with a shell fired from the big gun, a rebel sharpshooter who had concealed himself there, and had given much annoyance to us and the men of the battery, before his position was discovered. An old barn in our front, just inside the fort, served as a cover to the enemy, but the firing of the guns made it very unsafe for them, and it was completely riddled with shot and shell fired at it during the siege. Between our pits and the fort, just to the left of our position, was a mill used for grinding corn, to which the rebels occasionally came out at night during the first of the investment, but the battery by a few well-planted shells made it so warm for the "Johnnies" that it was abandoned by them.

A constant steady fire on the rebel works was maintained by our batteries, while on their side the rebels kept up a fire in reply to ours, and shot, shell, and bars of railroad iron were constantly whizzing and shrieking through the air. The firing was usually most severe at night and, lying on our backs, we would watch the bombs from our mortars as they flew through the air like revolving stars, or the shells from the fort as they shot towards our lines, the streaks of light from the fuses of the latter indicating when they were coming in our direction, and causing us to creep close under our earthworks at such times until their explosion showed the danger to be over for a time. They made a horrible sound, but nothing compared to the awful unearthly shriek caused by the bars of railroad iron with which we were occasionally favored. These were fired from a big gun in the fort, which we understood was mounted on a car and moved around the works on a railroad constructed for the purpose.

We had an enemy, a "gray-back" too, within the pits, more persistent and difficult to contend with than his namesake in the fort, the small insect which did much to make life almost unbearable, and a constant *skirmish* was necessary to keep us even partly free from these pests, the sand in the pits being almost alive with them.

The rations and coffee were cooked in the rear and carried to the men in the pits, and water also had to be brought by details made for the purpose. As a part of the line was exposed, these details and our company cooks had to pass across quite an open space, and it was amusing to see the dash made to get over it and under cover, frequently at the expense of much of the coffee or water, but fortunately without damage to the men.

The weather which had been steadily growing hotter was almost unbearable in the pits where was almost no shade, and for the greater part of the day we were exposed to the burning sun, obtaining shelter only by getting under the shadow of the breastworks, or crawling under a shelter made by raising our blankets on short sticks, but as this cut off the air we preferred to remain exposed. Fortunately the air would cool soon after sundown, so that we could, to some extent, recuperate from the effects of the heat of the day.

June 8th we were relieved during the night and again withdrawn a short distance to the rear where we were camped in a grove of high magnolia trees, the "Magnolia Grandiflora," the flowers on which were in bloom, and their fragrance filled the air. The whole place was covered with these noble trees, and the lovely white flowers showing through the rich dark bronze-green of the leaves were a beautiful sight. We did not appreciate them as we would have done had the surroundings been more peaceful, though we could not but notice their beauty and fragrance, which, with the grateful shade the great trees provided, helped to ameliorate our condition. June 10th we had heavy rain through the night. June 11th we resumed our position in the rifle pits. The same night a heavy skirmish line advanced in our front. June 12th, at midnight, the skirmishers again went out, our regiment furnishing a detail each night for the purpose. June 13th, at midnight, another advance was made by the skirmishers, who retained their positions through the day.

CHAPTER VII.

*Port Hudson, Louisiana — Assault, June 14, 1863 —
The Surrender — Our Losses during the Siege.*

JUNE 14th, at 1 a. m., we were silently and quietly withdrawn from the pits and marched back two miles. Preparations had been made for an assault on the works at daybreak, our division (Grover's), with two regiments of the Third Brigade, First Division, under Colonel N. A. M. Dudley, being ordered to attack the works on the right, in front of the position held by Colonel Dudley, while a similar attack was to be made by Brigadier-General Dwight on our extreme left, and a feigned attack which should be converted into a real one if opportunity offered was to be made by Major-General Augur in the centre. Our brigade, with the Second, was held in reserve as supports to the rest of our division, which was to advance as stormers, and at 3 a. m. we were marched to our position. It was yet very dark though we could see our way clearly, and all the movements were made as noiselessly as possible. The rumble of artillery and tramp of troops reached our ears as we stood in line awaiting orders. The assaulting column of our division had gone ahead and formed line of battle, preceded by a heavy line of skirmishers, then a body of men carrying bags of cotton and fascines with which to fill the ditch, to permit the stormers to cross readily, pioneers carrying axes, shovels, pickaxes, etc., to remove obstructions and level the works, followed by men with a pontoon bridge, for the passage of artillery, and was only waiting the signal to charge the works. At 4 a. m. the action commenced in our front, but owing to some cause the assaults were not all made together, the consequence being that the rebels were enabled to mass themselves at each point and successfully resist our attacks. Our guns in the meanwhile kept up a terrific fire on the rebel works. At 8 a. m. the reserve was ordered in. We marched through a ravine, which was in plain sight of the rebels and covered by their sharpshooters, and several of our men fell before we reached our position. We came at length to a hill on the crest of which were drawn up several regiments ready for a charge, and as we approached they made a gallant dash to the front. We followed to the top of the hill, when the command "Charge" was given, which we obeyed with a cheer and a rush down the hill into a ravine and up another hill to within twenty-five yards of the breastworks, beyond which it was impossible to advance, owing to the severe fire of the enemy. Here we lay until 12.30 p. m., our eyes saddened by the sight of our dead and our ears tortured with the groans of our wounded, when we were marched through another ravine and came out at the foot of a hill only fifteen yards from the fort. Here we were halted, and under a blazing sun without shelter we lay exposed to a constant fire until 9 p. m., when all the forces were drawn off, with the exception of the regiments left as pickets. We were relieved by a detachment of the First Louisiana Engineers (colored), which proceeded to fortify the position we had gained. Our loss was 14 men wounded and 2 men missing, a total of 16. The only advantage gained at the point of our assault was the holding the hill over which we charged and on which breastworks were at once thrown up, thus bringing our lines closer to the rebel works. June 15th we were relieved in the early morning, and marched back to our old position. That day was issued the following:

GENERAL ORDERS No. 49,
HEADQUARTERS DEPARTMENT OF THE GULF,
NINETEENTH ARMY CORPS,
Before PORT HUDSON, June 15th, 1863.

The commanding General congratulates the troops before Port Hudson upon the steady advance made upon the enemy's works, and is confident of an immediate and triumphant issue of the contest. We are at all points upon the threshold of his fortifications. One more advance and they are ours! For the last victory that duty imposes the commanding General summons the bold men of the corps to the organization of a storming column of a thousand men, to vindicate the flag of the Union and the memory of its defenders who have fallen! Let them come forward! Officers who lead the column of victory in this last assault may be assured of just recognition of their services by promotion; and every officer and soldier who shares its perils and its glory shall receive a medal fit to commemorate the first grand success of the campaign of 1863 for the freedom of the Mississippi. His name shall be placed in general orders upon the Roll of Honor. Division commanders will at once report the names of the officers and men who may volunteer for this service, in order that the organization of the column may be completed without delay.

By command of Major-General Banks.

RICHARD B. IRWIN,
Assistant Adjutant-General.

Colonel H. W. Birge, Thirteenth Connecticut, commanding our brigade, at once volunteered with every member of his staff, and was placed in command.

From our regiment eighteen volunteered.

First-Lieutenant JULIUS H. TIEMANN, Company B, Acting Aide to Colonel Birge.
Second-Lieutenant ALFRED GREENLEAF, JR., Company B.
Captain ROBERT McD. HART, Company F.
First-Lieutenant DUNCAN RICHMOND, Company H.

Sergeant MICHAEL HOGAN, Company C.
Sergeant JAMES T. PERKINS, Company E.
Sergeant GILBERT S. GULLEN, Company F.
Sergeant THOMAS BERGEN, Company K.
Corporal EDGAR HOLLENBECK, Company C.
Private AMOS HARK, Company B.
" GEORGE W. HATFIELD, Company B.
" HUGH MCELRAVY, Company B.
" JOHN TAYLOR, Company B.
" CHRISTIAN SCHNACK, Company C.
" JOHN THORP, Company E.
" BARTHOLOMEW DOSER, Company F.
" JAMES BRAZIER 2d, Company I.
" GEORGE W. SCHOFIELD, Company I.

Their services were not called for, however, as the fort surrendered, though the column was duly organized and ready for the work proposed to it; and no official recognition of their bravery has ever been taken or medals distributed as promised.

June 19th, Marshall A. Dunham, private, Company A, was promoted Sergeant-Major. Our regiment, with the others of our brigade, was ordered to the right with Nims' Massachusetts Battery to prevent the rebels cutting their way out, which it was reported was their intention. We suffered severely with the heat, which was very oppressive. June 29th, Major-General Banks delivered an address to the troops congratulating them on the coolness and steadiness displayed under fire. July 6th, heavy rain fell, the first for a number of days. We were detailed as pickets on the Jackson road, it being reported the rebels were to make an attack in the rear. There was a large rebel force at Clinton and in the vicinity, and the report came from one of their deserters. The day and night passed without incident.

July 7th, at 11 p. m., Major-General Frank Gardner, commanding Port Hudson, sent a flag of truce to Major-General

Banks asking for an official confirmation of the surrender of Vicksburg information of which had been given to the rebels by our troops. The news had reached us during the forenoon of the 7th that Vicksburg had been surrendered on the morning of July 4th to Major-General U. S. Grant, and had been celebrated by a grand fire of artillery along our whole line and from all the mortar and gun boats in the river, to which were joined the shouts and cheers of the soldiers and sailors. Major-General Banks at once sent an official copy of the report and, receiving this, Major-General Gardner asked for a commission of three officers to meet a similar commission appointed by him to arrange for the surrender of the position and garrison, which was complied with by Major-General Banks, and July 8th, at 6 a. m., all hostilities ceased. At 9 a. m. the commission met, the terms agreed to being "the unconditional surrender of Port Hudson and its dependencies with the garrison and material of war, and that the fort should be occupied and its garrison received as prisoners of war by the United States forces at 7 a. m. the next day." These terms were signed by Brigadier-General Charles P. Stone, Brigadier-General William Dwight, and Colonel Henry W. Birge on our part, by Colonel W. R. Miles, Colonel I. G. W. Steedman, and Lieutenant-Colonel Marshall J. Smith on that of the rebels, and were approved by Major-General N. P. Banks and Major-General Frank Gardner, the agreement being signed at 2 p. m. of July 8th; and at first it was agreed that the fort should be occupied at 5 p. m. of the same day, but this was afterwards changed and 7 a. m. of the 9th designated and agreed to.

July 9th, at 7 a. m., our forces marched in along the river front, the "Volunteer Stormers" under command of Colonel H. W. Birge leading the column, preceded by Brigadier-General George L. Andrews and the staff. The rebels, drawn up in line, were faced by our troops; they piled arms and colors, and the surrender was complete. Over 6000 prisoners with quantities of small arms and ammunition and 73 pieces of artillery fell into our hands. After the surrender the enlisted men were paroled to the number of 5935, and the officers, numbering 405, were sent to New Orleans and Vicksburg, showing a total of 6340. For forty-four days there had been constant fighting, and great was the rejoicing throughout the army that at last their privations and efforts had achieved so glorious a result.

Some time later the following General Orders and Resolution were issued, which, when received, were read to the regiment at dress parade.

GENERAL ORDERS } HEADQUARTERS DEPARTMENT OF THE GULF,
No. 57. } 19TH A. C.,
NEW ORLEANS, August 5, 1863.

The commanding General takes great pleasure in communicating to the troops of this department the contents of the following dispatch this day received from the General-in-Chief:

HEADQUARTERS OF THE ARMY,
WASHINGTON, July 23, 1863.

MAJOR-GENERAL BANKS, New Orleans.

General: Your dispatches of July 8th, announcing the surrender of Port Hudson, are received. I congratulate you and your army on the crowning success of the campaign. It was reserved for your army to strike the last blow to open the Mississippi River. The country, and especially the great West, will ever remember with gratitude their services.

Very respectfully, your obedient servant,
H. W. HALLECK,
General-in-Chief.

By command of Major-General Banks.
RICHARD B. IRWIN,
Assistant Adjutant-General.

GENERAL ORDERS } WAR DEPARTMENT, ADJUTANT-GENERAL'S
No. 41.   }   OFFICE,
                       WASHINGTON, February 1, 1864.

The following resolution of the Senate and House of Representatives is published to the Army:

I. PUBLIC RESOLUTION NO. 7.

A Resolution expressive of the thanks of Congress to Major-General Nathaniel P. Banks, and the officers and soldiers under his command, at Port Hudson.

Resolved by the Senate and House of Representatives of the United States of America, in Congress assembled, That the thanks of Congress are hereby tendered to Major-General Nathaniel P. Banks, and the officers and soldiers under his command, for the skill, courage, and endurance which compelled the surrender of Port Hudson, and thus removed the last obstruction to the free navigation of the Mississippi River.

Approved January 28, 1864.

By order of the Secretary of War:
E. D. TOWNSEND,
Assistant Adjutant-General.

Our total loss during the siege was 73: 15 men killed; 1 officer, 55 men wounded (4 mortally); 2 men missing. The following list is as near perfect as it can be made:

OFFICERS WOUNDED.

Company C.

Captain . . . . CHARLES LEWIS

KILLED.

Company A.

Col.-Corp. RACE, JONATHAN J.

Company E.

Corporal, CHRISTMAN, JACOB H.   Private,   PROPER, WILLIAM H.
Private, MAXWELL, JOHN   "   PUGH, WILLIAM

Company F.

Private, McCAULEY, JOHN

Company G.

Private, GALLAGHER, JOHN   Private, PULTZ, HARVEY G.

Company H.

Sergeant, COLWELL, THOS. E.   Private, McCORMICK, JAMES
Corporal, UGGLA, WILLIAM   "   ROSSITER, CHARLES
Private, DALEY, JOHN

Company I.

Private, COON, WILLIAM

Company K.

Private, BRIDGES, EDWARD

WOUNDED.

Company A.

Private, AKINS, THOMAS   Corporal, PEARY, SILAS W.
" HOWES, GEORGE   " SAGENDORPH, JACOB
" KEEGAN, PATRICK   Private, TATOR, JOHN
Corporal, MAURER, GEORGE

Company B.

Private, IRVING, ALEX. F.   Corporal, ROBERTS, WILLIAM
" JOY, JOHN   Private, WURTZ, BALTHAZAR
" McCARTNEY, THOMAS, mortally.

Company C.

Sergeant, HOGAN, MICHAEL   Private, SCHERMERHORN, JOHN
" NORMAN, SAMUEL A.   " STAATS, MYRON
Private, PATTERSON, JOSEPH   " TATOR, WILLIAM
Col.-Serg., SPANBURGH, WM. H.   " VAN VALKENBURGH, CORNELIUS

Company D.

Private, FURNESS, MICHAEL
" HANNOPHY, JOHN.
    mortally.
Sergeant, JENNINGS, JOHN F.
Private, MCKINLEY, DAVID
" NEVINS, THOMAS
Corporal, PEARSALL, ALANSON

Company E.

Private, MYERS, JOHN W.
" MCCRACKEN, ROBERT
" O'BRIEN, PATRICK J.
Private, PROPER, ROBERT
" RACE, ROBERT

Company F.

Private, BROKEE, JOHN R.,
    mortally.
" CALLAGHAN, WILLIAM
Corporal, FERGUSON, JOHN H.
Private, O'MARA, JOHN
Sergeant, TOMPKINS, SAM'L C.

Company G.

Private, BOLLINGER, JOHN C.
Corporal, GOSHIA, ANDREW
Private, LYNCH, JOHN
Corporal, RICHMOND, SILAS W.
Private, SHEA, THOMAS

Company H.

Private, BARRETT, THOMAS
" JACOBS, DAVIS
" MILLER, PETER
Private, MCGREEN, EDWARD
" PETTINGER, EDWARD
" PETERSEN, NIEL

Company I.

Private, BOGARDUS, FRED'K.
Corporal, BRAZIER, JAMES S.
" COSGROVE, EDWARD
Private, KELLERHOUSE, WM.
" VAIL, EDWARD

Company K.

Private, BRUSH, JOHN
" TRUMBULL, ALBERT C.,
    mortally.
Corporal, VANDERGAW, FRANCIS L.

MISSING.

Company I.

Corporal, COOK, JOHN

Company K.

Private, GARHOLT, AUGUSTUS

CHAPTER VIII.

Leave Port Hudson, La.—Donaldsonville, La.—Camp Kearny, Carrollton, La.—Thibodeaux, La.

JULY 10th orders were received to be ready to move at daybreak with five days' rations and one hundred rounds of ammunition per man. During the same night one brigade of our division with Nims' Massachusetts Battery embarked on the transport *Laurel Hill*, and July 11th Brigadier-General Grover and staff with the rest of the division marched through the fort and embarked on transports for Donaldsonville, our regiment going on the steamer *Iberville*. During the investment of Port Hudson the rebels west of the Mississippi had been concentrating under Lieutenant-General E. Kirby Smith and hoping to make a diversion had attacked several places, the forces being under the immediate command of Major-General R. Taylor. The rebels under Colonel Jas. P. Major attacked and captured Plaquemine, Bayou Goula, Paincourtville, and Thibodeaux at which place they captured Sergeant John Pelletrau, Company K, who had been sent on special duty to New Orleans and was on his way back to the regiment. June 20th they attacked La Fourche Crossing where a force of about 800 under Lieutenant-Colonel Albert Stickney was stationed, and were handsomely repulsed with severe loss. Another rebel force under Brigadier-Generals Mouton and Green crossed Berwick Bay in skiffs and rowboats and attacked Brashear City June 23d, which place they captured with most of the garrison and destroyed or carried off all the baggage belonging to our army which had been stored there at the beginning of the campaign in April. All the baggage of the officers of our regiment as well as the knapsacks of the men, with their contents, was destroyed. One of our men, Lawrence Martin, Company F, was killed there. He was in the invalid camp which had been established at this point, the convalescents doing duty as garrison guarding the stores of the Quartermaster's and Commissary Departments. Musician Henry C. Dunham and several others of our regiment were captured at the same time.

The rebels then joined forces and marched on Donaldsonville where was a small fort (Butler) garrisoned by 180 men, mostly convalescents, under command of Major Joseph D. Bullen, Twenty-eighth Maine, and the gunboat *Princess Royal* in the river to assist them. The rebels made the attack in the early morning of June 28th but were repulsed with a loss in killed, wounded, and prisoners of nearly double the number of the defenders. They lost 4 officers and 36 men killed, 4 officers and 110 men wounded, 9 officers and 121 men prisoners, while in the fort the loss was 1 officer and 7 men killed, 2 officers and 11 men wounded. The gunboat *Princess Royal* did good service and lost 1 killed and 2 wounded. The *Winona* also was engaged, having arrived at the fort about two hours after the engagement began, and it was largely due to the presence and aid of the gunboats that the gallant men in the fort won such a glorious victory. As the rebel army, reported ten thousand strong, still menaced the place and its capture would have seriously interfered with navigation of the river, and as the rebels also had approached within twenty miles of New Orleans, immediately after the surrender of Port Hudson all the troops available were despatched from there to drive them back. Arriving at Donaldsonville the division was placed in position to cover the town and fort. In advance on the levee road to the right of the Bayou La Fourche were the forces of Brigadier-General Weitzel. On the left bank the First Brigade of our division under Colonel Joseph F. Morgan, Ninetieth New York, was in advance. We arrived at Donaldsonville at 10 p. m. and were at once landed and marched to the front as pickets. We retained this position with a section of artillery, being reinforced July 12th by the Twenty-fifth Connecticut, until the forces of Colonel Morgan advanced beyond us. July 13th the enemy made an attack on both sides of the bayou driving back Morgan's forces with a loss of 465 killed, wounded, and missing, and two pieces of artillery. Charges were afterwards preferred against Colonel Morgan but the findings and sentence of the court-martial were disapproved by Major-General Banks.

Our brigade was thrown forward to cover the retreat, which however the rebels did not follow up, and our regiment was posted on the right in front, where it remained all night on picket. July 15th the rebels fell back and retreated west of the Atchafalaya river. Our force not being sufficiently strong could not follow them beyond Brashear City, which place was occupied by our troops under Lieutenant-Colonel Peck July 23d. July 15th Colonel Molineux, though not entirely recovered from his wound, rejoined the regiment after an absence of three months, and most sincere was the rejoicing to have him again in command though Lieutenant-Colonel Burt had proved himself an active, brave, and efficient officer and commander. July 16th our regiment was transported to the east bank of the Mississippi to cover and guard the crossing of the wagon trains coming down from Port Hudson. Camp duties were very light and we enjoyed the rest after the fatigue of the long siege. Not the least of our enjoyments was the feasting on muskmelons and watermelons of which there was a large field only a short distance from our camp. July 20th First-Lieutenant William F. Tiemann, Company A, was appointed acting aide on the staff of Colonel George B. Bissell commanding the Third Brigade but returned to the regiment early in the following month when Colonel Bissell was relieved. July 25th Thomas Bergen, First-Sergeant Company K, was promoted Commissary-Sergeant *vice* William F. French returned to Company G as Sergeant.

July 29th our regiment, with two batteries, was detailed as guard to the baggage train, and with one hundred baggage wagons marched down the road along the east bank of the river. We marched seventy-three miles to Carrollton, seven miles above New Orleans, which was reached August 2d, and encamped there to recuperate, the camp being called "Kearny" after the gallant general who had so lately laid down his life for his country. July 30th Captain William H. Sliter, Company G, and Captain Joe B. Ramsden, Company K, and July 31st Second-Lieutenant Edgar G. Hubbell, Company C, resigned and were discharged. August 5th, after a long spell of pleasant weather, we had rain and the day was very unpleasant.

August 15th, by S. O. 200, Headquarters Department of the Gulf, the Nineteenth Corps was reorganized with Major-General W. B. Franklin in command, and the brigade, comprising the Thirteenth Connecticut, Ninetieth New York, Ninety-first New York, One Hundred and Thirty-first New York, and One Hundred and Fifty-ninth New York, was constituted the First of the Fourth Division, designated as "Grover's," and the division assigned to the district "Defenses of New Orleans," with Brigadier-General William H. Emory temporarily assigned to command as Brigadier-General Grover was absent on furlough. August 16th Second-Lieutenant Robert H. Traver, Company E, was discharged. August 18th the following was issued:

GENERAL ORDERS } HEADQUARTERS 159TH REGIMENT
No. 8.   }   NEW YORK S. V.
CAMP KEARNY, CARROLLTON, LOUISIANA, August 18, 1863.

The Colonel commanding congratulates the regiment that its conduct during the late campaign in the TECHE COUNTRY and before PORT HUDSON has met with the approval of the commanding General, and that the honor of New York State has been fully sustained by both officers and men.

The regiment now bears an enviable reputation for endurance and courage, and full confidence is felt that, if called upon, it will continue to win fresh honors.

Among the many who have faithfully performed their duty, the names of the following officers and men are hereby published in these General Orders AS HAVING BEEN ESPECIALLY NOTED FOR SOLDIERLY CONDUCT AND VALOR IN THE FACE OF THE ENEMY. Many of these have fallen, and their loss we regret, as gallant and devoted soldiers of their country.

Lieutenant-Colonel GILBERT A. DRAPER, Irish Bend — killed.
Lieutenant-Colonel CHARLES A. BURT, Port Hudson, May 27 and June 14.
Adjutant ROBERT D. LATHROP, Irish Bend — killed.
Quartermaster-Sergt. JOHN H. CHARLOTTE, Irish Bend — wounded.

Company A.

First-Lieutenant JOHN W. MANLEY, JR., Irish Bend — killed.
Second-Lieutenant WILLIAM F. TIEMANN, Irish Bend, Port Hudson — wounded.
First-Sergeant EDWARD TYNAN, Irish Bend — wounded.
Private THOMAS DALEY, Irish Bend — wounded.

Company B.

Sergeant B. RANSOM, Irish Bend and Port Hudson.
Private THOMAS CARSON, Irish Bend.
    "   JAMES HANLIN, Port Hudson, June 14.
    "   AMOS HARK, Irish Bend and Port Hudson.

Company C.

Captain CHARLES LEWIS, Irish Bend, Port Hudson, June 14 — wounded.
First-Sergeant A. W. WENTZ, Irish Bend, Port Hudson.
Color-Sergeant WILLIAM H. SPANBURGH, Irish Bend, Port Hudson — wounded.
Private MORTIMER ROCKEFELLER, Irish Bend — wounded.
" AMBROSE COONS, Irish Bend — wounded.

Company D.

Sergeant JOHN PENDERGAST, Irish Bend — wounded.
" ISAAC L. ROSE, Irish Bend — wounded.
Corporal ALANSON PEARSALL, Irish Bend and Port Hudson — wounded.

Company E.

Captain WILLIAM WALTERMIRE, Irish Bend and Port Hudson, May 27 and June 14.
First-Sergeant SAMUEL B. MACY, Irish Bend — wounded.
Sergeant JAMES M. OSTRANDER, Irish Bend, Port Hudson.
Corporal DAVID E. WALTERMIRE, Irish Bend, Port Hudson.

Company F.

Captain R. MC D. HART, Port Hudson, May 27 and June 14.
Sergeant GILBERT S. GULLEN, Port Hudson.
Private ZEBULON V. FLOWERS, Irish Bend — killed.

Company G.

Lieutenant HERMAN SMITH, Irish Bend and Port Hudson.
" BYRON LOCKWOOD, Irish Bend — killed.
Corporal JOHN GALLAGHER, Port Hudson — killed.
Private HARVEY G. PULTZ, Port Hudson — killed.

Company H.

Captain WELLS O. PETTIT, Irish Bend and Port Hudson — wounded.
First-Lieutenant DUNCAN RICHMOND, Port Hudson.
Sergeant WILLIAM J. KENNEDY, Irish Bend — wounded.
Private ANDREW CANONIER, Irish Bend and Port Hudson.

Company I.

First-Sergeant MARK BAKER, Irish Bend — killed.
Sergeant THEODORE BOHRER, Irish Bend — killed.
Corporal WILLIAM H. HAWS, Irish Bend — killed.
Sergeant C. V. R. COVENTRY, Irish Bend and Port Hudson.
Private JAMES BRAZIER, Jr., Irish Bend and Port Hudson.
    " JOSEPH O. REED, Irish Bend — wounded.

Company K.

First-Lieutenant WILLIAM R. PLUNKETT, Irish Bend — killed.
Second-Lieutenant CHARLES P. PRICE, Irish Bend — killed.
First-Sergeant THOMAS BERGEN, Irish Bend and Port Hudson.
Corporal FRANCIS L. VANDERGAW, Port Hudson — wounded.
    " JOHN DAY, Irish Bend and Port Hudson — wounded.
Private JAMES CLOSE, Irish Bend and Port Hudson.
    " ALEX. TRUMBULL, Irish Bend and Port Hudson — killed.

The following volunteered for the FORLORN HOPE, upon the call of Major-General N. P. Banks:

Captain ROBERT McD. HART, Company F.
First-Lieutenant DUNCAN RICHMOND, Company H.
Second-Lieutenant ALFRED GREENLEAF, Jr., Company B.
Sergeant MICHAEL HOGAN, Company C.
    " JAMES T. PERKINS, Company E.
    " GILBERT S. GULLEN, Company F.
    " THOMAS BERGEN, Company K.
Corporal EDGAR HOLLENBECK, Company C.
Private CHRISTIAN SCHNACK, Company C.
    " JOHN THORP, Company E.
    " HUGH McELRAVEY, Company B.
    " AMOS HARK, Company B.
    " GEORGE W. HATFIELD, Company B.
      JOHN TAYLOR, Company B.

Private BARTHOLOMEW DOSER, Company B.
" JAMES BRAZIER, Company I.
GEORGE W. SCHOFIELD, Company I.
By command of
EDWARD L. MOLINEUX,
Colonel commanding 159th N. Y. S. V.
Lieutenant HERMAN SMITH, *Acting Adjutant.*

August 25th First-Lieutenant Henry M. Howard, Company F, was transferred to Company D, to take command, Captain Hatry, Company D, being under arrest awaiting court-martial. August 26th Colonel E. G. Beckwith assumed command of the division and defenses of New Orleans, Brigadier-General Emory having taken the field.

The weather being intensely hot and sultry, duties were made as light as possible, only those actually necessary being performed. We remained in Camp Kearny until August 29th, when our brigade, Colonel Birge in command, was ordered to garrison the district west of the Mississippi extending to Brashear City, the Second Brigade of our division with the artillery remaining at New Orleans. We were ferried over the river on the transport *Laurel Hill* to Algiers, directly opposite New Orleans, September 1st, where we took the cars and arrived at Terrebonne from which we marched three miles to Thibodeaux (fifty-five miles west of New Orleans), the headquarters of the district, the same day. The Thirteenth Connecticut and our regiment were assigned to garrison the town and do provost and picket duty, the other regiments being stationed at Brashear City and distributed through the district to cover and guard the railroad and crossings at the bridges over the bayous.

We were encamped just outside the town on Madame Guion's plantation, to the left of the Thirteenth Connecticut whose right extended to the Bayou La Fourche. We were

CAMP LIFE AT THIBODEAUX.

well situated and the men made their tents as comfortable as possible, raising them about two feet by a double row of boards as a foundation, and covering the ground with boards also. This gave room for raised bunks, which were more satisfactory than sleeping on the flooring. September 9th our chaplain, Isaac L. Kipp, resigned. September 24th, by S. O. 239, Colonel Molineux was detailed to the staff of Major-General Franklin commanding the forces in the field, as acting assistant Inspector-General, and September 27th Lieutenant-Colonel Burt assumed command of the regiment.

The duties of officers and men were very severe at first as there were many details made for guard and picket duty, some of the officers going on duty every other day, there being only four captains and five lieutenants present for duty. The time was employed in company and regimental drill and the men attained a high state of proficiency. Company inspection was held every Sunday morning, and it was rigidly required that arms and accoutrements should be in perfect order, clothing clean and in good repair, and the tents and company streets, as well as the parade, neatly kept. Guard mounting and dress parade were held daily, in both of which the men took the greatest pride and endeavored to appear to the best advantage. Our drum corps was most thoroughly drilled by Drum-Major Dayton assisted by Drum-Sergeant Dunham, and under their able supervision, with constant daily practice, became very proficient and was superior to any other in the department. October 8th, by S. O. 252, our brigade and the troops in the District of La Fourche were made a separate command under Brigadier-General Birge, who had received his well-merited promotion in September. October 9th Lieutenant-Colonel Burt assumed command of the district and Captain Hatry that of the regiment during the temporary absence of Brigadier-General Birge, which they retained until October

30th when he returned from New Orleans. October 10th Second-Lieutenant Alfred Greenleaf, Jr., Company B, was detached to the Second Louisiana Cavalry.

November 2d our surgeon, Charles A. Robertson, resigned. Colonel Molineux was appointed acting provost-marshal-general of all the forces in the field under command of Major-General Franklin, on whose staff he was serving as acting assistant inspector-general. November 3d Lieutenant George R. Herbert, Company H, acting signal-officer with Franklin's forces in the front, was captured at Carrion Crow Bayou. November 4th Martin Garner, Company C, who was with Colonel Molineux as orderly, was captured near Carrion Crow Bayou, together with a gray horse belonging to the colonel. November 10th Hospital-Steward Alfred H. S. Moore was discharged for disability. November 16th Captain Joseph A. Hatry, Company D, was dismissed the service by sentence of court-martial. November 20th Private Edward E. Baker, Company B, was promoted Hospital-Steward. The regiment was visited by Colonel Molineux on his way from the front to New Orleans.

November 26th was observed as Thanksgiving Day, there being relief from duty as far as possible and extra meals when they could be obtained. Our comrades of the Thirteenth Connecticut celebrated the day in good old New England style, the officers having a dinner where roast turkey and pumpkin pie were not wanting, and the men had blindfold and sack races, climbing a greased pole, chasing a greased pig, and other sports, in all of which our regiment was most cordially invited to participate.

December 2d First Assistant-Surgeon William Y. Provost was promoted Surgeon; December 5th Quartermaster Mark D. Wilber resigned. December 7th First-Lieutenant John W. Shields, Company I, was cashiered by sentence of court-martial. December 18th Charles H. Brundage, a private of the Seventh New York Heavy Artillery, commissioned Second-Lieutenant, joined the regiment and was assigned to Company K. December 22d Colonel Molineux was appointed commissioner for Major-General Banks to meet a commissioner for Major-General Taylor to arrange for exchange of prisoners. December 24 First-Lieutenant Julius H. Tiemann, Company B, who had been serving as acting aide on the staff of Brigadier-General Birge resigned and was discharged. December 25th Lieutenant George R. Herbert and Martin Garner were exchanged under the auspices of Colonel Molineux acting as commissioner for Major-General Franklin.

Christmas was observed as a holiday, the men being granted freedom from drills. December 26th William Prince was commissioned First-Lieutenant from civil life and was placed on the rolls of Company I. December 29th Colonel Molineux was relieved from the staff of Major-General Franklin and January 3d, 1864, assumed command of the district relieving Brigadier-General Birge who had been granted a furlough. The winter had been a very severe one, there having been several heavy frosts. January 4th a cold sleety rain fell day and night, and January 7th there was quite a snow fall, something very notable in the warm section we were supposed to be in.

January 7th Lieutenant-Colonel Charles A. Burt resigned on surgeon's certificate and Captain Hart took command of the regiment. January 10th Major Edward L. Gaul was promoted Lieutenant-Colonel. January 15th Captain Charles Lewis, Company C, was promoted Major of the One Hundred and Seventy-sixth New York and transferred, and Second-Lieutenant Herman Smith, Company G, was transferred to Company C. January 25th Quartermaster-Sergeant John H. Charlotte was promoted First-Lieutenant and Regimental Quartermaster. Corporal William A. Jaquins, Company C, was promoted Quartermaster-Sergeant. January 28th Principal Musician John W. Mambert, fifer, was reduced to the ranks and returned to Company G, and Musician Thomas B. Miller, Company A, was promoted First Principal Musician. February 3rd Second-Lieutenant Lambert Dingman, Company I, was discharged. February 10th Captain Charles C. Baker, Company I, was promoted Major of the Thirty-ninth New York ("Garibaldi Guards") and transferred. February 12th First-Lieutenant Crawford Williams, Company C, who had been on the staff of Colonel E. G. Beckwith and later on that of Major-General J. J. Reynolds as acting assistant-commissary subsistence was discharged. February 17th a political mass-meeting was held in the town at which addresses were made by Hon. Michael Hahn, Free State candidate for governor, and others, relieving the usual monotony of garrison duty by the excitement occasioned. February 20th First-Lieutenant Duncan Richmond, Company H, was promoted Captain Company K. February 23rd First-Lieutenant William F. Tiemann, Company A, was promoted Captain Company A. February 24th Bazillai Ransom, Sergeant Company B, and Color-Sergeant, who had distinguished himself at Irish Bend, was commissioned Second-Lieutenant but was not mustered and was discharged. Sergeant Andrew Rifenburgh, Company G, was promoted Second-Lieutenant Company G. February 25th Captain William Waltermire, Company E, was promoted Major and assumed command of the regiment.

March 2d, at New Orleans, before the Provost Court, ten men of our regiment were convicted charged with going on a plantation, breaking negro cabins, violating women, stealing money, clothing, and between 200 and 300 pounds of sugar, and were sentenced to Tortugas, one for life at hard labor with ball and chain, one for ten years at hard labor, and the remaining eight for three years. March 7th a brigade of cavalry under Colonel N. A. M. Dudley marched through the town on their way to the Red River. This and other indications led us to suppose that our own stay would not be much longer. March 12th Major Waltermire was relieved of the command of our regiment by Lieutenant-Colonel Gaul who returned that day having been absent on detached service in Albany, N. Y., since February, 1863. The same day a new company of 92 enlisted men, mostly veterans of the Fourteenth New York Volunteers, and 3 officers, Captain James S. Reynolds, who had been Second-Lieutenant in the Fourteenth New York Volunteers, First-Lieutenant E. Spencer Elmer, who had been Sergeant in Company K in the Fourteenth New York Volunteers, and Second-Lieutenant Peter R. Van Deusen, also joined the regiment and was designated " G ", the men remaining of old Company G being transferred to the other companies. First-Lieutenant George W. Hussey was transferred to Company B and Second-Lieutenant Andrew Rifenburgh to Company E.

CHAPTER IX.

Leave Thibodeaux, La.—Alexandria, La.—Red River Campaign.

MARCH 13th Brigadier-General Cuvier Grover, having been appointed to the command, arrived in Thibodeaux for the purpose of reorganizing the forces, his division, by S. O. 41, February 15th, 1864, being constituted the SECOND, and the brigade, by G. O. No. 1, the SECOND, comprising the One Hundred and Fifty-ninth New York, One Hundred and Thirty-first New York, Ninetieth New York, Thirteenth Connecticut, and First Louisiana, to be commanded by Brigadier-General H. W. Birge; and our regiment was thereafter until the close of the war part of the Second Brigade, Second Division, Nineteenth Army Corps. March 15th marching orders were received and everything was at once prepared for a move. March 19th Sergeant-Major Marshall A. Dunham was discharged for promotion having been commissioned First-Lieutenant, U. S. C. T.

March 19th we broke camp, marched at 6 p. m. to Terrebonne station three miles, and after much delay, owing to the inefficiency of the transportation, took the cars March 21st, reaching Algiers opposite New Orleans the same day, and March 24th were embarked on the transport steamer *James Battell*, sailing up the Mississippi and Red Rivers, and arriving at Alexandria, La., March 27th, where we disembarked and went into camp above the town just beyond the Bayou Rapides. The town is located on the south or right bank of the Red River two hundred miles from the mouth, one hundred and seventy miles in a direct line and three hundred and sixty miles by water northeast of New Orleans. It is two hundred and twenty-eight miles by rail from New Orleans. April 1st, with the other regiments of the brigade, we were drawn in nearer the town across the bayou. April 4th Brigadier-General Birge having returned assumed command of the brigade, relieving Colonel Molineux, who was thereupon detailed to organize the State troops, natives of Louisiana, numbers of whom were enlisting to support the cause of the Union. April 7th a very heavy rain fell. April 9th Captain Robert McD. Hart, Company F, was detached to serve as Ordnance Officer on the staff of Brigadier-General Grover. Sergeant William E. Palmer, Company D, was promoted Sergeant-Major. April 9th Second-Lieutenant Charles H. Brundage, Company K, who had been with the regiment only about four months, was cashiered by sentence court-martial. We had at this time only nine officers in all present for duty with the regiment.

The main army moved on towards Shreveport, leaving our division under Brigadier-General Grover to garrison and guard Alexandria which was held as a depot for supplies. April 11th part of our brigade was sent up the river on transports, and April 14th the remainder of our division was ordered to the front, Brigadier-General Grover accompanying it in command, leaving our regiment, with a squadron of cavalry and battery of artillery and the State troops, all under Colonel Molineux, to protect the stores which were in Alexandria. As the country was infested with "Guerrillas," or "Partisan Rangers," as the freebooting rebels were termed who owned to no allegiance to any disciplined body, we were liable to an attack at any moment and the utmost vigilance was necessary, so we were drawn into the town, throwing up breastworks and barricading the streets as well as our small force would permit, while the cavalry and State troops, who were mounted, were posted to cover all approaches and give due warning of any appearance of the rebels. There were also two gunboats in the river so placed as to cover the town and its approaches. Fortunately, though unexpectedly, this lasted but one day as April 15th part of our division reinforced us. April 18th First-Sergeant Christopher Branch, Company F, was promoted First-Lieutenant Company F. April 23d was wet and unpleasant with frequent heavy showers. April 24th Colonel Molineux resumed command of the regiment and orders were issued to prepare for a march which, however, were countermanded. April 26th the remainder of our division, with the main army, returned to Alexandria. Success had not crowned the attempt on Shreveport; it resulted in complete failure.

On April 7th the advance had met and driven a small force at Pleasant Hill. April 8th our cavalry under Brigadier-General A. L. Lee supported by Colonel Landram's brigade, Fourth Division Thirteenth Corps, and later by two other brigades of the same corps under Brigadier-General Ransom, met and drove the enemy to Sabine Crossroads where the main body of the rebels was met and our troops were obliged to retreat. The road being obstructed by the supply-train of our cavalry it was impossible to withdraw all the artillery, and many pieces with over one hundred and fifty wagons and some eight hundred men fell into the hands of the rebels, who pursued our retreating forces sharply three miles until met at Pleasant Grove by Emory's First Division Nineteenth Corps when the rebels were repulsed with severe loss and our army fell back to Pleasant Hill fifteen miles. April 9th the rebels attacked our force at Pleasant Hill, the First Division Nineteenth Corps, with a brigade of the Sixteenth Corps, supported by the remainder of the Sixteenth Corps, sustaining the attack which was very severe, repulsing the rebels handsomely and driving them until nightfall. Our army then fell back to Grand Ecore and from there to Cane River, where the rebels were strongly posted, which they reached April 23d, and an attack was made by a force comprising two brigades of the Nineteenth Corps with two divisions of the Thirteenth Corps, led by Brigadier-General Birge, who assaulted the position held by the rebels and drove them from it, thus securing the safe passage of our army which then continued the retreat until Alexandria was reached. In the meanwhile the gunboats, which had gone up Red River in support of the army, returned, but owing to the falling of the water in the river were unable to pass the rapids.

April 28th the whole army was drawn up in line of battle in two lines, the Nineteenth Corps on the inner one, our brigade near the center. We stood nearly the whole day expecting an attack but none was made. At night we saw the flames from a sugar-house about a mile from the town, which was burned by the rebels who were passing around us with the evident intention of endeavoring to cut off our retreat down the river or to prevent supplies from reaching us.

April 29th, just after dark, our regiment with the Thirteenth Connecticut, First Louisiana, a squadron of cavalry, and section of artillery, under Colonel Molineux, was crossed on a pontoon bridge and camped in Pineville, opposite Alexandria, on the left bank of the river, to cover and support the workers on a dam which Lieutenant-Colonel Joseph Bailey, Fourth Wisconsin, on Major-General Franklin's staff, undertook to build to raise the water sufficiently for the gunboats to pass the rapids. April 30th Colonel Molineux was placed in command of the brigade, relieving Brigadier-General Birge who was to command the post at Baton Rouge, and Lieutenant-Colonel Gaul assumed command of the regiment. We occupied a position to the right of the main road with a section of artillery on our left, the Thirteenth Connecticut and First Louisiana being on the left of the road. Breastworks were thrown up by our brigade and we stood under arms for an hour each morning just before light to be in readiness for any attack, as it was expected the rebels would attempt to defeat the undertaking and capture the gunboats. May 2d Second-Lieutenant Alfred Greenleaf, Jr., Company B, was discharged. May 4th heavy firing was heard on the right bank above the town. May 5th we heard heavy musketry and artillery firing down the river, and later learned that a large force of rebels with several batteries had established themselves at Dunn's Bayou thirty miles below Alexandria where they attacked the transport *John Warner*, loaded with cotton and with about four hundred men on board, convoyed by two small gunboats — *Signal* and *Covington*. They had disabled the *Warner*, and the two gunboats being also disabled the *Covington* was set fire to and blown up by her commander, while the *Signal* fell into the hands of the rebels who sunk her across the channel as an obstruction.

Although doubt was expressed as to its feasibility the dam was a success. Two wings were constructed, one from either shore, towards the centre of the river. From our side, the left bank, it was built of logs and large trees with the limbs closely packed down, and from the right bank with large crates filled with stones, and at the end of this wing several scows were filled with brick, stones and iron, obtained from sugar-houses in the vicinity which were torn down for the purpose, and sunk. May 9th the pressure of water was so great that two of the scows were forced from their position and swung in below the dam. The gunboats *Lexington*, *Neosho*, *Hindman*, and *Osage* passed through safely though it was a most exciting scene, the water rushing through the break like a boiling torrent, and the first two vessels were almost entirely submerged. As they righted themselves and floated into deep water below the rapids the whole army joined in shouts and cheers, and many were the words of praise spoken of Lieutenant-Colonel Bailey who had planned and superintended the construction of the dam. The water fell too rapidly to get the other boats over but several smaller dams were constructed above which raised the river sufficiently, and May 12th the *Mound City*, *Carondelet* and *Pittsburgh*, followed on the 13th by the *Louisville*, *Chillicothe*, *Ozark*, and two tugs, passed in safety.

CHAPTER X.

Leave Alexandria, Louisiana — Marksville, Louisiana — Mansura Plains, Louisiana — Arrival at Morganza, Louisiana.

MAY 2d Brigadier-General William H. Emory was appointed to the command of the Nineteenth Army Corps, which he assumed the same day. May 11th at 2 a.m. we were roused by firing, the rebels having made an attack on our cavalry pickets but they did not follow it up. We stood under arms until 6 a. m. when we crossed the river on the pontoon bridge, and having sent all our baggage on board the transports commenced our march from Alexandria by the road running parallel with the river on the right bank. We were in the advance, following directly behind our cavalry. The weather was very hot. After marching nine miles we were ordered back four miles by Brigadier-General Grover as the rest of the army was not ready to move. May 12th at 3 a. m. we were aroused quietly and stood under arms in line of battle until daybreak. At 7 p. m. we were startled by the long-roll, our cavalry picket having discovered a rebel regiment forming line. We quickly fell in and stood under arms two hours, and then as no attack was made though some shots were fired in the front we went back to our quarters. May 13th we broke camp and started on our march at 8 a. m., making nine miles. May 14th we marched at 6 a. m. We were passed by the transports and gunboats which had left Alexandria early that morning. They reported that the whole town had been destroyed by our forces. The weather was extremely hot. We marched fifteen miles that day, reaching the point where the rebels had attacked the *John Warner* and gunboats. The ground was covered with letters from the mail captured on the *Warner*. Camp fires not yet extinguished indicated the rebels were in close proximity. Our regiment was detailed as pickets and stationed about a mile from the river. May 15th at 8 a. m. we resumed our march and after going five miles were halted at Bayou Choctaw to permit the laying over of a pontoon bridge which delayed us an hour. We then moved on three miles through a heavy woods and came out on an open plain where at 3 p. m. the rebels formed line of battle to oppose our further progress, and our division was at once advanced, our brigade in front, in support of our cavalry which had been skirmishing with the rebels since early morning. As we came into the open they made a splendid charge and the rebels left in a hurry. We were suffering greatly as the heat was almost insupportable and water very scarce. We again took up our line of march and after going four miles were halted, as we supposed for the night, and the men commenced cooking their suppers but had hardly done so when we heard the call from Colonel Molineux, "Fall in, Second Brigade," "Hurry," "Hurry," which was taken up and repeated by the officers. Instantly the camp kettles and cups were emptied, the men hastily fell in and the order came, "By the right flank! Double quick! March!" and, our regiment in front, we went on a run through Marksville (which is three miles south of Red River and thirty-five miles southeast of Alexandria) near which we had halted, and passing the town two miles were filed to the right on an open plain and faced in line just to the rear of our cavalry which were heavily engaged and had lost some ground which they at once regained with our support; and after shelling us for several hours the rebels withdrew. A drove of hogs crossing our front suffered severely from the charge which was made on it the instant we had orders to break ranks. Fires were soon made, and after refreshing themselves with coffee and roast pork the men were soon enjoying their well-earned rest. We remained in the front all night, sleeping in line on our arms. We lost two men, Abner Staunton, Company D, and George W. Schofield, Company I, missing. Staunton died October 28, 1864, in Camp Tyler, Texas.

May 16th the rest of the army came up, and our brigade in advance, forming line of battle as the enemy were in strong force in our front, we marched over fences, through cane and corn fields for four miles when we came to Mansura Plains, seven miles south of Marksville, where the rebels made another stand, and as we approached opened on us with artillery. On a vast prairie, miles in extent, our whole army was drawn up in echelon of brigades, our brigade the left of the Nineteenth Corps in advance as the brigade of direction, the other brigades of the corps with those of the Thirteenth and Sixteenth Corps to our right and rear, the cavalry to the front, and on our flanks in the intervals the batteries, many of them hidden by the smoke from their rapid discharges; and a more glorious spectacle could not be imagined. As far as the eye could see, troops marching and taking position, cannon booming, flags flying, and the glistening of the rifles in the bright sunlight, with the soldierly bearing of the men, the charging of the cavalry, and the dashing into position of the artillery, while opposite were also the enemy in line in clear view, made a sight not often seen in a lifetime and never to be forgotten. It was grand to look along the lines and see the brigades in position with their commanders just to the rear surrounded by the staff, and to see the same with divisions and corps. Brigadier-General Grover came dashing to the front with a section of artillery, the horses at full gallop; they quickly wheeled into position which he indicated as he sat his horse

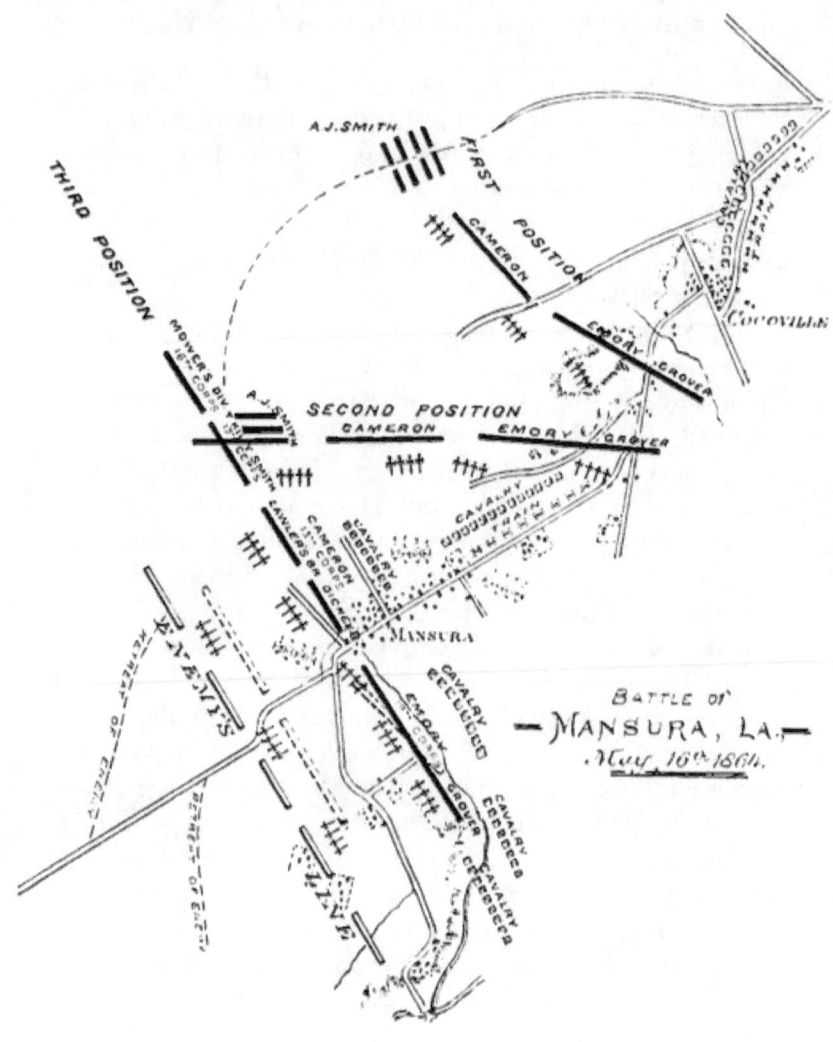

looking through his field-glasses at the enemy in our front, unlimbered, and in a moment opened on the rebels. After an artillery duel lasting nearly three hours our division was ordered in, but the enemy did not wait for us and almost immediately broke and commenced a rapid retreat. We hurried after them about four miles when, further pursuit being useless as they had succeeded in making good their escape, we were halted at Bayou Rouge. Resuming our march later we arrived at Bayou de Glaise, about eight miles from Simmsport, where we camped for the night. May 17th, marching at 7 a. m., we arrived opposite Simmsport, where we had been just a year before to a day, at 12 m., and there we were met by Major-General E. R. S. Canby who had as we understood taken command of the department by a general order issued May 11th.

May 18th at noon we were ferried over the Atchafalaya by transports, while the artillery, cavalry, and wagons crossed on an extraordinary and novel bridge, suggested by Lieutenant-Colonel Bailey, who had built the dam, made by placing the transport steamers side by side, and went in camp on the Semmes plantation, in Simmsport, in the same location we had occupied the year before. At 11 p. m., just after getting asleep, there was an alarm; we broke camp and marched three miles up the river where we went into camp again, but had hardly turned in when, May 19th, at 4 a. m., we were marched back to the crossing for the purpose of moving over to the support of Major-General A. J. Smith, Sixteenth Corps, who had been engaged on the 18th at Yellow Bayou, three miles from Simmsport, and had defeated the rebels. Our assistance was not needed as the rebels had retreated, and we were marched back up the river again six miles and went into camp. The fields were full of blackberries which the men gathered in bushels. May 20th at 6 p. m. we were started off and marched eleven miles halting at midnight. May 21st we were roused at 4 a. m. having had but four hours' rest, but did not start until 8 a. m. and were then marched twenty miles. It was terribly hot and several men were sunstruck. The dust which was ankle-deep rose in clouds at every step, and as the road was bordered much of the way on both sides with high bushes, preventing any circulation of air, it was almost impossible to breathe. The surgeons representing to Brigadier-General Grover that the men could not endure the fatigue in such heat, we were halted from 12 m. to 3. p. m. before resuming the march. May 21st First-Lieutenant George W. Hussey, Company B, was detached as A.A.D.C. on the brigade staff. May 22d we marched four miles starting at 4 a. m. and went into camp between the levee and river at Morganza Bend, on the west bank of the Mississippi fifty-one miles above Baton Rouge. As we came in sight of the river, tired and footsore though we were, the men broke out in loud cheers, and as soon as camp was made enjoyed a bath in its cool and refreshing waters. We here received a mail, the first for many days, and several recruits reported to the regiment. May 23d, Sergeant Edward Duffy, Company I, was promoted First-Lieutenant Company A. May 24th we had a slight shower which only served to intensify the heat. May 29th orders were received to be in readiness to move at a moment's notice, it being rumored that Taylor's forces had crossed the Atchafalaya and were about to attack Plaquemine just below Baton Rouge, but the report proved false and the orders were rescinded. June 1st Colonel Molineux, who was quite ill, went to New Orleans. June 2d Lieutenant-Colonel Edward L. Gaul was discharged, Major William Waltermire was promoted Lieutenant-Colonel, and Captain Robert McD. Hart, Company F, was promoted Major. June 2d with the Thirteenth Connecticut and First Louisiana we moved camp, the one we were in being a heavy sand-bank and the wagons made so much dust in passing over the road adjoining it that it was almost insupportable. It was a pleasant move. We encamped two miles below our old camp, in a charming spot, shady and cool, between the levee and river in a grove of young cottonwood trees. We thinned out the trees, cutting those in the company streets close to the ground, leaving stumps where the tents were to go of about five feet high, on which were erected the "dog tents," as the canvas shelter under which two men could barely crawl was called, and inside these were left shorter stumps on which the men erected bunks about two feet from the ground. This proved a good arrangement, as the next day and for ten successive days we had repeated and heavy showers with most terrific lightning and thunder. During one severe shower the water rose almost to the bunks, on which the men mounted for protection. Being so shady it took long to dry, and regular rations of whisky and quinine were issued by order of the surgeon. Our first camp had been all dust and this seemed destined to be all mud, but we infinitely preferred the latter, and when the rain was over were very comfortable. The weather being extremely hot but little drilling was done, but the daily details from the regiment for picket duty were heavy. At this time we had but five line officers for duty with the regiment, two of those present being on the sick list. June 8th, the Fourteenth New Hampshire, a new regiment seven hundred and fifty strong, arrived and were attached to the brigade, their Colonel, Robert Wilson, assuming command of the brigade by right of seniority. They were a fine looking body of men and in their clean new clothes presented a sharp contrast to us in our old, well-worn and rather dilapidated uniforms.

June 10th, Second-Lieutenant Andrew Rifenburgh, Company E, was promoted First-Lieutenant, Company E. June

11th at 4 p. m. the corps was reviewed by Major-General W. H. Emory. It was clear when we left camp but the rain fell in torrents just as the review began and every one was drenched. It ceased raining just as the review was over, while we were on our way back to camp. June 14th, another review of all the troops at Morganza was held by Major-General D. E. Sickles. The day was beautiful but intensely hot. June 15th, Joseph G. McNutt, commissioned Captain from civil life, joined the regiment and was assigned to the command of Company I. June 16th, the regiment was inspected by the Corps Inspector and highly complimented on the condition of the arms and accoutrements, the drill and general appearance of the men, Companies A and F being specially mentioned as the finest looking in every way the Inspector had seen in the whole corps. June 19th we received orders to prepare rations for ten days. The same night at 10 o'clock we embarked on the transport *Ohio Belle* with the Thirteenth Connecticut and a detachment of cavalry, and after a long delay caused in getting the rest of the division on other transports we finally started June 20th at 3 a. m.

The force numbered about five thousand infantry, five hundred cavalry, and four pieces of artillery, all under command of Brigadier-General Grover, and was sent to explore the river above us, it being reported the rebels had begun planting a battery there to obstruct navigation. We sailed up the river to Tunica Bend, fifteen miles above Morganza, on the east bank, where the cavalry and several regiments of infantry were landed and after a reconnaissance of fifteen miles returned with three prisoners. The troops reembarked at sundown and we steamed up the river again, arriving at Fort Adams, Mississippi, fifty-nine miles above Morganza, on the east bank, June 21st at 6 a. m. The troops were all disembarked and the cavalry went off on a scout, returning in the afternoon without having seen any rebels in the vicinity. The country at this place was beautiful, hilly with thick woods, a great contrast to Louisiana where everything was perfectly flat and level. Near by was a high hill on which had stood the old fort from which the place is named, from the top of which it was said the country could be seen for fifty miles around. We reëmbarked during the afternoon, and returning reached Morganza at 9 o'clock the same night. June 26th the Ninetieth New York and Fourteenth New Hampshire were transferred to another brigade, and the Third Massachusetts Cavalry (dismounted) attached to ours, Colonel Molineux resuming command July 5th.

CHAPTER XI.

Leave Morganza, La.—Presentation of Colors—Leave Louisiana for Virginia—Arrival at Bermuda Hundreds, Va., and Washington, D. C.—Our Bear.

JULY 2d at 10 p. m. the regiment broke camp, embarked on the transport *Lancaster, No. 4,* sailed down the river at 3 a. m. July 3d, and stopping at Port Hudson and Baton Rouge on the way arrived at Algiers July 4th at 6 p. m. after a very hot and tedious voyage, the steamer being crowded with troops and baggage. There was a brisk shower during the afternoon, the first for over three weeks. Landing that night we were quartered in the Belvidere Iron Foundry and the field adjoining. July 7th was almost unbearable, the heat was so intense.

July 8th a most interesting and pleasant event occurred, the reception of a stand of colors comprising the State and national flags, the latter inscribed "Irish Bend, La., April 14, 1863," "Port Hudson, La., May 25, June 14, 1863," and two guidons with the figures "159"—the whole of silk with heavy gold fringe—which had been presented to Colonel Molineux by the Twenty-third Regiment National Guard, of Brooklyn, together with a beautiful sword and equipments. The regiment was paraded, and in a few fitting and well-chosen words Colonel Molineux transferred the colors to the care and custody of the regiment. Immediately after the parade the officers met and drew up the letter shown in the following correspondence :

BROOKLYN, June 24, 1864.

Colonel EDWARD L. MOLINEUX, *159th Regiment N. Y. V.*, New Orleans.

Dear Sir: It becomes my privilege, as President of the Council of Officers of the Twenty-third Regiment, N. G. S. N. Y., to convey to you the expression of regard and honor for yourself, as a patriot and soldier, which this regiment has recently caused to be prepared for your acceptance.

With this will be forwarded a sword and equipments, together with a full stand of regimental colors, which I beg you to accept from the officers and men of the Twenty-third Regiment, your friends and former associates. The sword you will worthily wear in the cause of liberty and the defense of our beloved country. The colors will be safely borne, wherever duty may call, by the gallant command in whose honor they are inscribed with the names of battle-fields already won.

It would be a needless task to speak of the duty of the hour to soldiers in the field, whose deeds already attest their valor and devotion, but it is our hope that these gifts may help inspire them to future achievement, reminding them that the hearts of their countrymen at home are with them, that we are proud of their courage and their victories, and that we are not unmindful of our duty to encourage and sustain them to the end in their glorious work.

May the triumphant day soon come, when all shall rejoice in liberty, peace, and a reunited country — the recompense for these years of war and sacrifice.

Accept the good wishes of all the members of the Twenty-third Regiment, and the assurance of my personal esteem.

Yours very truly,
(Signed) JAMES H. FROTHINGHAM,
President of the Council, Twenty-third Regiment, N. G.

HEADQUARTERS
ONE HUNDRED AND FIFTY-NINTH REGIMENT, N. Y. S. V.
ALGIERS, LA., July 8, 1864.

JAMES H. FROTHINGHAM, Esq., President of the Council, Twenty-third Regiment, N. G.

Dear Sir: We have, this day, received from Colonel E. L. Molineux the beautiful stand of colors presented to him by the members of the Twenty-third Regiment, N. G.

When these elegant emblems of State and Country were unfurled to our view we felt indeed imbued with fresh patriotism, and, as a gift of a regiment which has already given its services to the country in time of need, we prize them still more highly.

It is not for us to speak of the inscriptions that were kindly placed thereon, but we will surely always endeavor to carry these colors to the point where they are ordered, and do it in such manner that it will not bring discredit either upon the givers or recipients.

We certainly feel inspired by this spirit which is shown us at home, and whenever we look upon these beautiful emblems we will think of our country and the kind friends who are ever watchful of our interests.

We join you most heartily in wishing that the day may soon come when we shall be permitted to again return to our peaceful vocations and with a united country.

Although we may regret the loss of dear friends, noble fellows who have fallen in this cause, yet the result will more than pay us for three years of war and sacrifice.

Allow us to thank the members for their beautiful present, trusting that they never will regret placing it in the keeping of the One Hundred and Fifty-ninth New York Volunteers.

We have the honor to be,
Your most humble servants,
(Signed) WILLIAM WALTERMIRE, *Lieutenant-Colonel,*
WILLIAM F. TIEMANN, *Captain,*
WILLIAM Y. PROVOST, *Surgeon,*
HERMAN SMITH, *Lieutenant and A.A., in behalf of the Regiment.*

HEADQUARTERS SECOND DIVISION, 19TH A. C.
U. S. Transport *Cahawba*, at Sea, July 20, 1864.

JAMES H. FROTHINGHAM, Esq., President of the Council, Twenty-third Regiment, N. G., S. of N. Y.

Dear Sir: I find some difficulty in expressing to you, the representative of the members of the Twenty-third Regiment, my feelings of gratitude for the elegant testimonial of friendship and regard which my old comrades have, in their kindness, presented to me.

However unworthy of such honor I feel myself to be, I can still assure you that it will prove an additional inducement to me, as a soldier, to prove worthy of such friendship. Devoted as we all may be to the interests of our beloved country, willing as we may be to suffer for the cause, yet nothing can warm our hearts more, or cheer us along in the discharge of arduous duties, than the knowledge that friends and comrades at home feel interested in our progress and fate, and a token of THEIR regard is doubly welcome, especially when it comes in such appropriate shape as that sent by you.

I can fully assure you that the splendid stand of colors will be nobly and bravely carried by the One Hundred and Fifty-ninth Regiment, and I sincerely pray to God that strength may be given me in every trial to be worthy of your sword and your esteem.

Uniting with you in the hope that the day may not be far distant when PEACE, honorable and permanent, may again shine over a united land,

I am your friend and comrade,

EDWARD L. MOLINEUX,
Colonel One Hundred and Fifty-ninth N. Y. V., Commanding.

These colors were carried by the regiment through all our succeeding campaigns and battles until our muster out of service, when the fragments, shot torn and riddled, were returned to Colonel Molineux.

July 15th was the hottest day we experienced in Louisiana. July 17th, Second-Lieutenant Peter Van Deusen, Company G, was discharged. The weather was intensely hot, and the city of New Orleans so near, being just across the river, that the men had a constant supply of rum, which did not serve to make them cool. On the contrary, rows were numerous, in one of which one man had a bayonet run through his arm, and our Assistant-Surgeon Briggs distinguished himself by knocking over one of the biggest and heaviest men in the regiment, who was drunk and disorderly and ventured some ill-timed remarks in relation to "pills!"

After waiting two weeks, July 17th at 8 p. m. we marched to the levee and were embarked on the steamer *Cahawba* with all our regimental property. Colonel Molineux and staff were on board, the steamer being headquarters of the brigade. The One Hundred and Thirty-first New York and Twenty-second Iowa were also on board. While lying at the levee we were almost devoured by the mosquitoes, which stung most venomously, seeming to realize our intended departure and wishing to make all they could out of us before we could get away. We sailed at 12 o'clock midnight, under sealed orders not to be opened for twenty-four hours after starting. Numerous guesses were hazarded as to our destination, Galveston and Mobile being the points most frequently named, but when opened we found our orders to be to proceed to Fortress Monroe and report. We were greatly crowded (1350 on board), but everything possible was done for our comfort and to keep the men contented, and there were few complaints and but little grumbling, quite a novelty when it is considered that is a soldier's principal prerogative, — at least he thinks so! We passed out of the mouth of the river, July 18th, in the evening, and July 20th passed Tortugas and Key West.

We arrived off Fortress Monroe, seventeen hundred and seventy-one miles from New Orleans, at 12 m., July 24th, after a quick passage of only six and one-half days and having had very pleasant weather. Colonel Molineux landed for orders and on his return we proceeded on and up the James River at 9 a. m., July 25th, and at 5 p. m. arrived at Bermuda Hundreds, Va., seventy-seven miles from Fortress Monroe and eighteen miles from Richmond, and disembarked immediately. It was currently reported that the Nineteenth Corps was all to be sent to Major-General B. F. Butler's command to enable him to extend his lines to the left, his forces occupying the position between the James and Appomattox Rivers with the right resting on the former. July 26th after unloading our regimental stores we moved six miles to the intrenchments in the front and were camped near Major-General Birney's headquarters, not far from Hatcher's house between batteries "five" and "six," one of which enjoyed the euphonious title of "Fort Slaughter" from its having proved so fatal to the rebels, who had made more than twenty assaults on it and had been repulsed with terrible loss each time. The defenses were breastworks of earth about seven feet high (with an inner platform of earth one foot high and two feet broad on which the men stood to deliver their fire), some five feet thick at the top and twelve or fourteen feet at the base. On top of the earthworks were sand-bags as a protection to our sharpshooters. At intervals of about two hundred and fifty yards were strong batteries numbered consecutively one, two, three, etc., in each of which were mounted ten to twelve guns, and opposite every other one, about one hundred yards in front, was thrown up a strong redoubt which was commanded by the battery in rear as well as those on either side. The works were built more strongly and with more art than those at Port Hudson but were not nearly as strong in reality, as Port Hudson was fortified naturally and the obstructions were much harder to overcome. The rebels were in strong force in our front, and the firing was incessant. The regiment was under fire in the trenches or on picket constantly, doing daily duty in one position or the other, and it seemed almost as if we must be in front of Port Hudson again. We moved camp every day during our stay which fortunately was a short one. July 27th at 3 a. m. we struck tents and at 9 a. m. marched one-half mile to the front and went in camp

July 27th at 7 a. m. we moved and camped near the bombproofs, going into the trenches at 8 p. m. July 29th at 5:30 a. m. we left the trenches and went back to camp, and at 9 a. m. struck tents and moved, camping directly behind the breastworks. July 30th at noon we struck tents and marched a mile to the left, camping a short distance back of the breastworks. We had hardly attained this position when orders came to move again, and July 31st at 2 a. m. we moved from the front, marched to the river, where we lay for two hours, and at 5 a. m. embarked on the steamer *Winona;* sailed in the afternoon, stopping at Fortress Monroe for a short time and then up Chesapeake Bay. August 1st at 6 p. m. we arrived at Washington, D. C., two hundred and sixty-one miles from Bermuda Hundreds, were at once landed, and marched up town through Pennsylvania Avenue to the "Soldiers' Rest" at the railroad depot.

One very important member of our regiment has been nearly forgotten. He had a "roll" of his own, not being on that of the regiment. During our campaign to Alexandria, La., in the spring of 1864, Governor Welles, of Louisiana, gave to Colonel Molineux, April 29th, a young bear cub, which the Colonel presented to the regiment. Bruin was placed in charge of the drum corps where he soon became a great favorite, and on the march his position was at the head of the regiment under the leadership and supervision of one of the drummers. He attracted great attention at all times, the regiment being known as the "bear regiment," or "Molineux's Bears," wherever it went, and especially so as he marched through Washington at the head of the column.

A great crowd gathered around him, in it being a very spruce and dandy darkey, and as it pressed in too closely and interfered with our march the bear's chain was let out, and the darkey, jumping aside to avoid the bear, stumbled and fell under a carriage, the wheels of which passed over him, fortunately without injury except to his clothes, and he was a most woe-begone and forlorn looking object as he limped away, the bear meanwhile plodding on perfectly unconcerned.

At the "Rest" we were provided with a bountiful supper and the men had a night's good sleep. All our baggage was loaded on the cars, and it was reported we were going to Chambersburg, Pa., which the rebels under McCausland had burned July 30th. August 2nd we were moved at 5 a. m., but instead of taking the cars were marched in column of companies up Pennsylvania Avenue past the Capitol, Treasury, and White House, and then by the flank to Tenallytown, D. C., six miles northwest of the Capitol, and camped in a beautiful spot on one of the hills which surround Washington, just within the chain of forts encircling the city. The rebel general, Early, with a large force, had crossed the Potomac and threatened the Capital, in defense of which we had been called from Bermuda Hundreds, other troops being hurriedly called from all points available for the same purpose. Finding the city too well defended for a successful attack, Early passed by, and after doing some damage in Maryland and Pennsylvania was forced back into the Shenandoah Valley.

August 5th the regiment was inspected by Major Hart, of Brigadier-General Grover's staff. August 6th we had a heavy thunder-shower, the first rain since leaving Louisiana. August 8th George B. Stayley, Sergeant in the Forty-eighth New York, promoted First-Lieutenant, joined the regiment for duty, and was assigned to Company H. August 9th we moved camp about one-quarter mile north of our old position to a high hill near Fort Gaines. The weather was intensely hot, the thermometer marking 98° in the shade during the afternoon. August 12th at 3 a. m. the regiment was detailed to cut down trees near Fort Bunker Hill, returning to camp at 5 p. m. of the 13th.

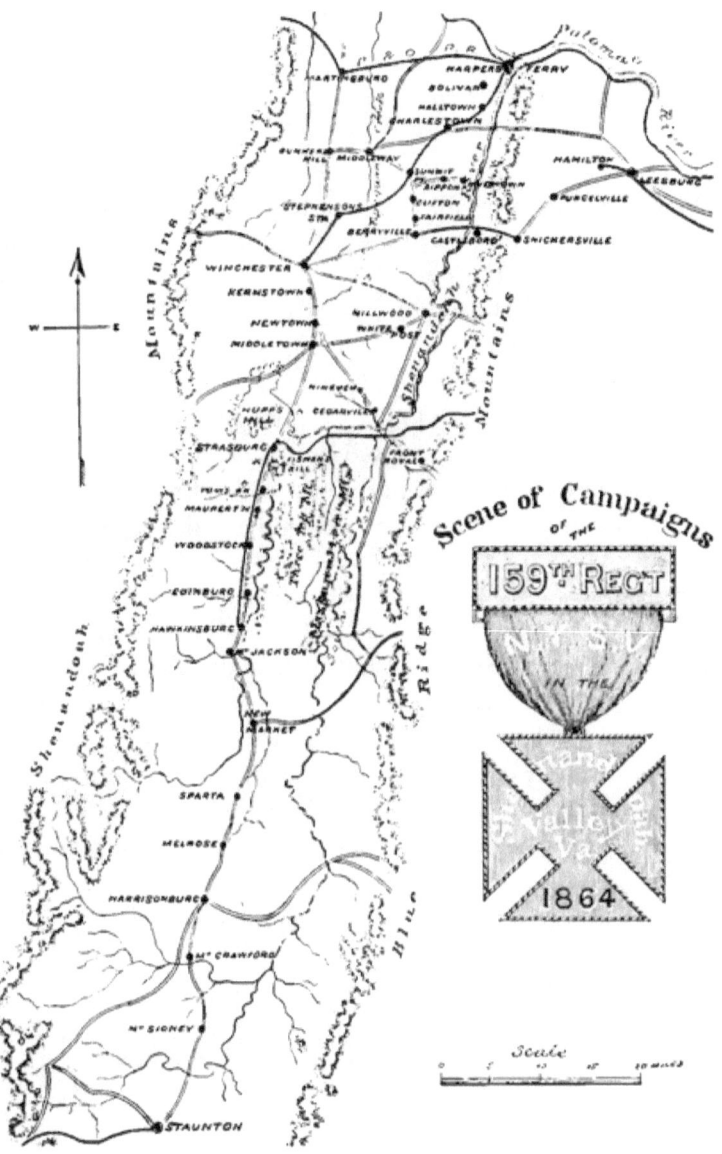

CHAPTER XII.

We join Sheridan's Command — Halltown, Virginia — Berryville, Virginia.

AUGUST 12th we received orders to move and were informed we were to join the forces under Major-General Phil. Sheridan in the Shenandoah Valley, where he was confronting the rebels under Early. Part of our corps had already joined him. August 13th, shortly after our return from the wood-cutting expedition, there was another severe thunder-storm, the rain falling in torrents.

August 14th we were roused at 1 a. m. and, getting breakfast, started over the Leesburg pike at 4 a. m. We marched nine miles to Difficult Creek, which we had to wade, camping after crossing. August 15th at 2 a. m. we moved, and at 7 a. m. passed through Drainesville, seventeen miles from Washington. Just before noon we crossed Broad Run, twenty-six miles from Washington, and camped. August 16th at 4 a. m. we resumed our march, crossing Goose Creek, four miles east of Leesburg, at 9 a. m., and arrived in Leesburg, thirty-six miles from Washington, at 12 m., going into camp a quarter-mile beyond the town. August 17th at 4 a. m. we started again, passing through Hamilton, four miles west of Leesburg, at 6 a. m., and Purcellville, fifty miles from Washington, at 10 a. m. At 10.30 a. m. we went into camp about four miles east of Snicker's Gap, but were ordered to strike camp at 5 p. m. and marched at once, reaching the Gap at 6.30 p. m. We were pressed forward as rapidly as possible, as it was reported the enemy was endeavoring to

cut us off from the Gap and prevent the junction of our
forces. At 9 p. m. we reached the Shenandoah River at
Castleborough, to cross which we had to strip off shoes,
stockings, and trousers, making the men look like a lot of
Highlanders. To add to our discomfort rain began to fall.
We reached Berryville, sixty-nine miles from Washington
and eleven miles east of Winchester, a march of thirty-three
miles in thirteen and one-half hours, actual time, at 12 p. m.,
and, footsore and weary, threw ourselves on the wet, muddy
ground without thought of blanket or covering, and were almost
instantly fast asleep, though it was raining heavily. August
18th at 5.30 a. m. we were started off without breakfast,
marching through Berryville and going four miles, where we
halted while the Sixth and Eighth Corps passed us, and were
permitted to get a mouthful to eat. Here we had a sight of
Major-General Sheridan, a short, stout, quick-moving man,
who looked as if he had determination enough for a dozen.
We liked his "general" appearance and thought he would
prove a good commander and a "man at a pinch," which, as
events proved, we were fully justified in thinking. After
the corps had passed, we marched again about four miles,
and late at night we went in camp in the woods about a
mile from the road. It had rained heavily all day and we
found it difficult to get any place to rest. August 19th we
remained in the woods, moving camp at sundown a short
distance further to the right. The day was very wet and
unpleasant. August 20th at 9 a. m. we were marched into
position, to the left of the road leading to Harper's Ferry,
about three miles south of Charlestown, where we rejoined
the rest of our brigade, which now comprised our regiment
with the One Hundred and Thirty-first New York, Third
Massachusetts Cavalry (dismounted), Eleventh Indiana, and
Twenty-second Iowa, Colonel Molineux in command, being
still the Second Brigade, Second Division, *Detachment* of the

Nineteenth Army Corps—the last designation, because part of the corps had remained in Louisiana. We also had with us a small detachment of the Thirteenth Connecticut as part of the brigade. The rain still fell and made things very unpleasant. August 21st we had regimental inspection and battalion drill. Heavy firing was heard in the direction of Summit Point, just south of us, and soon troops were moving taking position in line, as the enemy were in force and our cavalry falling back. We were posted on the crest of a hill and at once put to work throwing up breastworks. We were in line until 9.30 p. m., when we received orders to move, and at 11 p. m. marched towards Harper's Ferry, the Nineteenth Corps being in the rear covering the movement, our brigade holding the extreme rear. The rain had ceased during the early morning and the day was pleasant.

August 22d at 1.15 a. m. we marched through Charlestown, ten miles south of Harper's Ferry, memorable as the scene of the hanging of John Brown. At 3 a. m. we reached Halltown, six miles from Harper's Ferry, where we were halted and camped on the heights to the right of the village. The enemy had been following us closely. At 4 a. m. skirmishing began again, and at 5.30 a. m. we marched out of camp down the hill into an open field to the left of the road, when we deployed as skirmishers, advancing about one-quarter mile where we threw up breastworks, acting as pickets for our division. During the afternoon and night it rained heavily. We remained on the lines until 5 a. m., August 23d, when we were relieved by another regiment of our brigade and we went into camp at Halltown. August 24th during the forenoon we moved camp to the left behind breastworks. In the afternoon our regiment, with the Twenty-second Iowa and Eleventh Indiana, under command of Colonel Daniel McCauley of the latter regiment, was marched out for a reconnaissance. Reaching the picket line, which was posted in the outskirt of a wood, our regiment was deployed as skirmishers, three companies in reserve. The regiment advanced across an open field in front of the woods and was engaged almost immediately with a heavy picket line of the enemy, which was soon strongly reënforced. Our men pressed forward bravely and the roar of the musketry was almost incessant. They drove the rebels for some distance through the woods in the edge of which they had held their position, until the heavy firing showed the presence of a large force, and then orders were given to fall back. This was even more difficult than the advance, as the rebels, now in large numbers, pursued as closely and rapidly as possible; but the retreat was executed in good order, the men being very deliberate in the movement, falling back quietly with the utmost coolness, and the regiment was soon within our lines again. Captain Wells O. Pettit, Company H, was severely wounded, and nine men were wounded, two fatally. One of the wounded was captured by the rebels.

Private JAMES J. LENFESTY, Company B, mortally.
Corporal MARTIN SMALIX, Company B.
Private WILLIAM SHERMAN, Company B, prisoner.
    " CHRISTIAN SCHNACK, Company C.
Sergeant EGBERT S. COVEY, Company G.
    " FRANK W. KURTZ, Company G, mortally.
Corporal NICHOLAS R. SHULTIS, Company G.
Private RUSSELL VAN DEUSEN, Company G.
Corporal JOSEPH O. REED, Company I.

The three companies in reserve were deployed to strengthen the pickets, but as the rebels did not advance beyond their first line they were drawn in and rejoined the regiment which then returned to camp. The whole conduct of the regiment was highly spoken of by the officers who witnessed the engagement and also in the report made by Colonel McCauley.

August 25th J. Anthony Tiemann, Sergeant, Company B, was promoted First-Lieutenant, Company F. August 25th we were aroused at 4 a. m. and stood under arms until daybreak. This was repeated August 26th. August 27th we again stood under arms. During the day we received orders to move. We were roused at 3 a. m. August 28th, struck tents and moved at 7.30 a. m., and marched ten miles from Harper's Ferry to just south of Charlestown, where we were posted behind strong breastworks to the right of the road near the position we had occupied on the 20th, the rebels having fallen back to Bunker Hill west of the Opequan.

August 29th part of the Eleventh Indiana left for home, the term of its service having expired.

During the day there was an alarm, the rebels having attacked and driven our cavalry for some distance towards our position, but they were driven back again and the lost ground regained. Each morning at 3 o'clock we were formed in line and stood under arms until 5.30 a. m. We had drill daily, besides which we furnished details for picket and to repair the breastworks. We had very little to eat except green corn, which we roasted, and green apples, which we ate raw. The change of climate caused us much suffering, as we felt the cold weather greatly, the nights and early mornings being much colder than we had experienced in Louisiana. September 2d First-Lieutenant George W. Hussey, Company B, was promoted Captain, Company F, and Sergeant John Day, Company K, to First-Lieutenant, Company B. September 3d, First-Lieutenant William Prince, Company I, was discharged to accept appointment as Ordnance Officer. Though borne on the rolls, he had never served with our regiment. September 3d we were roused at 3 a. m. and struck tents, and at 6 a. m. marched up the valley twelve miles where we were halted in a large field to the left of the road, taking position in the corps line just west of Fairfield, the Sixth Corps being on the right towards Clifton, and the Eighth Corps on the left towards Berryville, the Nineteenth Corps occupying the center. We had been in camp but a short time, when, at 5 p. m., heavy firing was heard in front and we were marched out and formed in line across the pike about a mile from Berryville. The firing grew quicker and more heavy, and our regiment, with the Twenty-second Iowa and Thirteenth Connecticut, which had rejoined the brigade that day from veteran furlough, together with the Third Brigade was ordered to the scene of action. Line was formed with our regiment on the left just to the right of the Eighth Corps, and we then marched forward under a heavy artillery fire to within short musketry range of the rebels, and occupied the crest of a hill. As it was growing dark and the firing began to slacken we were halted and ordered to take what rest we could in line, but it was quite impossible to sleep, as it was raining heavily and the night was bitterly cold. For some time the rebels kept up a firing by file, and as the bright flashes ran along their line they looked like myriads of fireflies illumining the woods. During the night they opened fire with artillery on our ambulances, which were moving in our rear, and one of our men, Stephen Morey, Company C, was wounded by a piece of shell, a number of which fell and exploded unpleasantly close. The firing was stopped as soon as the rolling of the ambulances ceased. September 4th the other regiments were drawn in, leaving ours on the line as pickets. The rebels shelled us and killed one man, Henry Karcher, Company G. It was rainy all day and our position was anything but comfortable. We were relieved at 7 p. m. and marched back about half a mile. September 5th breastworks were thrown up on the line we held. It rained heavily all day and night.

September 6th Edward Tynan, who had been First-Sergeant, Company A, and discharged in consequence of a severe wound received at Irish Bend, La., April 14, 1863, was commissioned First-Lieutenant from civil life, and joining the regiment was assigned to Company I. The rain which had continued steadily ceased at noon and the afternoon was very pleasant. September 7th our entire brigade, with Colonel Molineux in command, left the camp at 10 a. m. and, moving parallel with the breastworks on the outside, marched to the Winchester pike. The Third Massachusetts was deployed as skirmishers across and beyond the pike on either side, our regiment to the left of the road. We went up the valley six miles when videttes of rebel cavalry were seen, one of whom was wounded by one of our sharpshooters but made his escape. Learning the rebels were in strong force a short distance beyond we marched back to camp, which we reached at 5.30 p. m.

September 8th heavy rain fell, and a ration of whisky was issued by order of the surgeon. September 9th we had a very heavy thunder-storm at midnight. September 10th was rainy and disagreeable. Sunday, September 11th, having been appointed by President Lincoln a day of thanksgiving and praise for the victories at Mobile and Atlanta, the regiment was marched to brigade headquarters where divine service was held, the chaplain first reading the proclamation of the President. It rained before the service was over, and in the afternoon there was a heavy hail-storm. September 12th drill was resumed and we had dress parade at sundown.

September 13th our regiment furnished a large detail for picket duty, and as our cavalry had that day captured the Eighth South Carolina Infantry with all its officers and its battle flags, extra precautions were taken as it was supposed the rebels would attempt a reprisal, but the night, which was a beautiful one though intensely cold, passed very quietly, the enemy making no demonstration. September 14th was showery, and heavy rain fell at intervals.

CHAPTER XIII.

Winchester, Virginia—Our Losses—Fisher's Hill, Virginia.

SEPTEMBER 16th we had brigade drill, the first in months, and as all the forces were having the same it was generally thought a move was in contemplation. September 17th we heard that General Grant was visiting General Sheridan, which served to confirm the thought, and it was soon made a certainty, as September 18th orders were received to move at 2 a. m. the next day without wagons or baggage. The day was cloudy and cold with light showers.

September 19th at 1 a. m. a general forward movement of the whole army commenced. We marched at 2 a. m. up the pike towards Winchester, thirty-two miles south of Harper's Ferry, where the enemy were rumored to be in strong force. In the early morning we heard heavy firing in our front. Baggage-wagons and artillery filled the road and caused a long delay until they were hauled out to either side and allowed our passing. Pressing on we soon passed hospital tents on the roadside, where already the surgeons were busy caring for the wounded, who were rapidly being brought in. At 9 a. m. we were marched under the crest of a hill to the right of the pike, crossing the Opequan, where we filled our canteens; and shortly after line of battle was formed, the First and Third Brigades of our division (Grover's) in front, the Fourth and our brigade being in the rear of the first line at supporting distance. We were then moved forward to the top of a hill, from which we had a view of the field beyond, our forces in front pressing forward under a heavy

SKETCH BY COLONEL E. L. MOLINEUX, COMMANDING BRIGADE.

fire from the rebels. The brigades in our front inclining to the right as they advanced, and the brigade of the Sixth Corps, which was on their left, keeping too much to the left, made a gap in our front line, which our brigade was ordered forward to fill. It was about 11.30 a. m. when the order was received. We went down the hill and across the field, passing a ravine, and then mounted a slight eminence directly in front of a rebel battery posted on a hill opposite our position, which was shelling us as fast as the pieces could be loaded and fired. To our right and left our forces were retiring before the enemy, while in our front the rebels were coming on in columns, and receiving the order "Commence firing" we became engaged immediately. The regimental line was perfect, the men marching with precision and keeping well dressed on the colors, though the rebel fire of artillery and musketry was terrific. We were halted, and kept up a steady fire for some time; then came the order "Cease firing," and shortly after this Lieutenant Handy, an aide on the staff of Colonel Molineux, dashed across the field just in our rear, his horse at full gallop, and shouted " Retreat! Retreat!!" Looking to our right we saw our forces rapidly falling back before heavy masses of the rebels, who were following them closely, and the order was at once obeyed. When we reached the ravine, but a short distance in rear of the eminence from which we had been driven, an order was given to rally, but such was the impetuosity of the rebel charge that our lines were swept back, and one officer and nineteen men of our regiment were captured. It was difficult to restore order, but being re-formed and the lines adjusted our regiment was again ordered forward with the other regiments of our brigade Dwight's division, which had been in the rear in support, had in the meanwhile advanced, and the Eighth Corps coming in on their right, on the left flank of the enemy, the rebels were forced back, and after a long and obstinate struggle lasting until late in the afternoon, Early with his army was driven in full retreat from Winchester with our forces in hot pursuit.

Lieutenant Herman Smith, Company C, Acting-Adjutant, was mortally wounded, and died October 4th. Enlisting in Company H, enrolled as Sergeant, he had been promoted to Sergeant-Major and Second-Lieutenant, and by his kindly manner and bravery in action had endeared himself to all, and his loss was severely felt by the regiment. Lieutenant Edward Duffy, Company A, Lieutenant Henry M. Howard, Company D, and Captain Joseph G. McNutt, Company I, were wounded. Captain William F. Tiemann, Company A, was captured by the rebels. Our regiment lost in the battle 78: 5 men killed, 4 officers (1 mortally) and 49 men (4 mortally) wounded, 1 officer and 19 men prisoners.

The following list is as near perfect as it can be made:

WOUNDED.

Company C.

Second-Lieutenant . . . . HERMAN SMITH, Acting-Adjutant, mortally.

Company A.

First-Lieutenant . . . . EDWARD DUFFY

Company D.

First-Lieutenant . . . . HENRY M. HOWARD

Company I.

Captain . . . . JOSEPH G. McNUTT

MISSING.

Company A.

Captain . . . . WILLIAM F. TIEMANN

KILLED.

Company A.
Corporal, TATER, JOHN D.   Private, VAN DEUSEN, DELBERT

Company C.
Sergeant, WENDT, AUGUSTUS

Company D.
Private, FITZGERALD, PATRICK

Company H.
Private, LANDER, HENRY E.

WOUNDED.

Company A.
Private, JENNINGS, DANIEL   Corporal, OSBORNE, HENRY A.

Company B.
Private, LAWRENCE, FRED'K J.   Private, RICHMOND, SILAS W.
" LOUGHLIN, STEPHEN

Company C.
Private, EDWARDS, A. EUGENE   Private, STAATS, MYRON
Sergeant, FITZGERALD, JAMES   " SCHNACK, CHRISTIAN
Private, GAILOR, AUSTIN   " SCHERMERHORN, JOHN
Sergeant, KELLERHOUSE, JONAS A.   " WHEELER, FREELAND
Private, SHUFELT, WILLIAM

Company D.
Private, KISTERS, FRANK W.   Private, SMITH, CONRAD
" MORRIS, ISAAC

Company E.
Private, ALMSTEAD, JOHN W.   Private, DECKER, JAMES
" BENZIE, GEORGE A.   " PROPER, ROBERT
" COYLE, WILLIAM H.

Company F.

Private, COLGAN, WILLIAM, mortally.
Corporal, CALLAGHAN, WILLIAM
Corporal, MACKEY, TERENCE
Private, NICHOLS, FLOYD C., mortally.

Company G.

Private, COE, JAMES H.
Corporal, HALLENBECK, JACOB
Private, MICHAEL, ANTHONY M.
Corporal, POST, DAVID
Private, SHEEHAN, DENNIS
" TOOMEY, JOHN

Company H.

Private, ADAMS, WASHINGTON, mortally.
" FRIER, WILLIAM H.
" HURLEY, ROBERT
Private, JENKINS, AUGUSTUS G.
" LEONARD, BENJAMIN
" POWELL, CHARLES
Sergeant, TRAVER, MARTIN

Company I.

Private, CORY, EUGENE A.
" HOUCK, WALTER C.
Private, WAGONER, WILLIAM H.

Company K.

Private, BROPHY, EDWARD
" COUGHLAN, JOHN
" HOFFMANN, GEORGE A.
" HAHN, HENRY
Private, KANE, JOHN
" KEWAN, JOHN M.
" TANNER, WILLIAM D.

MISSING.

Company A.

Corporal, PEARY, SILAS W.
Private, WARD, THOMAS, died in Salisbury, N. C.

Company B.

Corporal, HATFIELD, GEORGE W.

Company C.

Private, DEWITT, DORR, died in Richmond, Va.
Private, SMITH, GROSVENOR

Company D.

Private, TREITLEIN, JOSEPH,
    died in Salisbury, N. C.

Company E.

Sergeant, MCNEILL, DEWITT

Company F.

Corporal, DOSER, BARTHOLOMEW, Private, MOTT, CHARLES W.
    died in Salisbury, N. C.

Company G.

Private, BRADY, CALEB   Private, SHERMAN, HENRY,
"   MEAGHER, JEREMIAH   died in Salisbury, N. C.
                                      "   SPAULDING, SABOR S.

Company H.

Private, LOUGEA, JOHN L.,   Private, MILLOTT, GEORGE
    died in Salisbury, N. C.

Company I.

Private, SCOTT, THOMAS

Company K.

Private, DOOLIN, BERNARD,   Private, GOSHIA, ANDREW,
    died in Salisbury, N. C.   died in Salisbury, N. C.
"   DOLAN, TIMOTHY

The enemy was closely followed by our army. Early made a stand three miles from Strasburg, at Fisher's Hill, which was strongly fortified, his lines extending from the Shenandoah River on his right to North Mountain on his left. The Valley pike, up which part of our brigade made its way later during the assault, extends for some distance nearly parallel with the river and in full view from the hill, then branches to the right for a short distance to Tumbling Run, which flows along the base of the hill and which is crossed by a narrow stone bridge, and turning to the left again goes on over the hill, flanked on either side by steep and precipitous rocks, except just to the right, where is a narrow and very deep ravine. Strong rifle pits were constructed by the rebels on either side of the road down to the run, covering it completely, while a strong earthwork was erected along the crest of the hill, which gave them full command of the road and approaches beyond.

September 20th the regiment marched at 5 a. m. with the rest of the brigade, camping near the ford at Strasburg, twenty miles south of Winchester. September 21st we moved our camp to the right of the Strasburg pike. In the early morning with our brigade we marched towards the right of our line and were formed in line of battle in rear of the First Brigade, occupying a knoll directly facing the mountain on which the main works of the rebels were constructed and from which they were maintaining a continuous steady fire on our position. At 8.30 a. m. we were moved out to the left of our line, and posted in an orchard near to and commanding the Strasburg pike, and were ordered to construct breastworks, which we did, and were then ordered to support the Fifth New York Battery which came into position on the Strasburg road to our left. At 1 p. m. we were moved out in support of a skirmish line to our right, but had hardly marched into position when we were moved still further to our left in support of the Seventeenth Indiana Battery. At 4.30 p. m. we were ordered to commence firing, and at 5 p. m. we advanced to support a line in our front, charging up the hill on the works, from which the rebels were quickly driven, and we soon occupied the crest. Our regiment was then detailed to take charge of the prisoners, then some two hundred in number, and follow our brigade, which led the advance in pursuit of the rebels, who were in full retreat. The pursuit

was kept up all night. At 9.30 p. m. our brigade skirmish-line was fired on by the rebels, and the forces in our rear by some mistake opened fire on our brigade. This mistake was repeated about a mile further on. The pursuit was kept up until 3.30 a. m., September 23d, when our advance was halted just south of Woodstock, twenty-nine miles from Winchester, and sixty-one miles from Harper's Ferry. Our regiment, in charge of the prisoners, a number of whom we had secured on the march, reached the brigade at 9.30 a. m. A quantity of small arms, several pieces of artillery, horses, wagons, and about one thousand prisoners, were captured, which, with a large wagon-train, the regiment was detailed to take charge of and convoy to Winchester. Leaving Woodstock at 5 p. m. September 23d, delivering the prisoners and property at Winchester September 25th, the regiment at once started back again in charge of a supply train, reaching the front and rejoining the brigade at Harrisonburg, sixty-eight miles from Winchester, at 3 p. m. September 27th, having marched ninety-seven miles in the four days. During the following three days we fed on green corn and apples, there being no rations issued. The weather was rainy, cold, and very unpleasant. September 28th we advanced to Mount Crawford, eight miles south of Harrisonburg, with the other troops in support of a movement by the cavalry, and September 30th we returned to Harrisonburg. October 3d we received orders to move, and struck tents at 5 a. m., but the orders being countermanded we went into camp again. The days and nights were rainy and very cold, it having continued to rain since the 1st. October 6th we struck tents and moved at daylight, marching twenty-three miles to near Mount Jackson. October 7th, with three days' rations, we moved at 7 a. m., and after marching a short distance went in line of battle. After a short delay the march was resumed, and passing through Mount Jackson,

Edinburgh, and Woodstock we camped two miles from the latter, having marched twenty miles. Rain fell during the night. October 8th we moved at 6 a. m. Twice we stopped and formed line of battle. We marched until 4 p. m., when we went into camp in a ravine near Fisher's Hill, nine miles from our starting place. October 9th at 9 a. m. we moved half a mile to the left. This day the rebel General Rosser, with a large cavalry force, was thoroughly and effectually whipped by our cavalry under General Torbert, with the loss of a number of killed, wounded, and prisoners, and nearly all his artillery. October 10th we moved at 2 p. m., crossing to the north of Cedar Creek, fourteen miles south of Winchester, and went into camp to the left of the road, after a march of five miles. The construction of earthworks was at once begun. October 11th Barzillai Ransom, who had been Sergeant, Company B, commissioned Second-Lieutenant, and discharged in February owing to insufficiency of men to permit his muster in, having been commissioned First-Lieutenant from civil life, joined the regiment and was appointed to command Company C.

Early having received reinforcements, had followed up our army, and October 13th made an attack in force on the Eighth Corps at Hupp's Hill, the fight being visible from our position. We were formed in line with the rest of the army, two regiments of our brigade being marched to the front to strengthen our picket line, but the rebels fell back to Fisher's Hill, their movement having been a reconnoissance to discover our position and force. At 4 p. m. we struck tents, and marched to the left at 10 p. m., where we remained all night on picket. October 14th at 10 a. m. we marched back to our old camp. October 16th at midnight the regiment was aroused and at once put to work throwing up breastworks. The night was intensely cold. October 17th the work of throwing up the breastworks was completed.

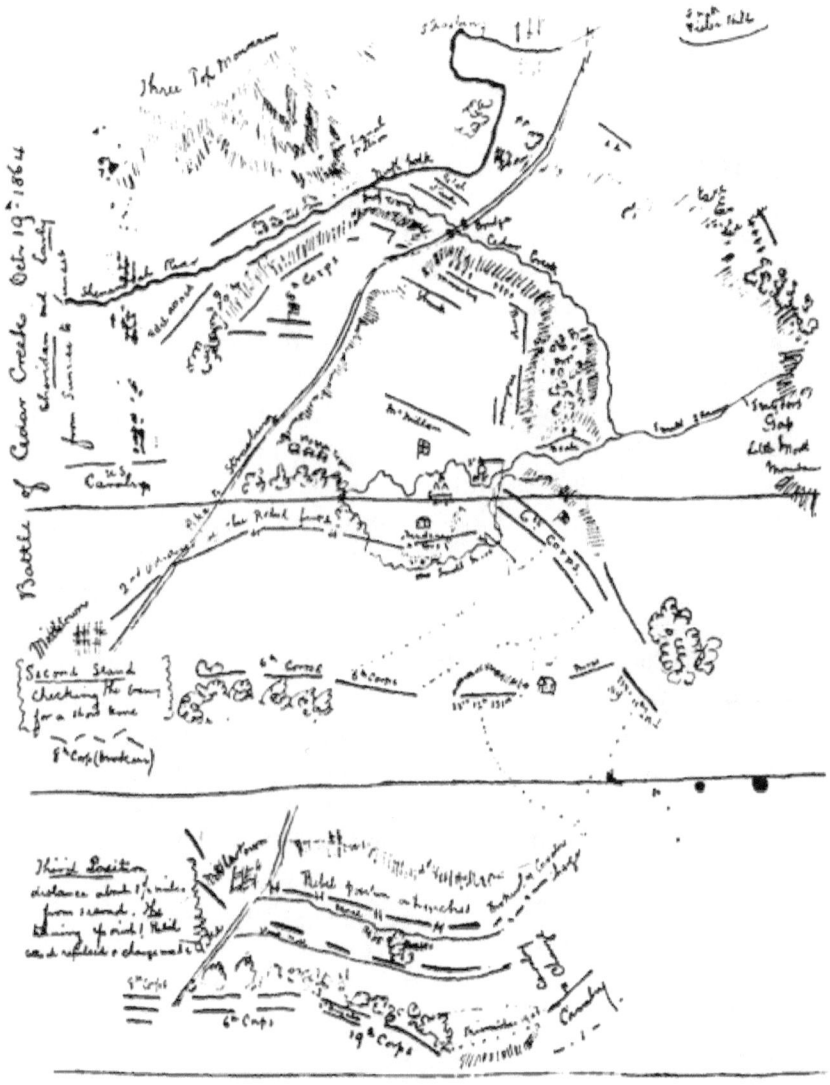

SKETCH BY COLONEL E. L. MOLINEUX, COMMANDING BRIGADE.

CHAPTER XIV.

Cedar Creek, Virginia — Our Losses.

OCTOBER 18th Colonel Molineux received orders to hold the brigade in readiness to move at daylight on a reconnoissance to Strasburg, it having been reported that the rebels had moved from our front, and we were ordered to be ready to march at 5:30 a. m. October 19th our regiment, with the others of the brigade, had breakfasted and was in line awaiting orders. Just before 6 a. m. the sound of heavy firing was heard on the left, and we were at once marched into the breastworks, and soon after the troops of the Eighth Corps were streaming past, followed by the yelling rebel host. Early had planned and executed a daring and brilliant move. Posting part of his army with the artillery in front of our forces to be ready at the desired moment, he had marched a large force during the night of the 18th under the base of Massanutten Mountain, fording the Shenandoah twice, and gained a position to the rear and on the left of the Eighth Corps, his movement being concealed in part by a dense fog which arose in the early morning. Our troops, all unprepared and unsuspecting such an attack, were quickly aroused from their slumbers by the volleys of musketry and the yells of the rebels as they advanced to the attack. At the same time the enemy in our front moved forward to the assault, and caught between the two fires our army was forced back. Our regiment, with the others of the brigade remaining, two having just been detached, was formed in line in front of the rifle pits to oppose the attack in the rear; but it was impossible to resist the rush of the rebels, who had driven the Eighth Corps from its position, and to sustain the murderous fire from those advancing in the front, who threatened to hem us in, and filing to the right we fell to the rear for a short distance, forming line facing the enemy to the left of the Sixth Corps, but were shortly afterwards ordered back about one hundred yards in support of a battery, which, however, retreated without firing a shot. We held the hill on which we were posted for some time and were then moved to the right near a belt of woods held by the rebels, where we were soon very actively engaged endeavoring to hold them in check. The whole line gradually fell back, retiring about four miles to just beyond Middletown. Up to this time the army had been under command of Major-General Wright of the Sixth Corps; Major-General Sheridan was absent, having gone to Washington on the 15th, and returning he reached Winchester on the day preceding Early's attack. Here, in the early morning, was heard the sound of artillery firing, but it was not at first supposed there was a battle going on. Leaving Winchester about 9 a. m., General Sheridan met a part of the retreating force just beyond the town. This and the heavy firing now distinctly audible showed him a general engagement was in progress. Dashing forward at top speed he met crowds of stragglers and demoralized troops whom he halted, and by his presence and cheering words soon infused new life and energy in the disheartened men, and with earnest resolve that his promise, "We shall occupy our old lines again to-night," should be true, the broken lines were re-formed, and with renewed vigor they marched to meet the enemy. At noon our brigade was advanced in line on the left of the Sixth Corps to a wood where a breastwork of rails was thrown up. Here the rebels made a charge on us, but were quickly repulsed, but to our sorrow we lost here the brave Captain Richmond. At 3.30 p. m., with the Sixth Corps on the left, the Nineteenth Corps on the right, and the Eighth Corps in support, our troops pressed forward after the rebels, who had now commenced to fall back. The Nineteenth Corps was strongly resisted, but gallantly advancing under the personal observation of General Sheridan the rebels were quickly driven from the positions they had stubbornly attempted to hold behind stone walls and fences, and they were soon fleeing before our victorious troops, who followed in close pursuit. Our brigade was on the extreme left of our corps next to the right of the Sixth Corps, the Thirteenth Connecticut deployed as skirmishers, our regiment the fourth from the left of the brigade. The rebels in our front were in two lines, strongly posted behind a stone wall and on the crest of a hill with a battery in position. After delivering our fire a charge was ordered and the rebels were driven from the hill, our colors being the third to be planted on its crest. We captured in the charge three officers and thirty-one men of the rebels. Halting here for a short time only, we pressed forward again until at Cedar Creek we halted and finally camped in our old quarters. General Sheridan had proved himself the "man at a pinch" we had thought him to be when we first saw him, and had nobly kept his glorious promise. Throughout the entire fight our regiment, with all those of our brigade, maintained its organization and moved from point to point as it was ordered.

Major Robert McD. Hart of our regiment, serving on Brigadier-General Grover's staff, was severely wounded and captured by the rebels while striving to rally one of our batteries. He was recaptured in the afternoon, but owing to the length of time during which he had no proper attention, though the rebels had treated him with the utmost kindness in their power, as he himself testified, the loss of blood was so great as to cause his death from exhaustion the same night. No officer possessed greater bravery or more of the spirit of a true soldier. He was a firm disciplinarian and exacted implicit obedience from his men, but no one cared more for or looked more closely to their interests than did he. A member of Company C, Seventh N. Y. S. M., he had recruited Company F of our regiment, of which he was Captain prior to his promotion, and had served with the company until appointed to the staff of our division commander, where he served with distinguished credit to himself until his untimely death.

Captain Duncan Richmond, Company K, who had been with us from the first, having helped to recruit the same company as Second-Lieutenant, and who was promoted to be its commanding officer and had been present in every engagement in which we had participated, was also killed, and the loss was most severely felt by the entire regiment. Pleasant and genial in his manner, kind to and thoughtful of his men, brave as the bravest, we could ill afford to lose so gallant an officer. He fell just as success was assured to our arms. None more worthy gave his life for his country.

First-Lieutenant Barzillai Ransom, Company C, was wounded.

Our loss was 22: 2 officers, 2 men killed; 1 officer, 12 men wounded (1 mortally); 5 men missing.

The following list is as near perfect as it can be made.

KILLED.

Major . . . . Robert McD. Hart,
                                       A. O. O. & I., 2d Div'n.

Company K.

Captain . . . . Duncan Richmond

WOUNDED.
Company C.
First-Lieutenant . . . . Barzillai Ransom

KILLED.

Company A.
Private, Morrin, Lewis

Company E.
Private, Perkins, James T.

WOUNDED.

Company A.
Private, Lown, John S.

Company B.
Private, Murray, Michael

Company C.
Private, Tater, William

Company D.
Private, Brown, John J., mortally.
" Furness, Michael
" Miller, George H.

Company E.
Private, Proper, George

Company G.
Private, Rowlinson, Elliott

Company H.
Private, Herbert, William

Company I.
Private, Devlin, John
Private, Edson, Almon

Company K.
Private, Leonard, James S.

MISSING.
Company A.
Private, Clearwater, Joseph

Company B.

Private, CAVANAGH, THOMAS
" DAILY, JOHN,
    died in Salisbury, N. C.

Private, SCHNEPF, GOTTLIEB,
    died in Salisbury, N. C.

Company I.

Private, MORTON, JAMES,
    died in Salisbury, N. C.

October 20th our regiment moved up the valley to Strasburg with the rest of our brigade, guarding for the night the ford on the left. Through the foresight and thoughtfulness of Colonel Molineux we were much better off than most of the troops, as he had permitted us, when the attack of the 19th was commenced, to strike our tents and secure our blankets; and these were now of good service as the night was piercingly cold. October 21st at 5 a. m. we marched back to our old camp. Rain fell during the night. October 23d the night was rainy and intensely cold. October 24th the congratulations of President Lincoln were read to the troops.

                      EXECUTIVE MANSION,
                      WASHINGTON, October 22, 1864.

MAJOR-GENERAL SHERIDAN.

With great pleasure I tender to you and your brave army the thanks of the Nation, and my own personal admiration and gratitude, for the month's operations in the Shenandoah Valley: and especially for the splendid work of October 19, 1864.

                      Your obedient servant,
                          ABRAHAM LINCOLN.

The day was intensely cold and there was heavy frost that night. October 26th was cloudy; the night was rainy and cold. October 27th was cold, cloudy, and unpleasant, with rain during the night. November 3d and 4th were rainy and cold. November 6th and 7th were wet and very cold. November 8th marching orders were received and tents struck at 4 a. m. We lay in the rain all day, and at night put up our tents again. The rain continued through the night. November 9th we struck tents at 5 a. m. We started at 9.30 a. m. and, passing through Middletown and Newtown, marched about five miles back of the creek, and camped on a hill to the right of the pike two miles north of Newtown. November 10th we moved camp to the left about half a mile. November 11th the rebels attacked our cavalry, and after a severe skirmish drove them back. At noon we struck tents ready to move, but the rebels were repulsed and we formed camp again. In the afternoon the regiment began the construction of breastworks. November 12th heavy firing was heard in the front. We struck tents at daylight and then again formed camp, without moving, at sunset. We finished the breastworks in our front, which we named "Fort Waltermire —Bears' Retreat, or a rough hug for rebs." The night was rainy and cold. November 20th and 21st were rainy and cold. November 24th was observed as Thanksgiving Day, and no duties except those absolutely necessary were performed. November 28th orders were received to go into winter quarters. November 29th we moved camp to the left of the Front Royal road, and began the erection of log huts, in which we were housed during the winter and made as comfortable as possible, and with a plentiful supply of fuel had little trouble to keep warm, though the climate was so much colder than in Louisiana. The winter was a very severe one, there being numerous snow-storms which covered the ground to the depth of several inches, and the streams in the vicinity were frozen over solidly. December 1st and 7th it rained all night and was very cold. The intermediate days were pleasant but cold. December 9th, at sunset, snow commenced to fall and continued all night. December 16th all the batteries fired salutes in honor of the victory obtained by General Thomas over General Hood at Nashville. December 17th salutes were again fired in honor of General Sherman's victory at Savannah and General Thomas again defeating General Hood. Colonel Molineux was promoted Brevet Brigadier-General, with rank from October 19th, for "gallant and meritorious conduct at the battles of Opequan, Fisher's Hill, and Cedar Creek." His regiment rejoiced with him that at last this well-merited honor had been conferred. December 20th First-Lieutenant Henry M. Howard, Company D, was discharged for disability, having been severely wounded at Winchester. December 25th, CHRISTMAS DAY, was duly celebrated, and the enjoyment of all made the greater by the reception of boxes from home. December 26th a salute was fired in honor of the capture of Savannah by General Sherman. We had heavy rain that night. December 29th we received marching orders to be ready to move early next morning.

CHAPTER XV.

Leave the Valley for Baltimore, Maryland — Savannah, Georgia — Morehead City, North Carolina — Augusta, Georgia — Madison, Georgia.

DECEMBER 30th, at 8 a. m., our regiment marched from its comfortable quarters, going nine miles to Stephenson's Depot, the terminus of the Harper's Ferry and Winchester Railroad, nineteen miles from Cedar Creek. We went into camp in a rough, uneven spot, and that night the snow fell heavily. December 31st was the most intensely cold day we had experienced, and in the afternoon snow again fell. We had no fires and no wood until night, when the teams brought boards from our old camp and we floored our tents and started fires. January 1, 1865, New Year's Day, opened cold and cheerless with the snow still falling heavily. The ground was covered deeply, and with our thin tents it was very uncomfortable. January 2d was pleasant and cold, but January 3d and 4th snow fell again. January 4th First-Lieutenant J. Anthony Tiemann, Company F, was discharged. Captain George W. Hussey, Company F, was relieved from duty on the brigade staff and rejoined the regiment. January 5th, at sunset, we received orders to be ready to move next day. January 6th, at 6 a. m., in a pouring rain we struck tents, and taking cars at the depot left at 9 a. m. for Harper's Ferry, eight miles distant, which we did not reach until dark. We were packed closely in dirty box-cars, some of the brigade, not so fortunate, having open platform-cars until their arrival at the Ferry. We remained in the cars all night, the rain continuing steadily, freezing as it fell; and January 7th, at 2 a. m., we started, arriving in Baltimore, Md., eighty-one miles from Harper's Ferry, at 9 a. m., where we were quartered in barracks at Camp Carroll on Carroll Hill, a mile from the city. The rain continued until late in the afternoon. Here we suffered the utmost discomfort, the barracks being overcrowded and excessively dirty.

January 10th rain fell heavily all day. January 11th part of our brigade left. January 12th we received orders to be ready to move next day. January 13th, at 2 p. m., we thankfully quitted the barracks, marching through Baltimore to the foot of Fell street. Our bear attracted great attention and was constantly surrounded by an admiring crowd. Arrived at the wharf we embarked on the transport *Suwo Nada*, which lay there waiting for us. January 14th we sailed at 5 p. m., arriving in Hampton Roads at 10 p. m., where we dropped anchor between Fortress Monroe and the Rip Raps, awaiting orders. General Grover and staff were on our steamer, and also the One Hundred and Twenty-eighth New York and Twenty-second Iowa, as well as the division hospital. January 15th, at noon, we hauled in alongside the pier and took in provisions, and at sundown started off again. January 18th we spoke the *Illinois* with General Molineux and staff and the other regiments of our brigade on board. They reported being unable to obtain a pilot, and were ordered to follow our steamer. We arrived and anchored in Warsaw Sound, seven hundred and nine miles from Baltimore, where a small steamer came alongside on which General Grover and staff embarked and proceeded up the river. January 19th we lay at anchor. Rain fell heavily all day. January 20th, at 9 a. m., orders were received to proceed up the river. We were transferred to the steamer *George Leary* in a pouring rain, and taken fifteen miles up to the city of Savannah, Ga., where we landed at 3 p. m. and were marched to and quartered in the depot of the Georgia Central Railroad.

January 21st our bear was weighed and found to weigh two hundred and six pounds. He was growing very large, and was very strong and not of as amiable a temper as he had been. January 23d, after continuing steadily six days, the rain ceased at sunset and we had clear weather. January 26th, at 8 a. m., we marched through the city two miles out to the fortifications on the west side near the Ogeechee road. January 27th, at night, there was a great fire in the city, caused by the burning of a magazine. Powder and shell exploded continuously, doing fortunately but little damage. January 28th, at 2 a. m., we were ordered to fall in ready to move if called for, but our services were not needed, the fire being checked without our aid. February 3d to February 7th we had rain steadily until the afternoon of the latter day. February 14th it rained all day and all night. February 22d, Washington's Birthday, was duly celebrated by the bands playing and the firing of salutes by our batteries.

From February 24th to the 28th we again had continuous rain. March 4th Captain George W. Hussey, Company F, was detached and assigned to the division staff. March 7th the regiment and quarters were inspected by General Williams. March 8th marching orders were received, and preparations were at once made for a move. At 9 p. m. the baggage was started off on the wagons. March 9th, starting at 4 a. m., the regiment was marched through the city and embarked on the steamer *U. S. Grant*. We sailed at 10 a. m., stopping at Fort Pulaski, and at 7 p. m. arrived at Hilton Head, fifty miles from Savannah, where we disembarked and went into barracks. We had steady rain from the 7th to 10th of March, clearing off cold and pleasant early in the morning. March 15th orders to move were received; at 6 p. m. we marched to the wharf, and at 9 p. m. were transferred by a small tug to the transport *New York*, which was anchored outside. March 16th our steamer weighed anchor and sailed at 7 a. m., arriving at Charleston, South Carolina, eighty-four miles from Hilton Head, at 1 p. m., passing as we entered the harbor Forts Sumter, Moultrie, Wagner, Gregg, Johnson, and Castle Pinckney, and dropped anchor in the river. March 17th the Twenty-eighth Iowa, Fifty-second Pennsylvania, and a detachment of the Fifty-fourth New York were taken on board, the embarkation occupying the entire day. March 18th we sailed at 10.30 a. m. with over sixteen hundred on board, under sealed orders. After getting to sea the orders were opened by Lieutenant-Colonel Waltermire directing him to report to Major-General Schofield at Wilmington, North Carolina. At 11 p. m. we hove to and dropped anchor. March 19th we started at 9 a. m. and dropped anchor off Fort Fisher, North Carolina, one hundred and thirty-four miles from Charleston, at 10 a. m. A boat came off with orders for us to proceed to Morehead City. We sailed at noon and arrived off Beaufort at sunset, where we dropped anchor. March 20th we sailed at 11.30 a. m., passing over the bar and into the harbor, and dropped anchor off Fort Macon. March 21st the steamer *H. M. Wells* came alongside, and our regiment, with the Fifty-fourth New York, was taken on board at 7.30 a. m., and we were landed at the railroad wharf, Morehead City, North Carolina, sixty-three miles from Fort Fisher. We were marched inland about a mile, and camped to the right of the railroad. March 22d orders were received to go to Newbern, and preparations for a move were made. March 23d the marching orders were countermanded. We moved our camp back a short distance to a more pleasant location. The wind, which had been blowing heavily ever since our arrival, rose to a gale, driving the sand in such volumes as almost to blind us. During the night the wind fell and the weather was much more pleasant.

March 26th a fire broke out in a house adjoining the government storehouse, and our men lent efficient aid in removing the stores and helping to extinguish the fire. In the afternoon dense smoke was seen in the direction of Newbern. A report was brought in that the rebels had fired the government barracks at Newport, twelve miles distant. The regiment fell in and stood under arms until 5 p. m. The same day a large fire occurred in Beaufort. March 28th Lieutenant-Colonel Waltermire sent a challenge to Lieutenant-Colonel Lewis of the One Hundred and Seventy-sixth New York, to play a game of base-ball between picked nines of the two regiments. The One Hundred and Seventy-sixth won by nineteen runs to seventeen for our regiment. March 29th and 30th heavy rain fell. April 6th rumors of Grant's success at Petersburg reached us. April 7th we received confirmation of the news, and the rejoicing was very great. Salutes were fired and the bands played. Heavy rain fell during the night. April 11th the return match was played between the two regiments, resulting in a victory for ours by seventeen runs to sixteen for the One Hundred and Seventy-sixth New York. At 11.30 p. m. news was received of Lee's surrender. No words can depict the deep feeling and intense enthusiasm this news elicited. The men cheered until they were hoarse, the drums beat, and cannon were fired all night. It was the "dawn of peace." April 13th, 15th, 18th, 20th, and 21st, we had heavy showers. April 23d General Grant arrived and took the cars for General Sherman's headquarters. There was great cheering by the troops when his presence was known.

April 29th Captain William F. Tiemann, Company A, who had been a prisoner to the rebels for over five months, reported to the regiment and resumed command of his company. May 2d we received orders to move next day to report to General Grover at Savannah, and preparations were at once made for the march. During our stay we had been guarding commissary stores and furnishing details to guard the trains carrying the stores and other materials to Goldsboro and Raleigh. May 3d we struck tents at 3 a. m. and marched at 2.30 p. m., but after going a short distance were ordered back to our camp again, where we remained until 8 p. m., when we marched to the pier and embarked on the transport *Star of the South*, on which Brigadier-General Birge with his staff and the One Hundred and Thirty-first New York was already on board. We were packed in like sheep, and the men found it most difficult to get any place to sleep. May 4th we sailed at 1 p. m., arriving off the mouth of the Savannah River at 5 p. m., May 6th, having stopped for a short time off Charleston harbor. Taking a pilot from an outward-bound steamer, we sailed up the river, and when arrived within a mile of the city our steamer grounded. General Birge and staff landed in a tug which came alongside. May 7th at 6 a. m. we got off and proceeded up the river, but grounded again just off the wharf. A small steamboat came alongside on which we embarked and were landed at the foot of Bull Street, Savannah, Georgia, two hundred and forty-four miles from Morehead City, and marched up in the city and camped near our old quarters on the west side. May 8th we had heavy rain. May 10th marching orders were received. May 11th at 2 a. m. we struck tents, and at 9 a. m., with the other regiments of the brigade, under command of Colonel Graham, left Savannah, our regiment guarding the wagon train. We marched fourteen miles. We went into camp in a newly plowed field, and, rain falling heavily, it was soon all mud. May 12th we started at 4.30 a. m., leading the advance of the column, and marched seventeen miles. May 13th we started at 4.30 a. m., marching eight miles and going into camp near Sister's Ferry. May 14th we marched at 4 a. m., going twenty

OUR ARRIVAL AT AUGUSTA.

miles. May 15th we started at 4.30 a. m. and marched eighteen miles. That night orders were received for our regiment with the One Hundred and Thirty-first New York and One Hundred and Twenty-eighth New York to press forward with all speed to Waynesborough. May 16th at 4 a. m. we started, and marching twenty-eight miles reached Waynesborough at sunset, where we at once took the cars, starting at 9 p. m. We reached Augusta, Georgia, one hundred and thirty-five miles from Savannah, at midnight, and were camped in a field near the railroad. We found Brigadier-General Molineux in command; he having been assigned to the duty May 3d and had formally taken possession of the city May 8th. May 18th and 19th were rainy and uncomfortable. May 20th we struck tents, and at 10 a. m. were marched through the city to the old City Hotel on Broad Street, where we went into very comfortable quarters, rooms being assigned to the different companies.

Lieutenant-Colonel Waltermire was appointed Supervisor of Trade, Captain Wells O. Pettit and Captain William F. Tiemann were appointed Assistant Provost-Marshals, Captain James S. Reynolds, Chief of Police; Lieutenant Barzillai Ransom and Lieutenant Edward Duffy were placed in charge of the jail. First-Lieutenant E. Spencer Elmer, Company G, was placed in command of Company K. May 24th Captain Wells O. Pettit, Company H, who had been severely wounded at Halltown, rejoined the regiment and at once assumed his duties as Deputy Provost Marshal. May 25th, 26th, and 27th we had heavy rains. May 29th there was regimental review by General Molineux, but as it commenced to rain heavily we marched around one square only and returned to quarters. May 30th we had regimental inspection. Just after forming line the rain poured in torrents. We were marched to the railroad depot and inspected, and then returned to our quarters. June 6th all the troops in Augusta were reviewed by General Molineux. It was fine when we started, but rain fell heavily just before the review was over, and we were all thoroughly soaked. June 22d Sergeant E. Parmly Brown, Company I, was promoted First-Lieutenant, Company D. July 4th was patriotically kept, many of the men imbibing more peach brandy than was good for them, the consequence being what threatened to be a serious disturbance, which, however, was quelled by the provost guard.

With the few exceptions noted, the two months of our stay passed uneventfully. The men of the regiment were drilled as much as could be, but being constantly on guard very few could be assembled for the purpose. Guard mount was a great attraction and daily drew great crowds of citizens, who most enthusiastically applauded the appearance of the men and their perfect drill and discipline. It was a real pleasure to see what pride they took in looking neat, and their clothing, arms, and accoutrements were most carefully looked after. The thought of home-going was in each mind, and it was partly in anticipation of this that extra care was taken of all their belongings. July 21st the regiment was relieved from provost duty by the Nineteenth United States Infantry (regulars), and was marched two and a half miles from the city to the Sand Hills and camped in the old United States Arsenal grounds.

July 21st Captain Joseph G. McNutt, Company I, was dishonorably dismissed by sentence of court-martial. July 23d Surgeon William Y. Provost resigned and was discharged. He had served for some time as Medical Director on the staff of Major-General Wm. H. Emory, and also on the staff of Major-General Grover. July 29th General Molineux resigned, and Brigadier-General J. H. King was appointed to command the department. Before his departure he issued the following letter to the regiment:

GENERAL MOLINEUX'S FAREWELL TO THE REGIMENT.

HEADQUARTERS DEPARTMENT OF AUGUSTA,
FOURTH DIVISION DEPARTMENT OF GEORGIA,
AUGUSTA, GEORGIA, July 29, 1865.

Officers and Soldiers of the One Hundred and Fifty-ninth New York State Volunteers:

Having tendered my resignation from the United States service I shall soon no longer bear the honored title of your commanding officer.

The war is ended, and it will not be long before you return to your Northern homes; but in parting from you at the present time, my feelings impel me to say a few words in farewell greeting, both as an officer and a brother soldier.

We enlisted together at a time when the fortunes of our country were dark; many brave comrades have fallen from our ranks on the field and by disease, but we, the survivors, may return thanks to God that their deaths have not been in vain, and that our labors have been crowned with success.

As a regiment you have won an enviable reputation for steady, persistent bravery on the field, and for good order and conduct in the discharge of any and every duty.

Since my connection with you I have kept firmly to the rule that my conduct should do you no discredit and that the reputation of the One Hundred and Fifty-ninth New York Volunteers should be second to none.

I am proud of you, and am grateful for the cheerful obedience which you yielded to strict discipline. It is this which has rendered you successful, and those of you who have at times thought the discipline severe and rigid must remember that it was necessary, and that although at times the voice may have been harsh yet the heart has always been warm towards you.

Recollect, comrades, whenever and wherever we may meet, I shall always be glad to greet you, and ready to assist you in any way in my power.

(Signed) EDWARD L. MOLINEUX,
*Colonel, One Hundred and Fifty-ninth New York Volunteers,
Brevet Brigadier-General United States Volunteers, Commanding.*

August 1st General Molineux left for home, and his departure was most severely felt. The organizer of the regiment, he had as its commander endeared himself to all the men by his care for them, and by his careful discipline and personal bravery had proved himself one of the best soldiers the war produced. He went home followed by the regrets and well-wishes of every man of the command.

August 3d John W. Coon, Company I, was accidentally shot and killed. August 7th Sergeant-Major William E. Palmer was discharged for disability. August 16th Gilbert S. Gullen, Sergeant, Company F, was promoted Sergeant-Major. Second Principal Musician George D. Dayton was reduced to the ranks and returned to Company B, and nearly every sergeant and corporal in the regiment were reduced to the ranks the same day for breach of discipline in being absent without leave. August 22d Quartermaster John H. Charlotte resigned and was discharged.

August 29th the regiment received orders to move, being detailed to garrison the "Sub-District of Madison," comprising Morgan, Jasper, Putnam, Newton, and Walton Counties. August 30th First-Lieutenant Edward Duffy was dishonorably dismissed by sentence of court-martial. August 31st we moved by rail one hundred and four miles to Madison, Georgia, the capital of Morgan County, where headquarters were established, Lieutenant-Colonel Waltermire commanding the sub-district, the companies being posted in the different towns on provost duty. Lieutenant John Day, with Companies B and F, was sent to Covington, Newton County; Lieutenant Andrew Rifenburgh, with Company E, was sent to Monroe, Walton County; and Captain James S. Reynolds, with Company G, to Monticello, Jasper County; the other companies being retained at Madison. September 6th Captain William F. Tiemann was relieved as Assistant Provost-Marshal, Augusta, and, rejoining the regiment, was assigned to duty as Assistant Provost-Marshal, Jasper County, relieving Captain James S. Reynolds, who was detailed on general court-martial. Captain George W. Hussey, Company F, was relieved from duty on the division staff and rejoined the regiment, and was then detailed on general court-martial, his company remaining under command of Lieutenant Day. September 26th a sad occurrence took place at Monticello. Franklin Miller became drunk and disorderly, and attempted the life of the commanding officer of the post. He was arrested and confined in the guard-house, but during the night was liberated by the corporal of the guard and, with several others, went to a house where a fracas occurred, during which Miller was stabbed in the bowels by Sergeant Robert C. Bruce of his company, and died in the early morning of September 26th. He was buried the same day, the minister of the Methodist church officiating. Bruce escaped and was never apprehended.

CHAPTER XVI.

Muster Out — Death of Our Bear — Leave for Home — Final Discharge — Recapitulation.

SEPTEMBER 28th orders were received to prepare the muster-out rolls of the regiment and to report in Augusta by October 13th. The companies were at once concentrated in Madison, and October 5th were moved by rail to Augusta, where the regiment was quartered in the old railroad shops, which had been used by the rebels as a machine shop during the war. The buildings were of wood, forming three sides of a square with a large vacant yard in the center. The floor was saturated with oil and grease, and the whole building was of the most inflammable character. During the early morning of October 9th a fire was started in the guard-house at one end of the building, as was generally supposed by some prisoners to liberate themselves. Like a flash of lightning the fire darted from one end of the building to the other, and almost immediately the whole structure was a raging mass of flame. The men had barely time to remove their arms and equipments, so rapidly did it spread, and most of them, as well as the officers, lost all their clothing except such as they had on. The officers, who were busy at the Court House working on the muster-out rolls, lost all their baggage, many of their company and private papers, and the relics they had collected and gathered during their service. One man, Alexander Keist, Company C, was missing and is supposed to have perished in the fire. Our poor bear, which had been with us so long and to which the men had become greatly attached, was fastened to a post in the vacant square, but so great was the heat it was impossible to get him out, and he was slowly roasted to death. Some of the darkies made a feast on his remains after the fire was over and the ruins cool enough to get through. Twice now had all our belongings been destroyed by fire, and almost nothing was left to us. The last was the worst, as high anticipations were enjoyed of our reception when we should arrive at home, and most earnest preparation had been made to appear at our very best. Under the depressing circumstances we gave up every thought of the public parade we had premeditated and arranged for.

October 12th the regiment was assembled, and by virtue of S. O. 36, Headquarters Department of Georgia, was mustered out of the service of the United States by Lieutenant S. S. Culbertson, United States mustering officer.

October 13th we turned our faces homeward, marching out of Augusta in the early morning, and October 15th reached a small station on the Central Railroad fifty-two miles from Augusta. Here we remained overnight, and October 16th proceeded by rail to Savannah, where we arrived at 3 p. m. the same day. Here we were camped within the city limits awaiting transportation, until October 18th, when we were marched through the city to the river wharf and embarked on the transport *Varuna*, which sailed October 19th, arriving at New York, eight hundred and seventeen miles from Savannah, October 22d. We were at once landed and marched to the Battery, and at 4 p. m. were embarked on a small steamer and transported to Hart's Island in the Sound, about twenty-four miles northeast of New York. Here were made up the final accounts of Quartermaster and Ordnance stores, and the pay rolls of the regiment.

Wednesday October 25th we were mustered out of the State service and received our final pay and discharge; and, leaving the island the same day, were landed at Peck Slip, New York, at 8 p. m., when, after a service of over three years, we disbanded, and the members from Brooklyn returned to their homes. The Columbia County companies left New York October 27th by rail, and were accorded a most hearty public reception at Hudson, after which they too separated, and the regiment as a body became a thing of the past.

The officers who returned with the regiment were :

Lieutenant-Colonel WILLIAM WALTERMIRE, commanding.
Assistant-Surgeon CALEB C. BRIGGS.
Acting-Adjutant GEORGE B. STAYLEY, *First-Lieutenant* Company H.
Captain WILLIAM F. TIEMANN, Company A.
First-Lieutenant JOHN DAY, Company B.
First-Lieutenant BARZILLAI RANSOM, Company C.
First-Lieutenant E. PARMLY BROWN, Company D.
First-Lieutenant ANDREW RIFENBURGH, Company E.
Captain GEORGE W. HUSSEY, Company F.
Captain JAMES S. REYNOLDS, Company G.
Captain WELLS O. PETTIT, Company H.
First-Lieutenant EDWARD TYNAN, Company I.
First-Lieutenant E. SPENCER ELMER, Company K, *Acting-Quartermaster*.

Of these, only four—Lieutenant-Colonel Waltermire, Assistant-Surgeon Briggs, Captain Pettit, and Captain Hussey—had been commissioned officers at the muster in of the regiment in 1862. Three who were mustered in as enlisted men and served continuously with the regiment—Captain Tiemann, Lieutenant Day, and Lieutenant Rifenburgh—were promoted from the ranks ; and two who, originally enlisting with the regiment, had been discharged for some months—Lieutenant Ransom, formerly Sergeant, Company B, and Lieutenant Tynan, formerly Sergeant, Company A—were commissioned from civil life. Lieutenant Brown joined as a recruit in November, 1863, and was promoted from the ranks. Captain Reynolds and Lieutenant Elmer joined the regiment with a company of recruits in March, 1864, and Lieutenant Stayley, commissioned from the ranks of another regiment, joined in August, 1864.

The following commissions were conferred on those named, but they could not be mustered in the grade specified owing to the numerical strength of the regiment being less than was required to entitle them to muster, except in the cases of Sergeant Spanburgh, who was discharged for wounds at Port Hudson, and Private Perkins, who was killed in action at Cedar Creek, Va.:

Lieutenant-Colonel WILLIAM WALTERMIRE, as *Colonel* from August 4, 1865.
Captain WELLS O. PETTIT, as *Major* from February 28, 1865, as *Lieutenant-Colonel* from August 4, 1865.
Captain JOSEPH G. McNUTT, as *Major* from October 19, 1864.
Captain WILLIAM F. TIEMANN, as *Major* from August 4, 1865.
Assistant-Surgeon CALEB C. BRIGGS, as *Surgeon* from August 8, 1865.
First-Lieutenant CRAWFORD WILLIAMS, as *Captain* from July 30, 1863.
First-Lieutenant E. SPENCER ELMER, as *Captain* from December 10, 1864.
First-Lieutenant EDWARD TYNAN, as *Captain* from August 4, 1865.
First-Lieutenant GEORGE B. STAYLEY, as *Captain* from August 4, 1865.
First-Lieutenant ANDREW RIFENBURGH, as *Captain* from August 4, 1865.
Sergeant WILLIAM A. JAQUINS, as *First-Lieutenant* from August 1, 1865.
Sergeant THOMAS BERGEN, as *First-Lieutenant* from August 1, 1865.
Sergeant WILLIAM H. SPANBURGH, as *Second-Lieutenant* from July 31, 1863.
Private JAMES T. PERKINS, as *Second-Lieutenant* from August 2, 1864.

The following commissions were issued to persons not connected with the regiment, but were declined :

Captain — WILLIAM F. FARNHAM, January 25, 1864.
Second-Lieutenant — JAMES S. CORNELL, *Private* One Hundred and Twenty-seventh New York, November 13, 1863.

At the muster out of the regiment there were 13 officers and 333 men borne on the rolls. Of these, 8 men were on detached service, 24 absent sick in hospital, 2 prisoners of war, 3 missing (2 of whom were supposed to be deserters), and 6 in confinement by sentence of court-martial, making the actual number present 13 officers and 290 men. Of these, 6 officers and 67 men had joined as recruits, leaving 7 officers and 223 men who had been with the regiment since its organization.

The regiment participated in seven general engagements :

Irish Bend, Louisiana	April 14, 1863.
Port Hudson, Louisiana	May 27, 1863.
Port Hudson, Louisiana	June 14, 1863.
Mansura Plains, Louisiana	May 16, 1864.
Opequan, Virginia	September 19, 1864.
Fisher's Hill, Virginia	September 22, 1864.
Cedar Creek, Virginia	October 19, 1864.

In these the loss of the regiment was:

	Officers.	Men.	Aggregate.
Killed	6	45	51
Mortally wounded	3	18	21
Wounded	7	168	175
Missing	1	39	40
Total	17	270	287

It was under fire in skirmishes at Indian Bend, Vermilion Bayou, Port Hudson, Donaldsonville, Marksville, Bermuda Hundreds, Halltown, Berryville, Woodstock, and other places, in which it lost:

	Officers.	Men.	Aggregate.
Killed	—	3	3
Mortally wounded	—	3	3
Wounded	1	8	9
Missing	—	2	2
Total	1	16	17

Not in battle alone were our numbers depleted, but many of our gallant comrades fell overcome by the exposure and fatigue of the camp and march. We lost from death and disease:

	Officers.	Men.	Aggregate.
Died	1	107	108
Discharged	7	158	165
Total	8	265	273

Those who thus died gave their lives to their country as truly as did others in the shock of battle, and their memories should be cherished with the thought, "THEY FELL AT THEIR POST."

By resignation, honorable discharge, and transfer we lost:

Officers, 18; men, 43; aggregate, 61.

Several of our officers and men were honored with commissions in other regiments. The number thus favored whom we lost was:

Officers, 2; men, 5; aggregate, 7.

While in Louisiana a call was made for volunteers to the Navy, and the regiment contributed 7 men.

There was another class by which the regiment lost heavily, whose names should be held in obloquy and their memories blotted out—*the deserters.* The number of those who betrayed their colors and forsook their comrades, most of whom deserted before we left New York, though there were also some who went with the regiment and deserted later, was 197.

RECAPITULATION.

STRENGTH AT MUSTER IN, AND GAINS.

	Officers.	Men.	Aggregate.
Original strength	38	802	840
Promoted from ranks	13	—	13
Promoted by appointment	12	—	12
Recruits	—	175	175
	63	977	1040
Less promoted from ranks	—	13	13
Total in regiment	63	964	1027

The total losses from all causes were:

	Officers.	Men.	Aggregate.
Died	10	176	186
Discharged	35	201	236
Transferred	—	38	38
Dishonorably dismissed	5	—	5
Deserted	—	178	178
Unaccounted for	—	38	38
Total	50	631	681

PARTICULARS OF LOSSES.

The particulars of these losses are as follows:

		Officers.	Men.	Aggregate.
Discharged:	Promoted to other regiments	2	5	7
	Honorably by resignation	16	—	16
	Dishonorably by court-martial	5	—	5
	Wounds / Disability	7	158	165
	Expiration of service	—	29	29
	Other causes	10	9	19
	Total	40	201	241
Transferred:	Veteran Reserve Corps	—	29	29
	Navy	—	7	7
	Other	—	2	2
	Total	—	38	38
Died:	In battle	6	48	54
	Of wounds in battle	3	21	24
	Prisoners of war	—	12	12
	Disease and unknown	1	91	92
	Other causes, accidents, etc.	—	4	4
	Total	10	176	186
Deserted (less apprehended, 19)		—	178	178
Not accounted for at muster out		—	38	38
	Total of losses.	50	631	681

STRENGTH AT MUSTER OUT.

	Officers.	Men.	Aggregate.
Present	13	290	303
Absent: Prisoners of war		2	
Sick		24	
Detached		8	43
Missing		1	
In confinement		6	
Without leave		2	
Total mustered out on rolls	13	333	346

From the time we left New York until our return we journeyed:

By transport	7491 miles
By rail	508 "
On foot	1333 "
A total of	9332 miles

and this does not include the changes in camps, which involved marches of one to four miles, and would aggregate at least two hundred miles to be added to the above.

We campaigned or were stationed in the States of Louisiana, Mississippi, Maryland, Virginia, North Carolina, South Carolina, and Georgia, and marched through or were quartered in over ninety cities, towns, and villages.

Through the heat and rain of the extreme South, the frost and snow of the more northern States, and the dust and mud of both, the regiment faithfully fulfilled its service, and was ever ready at the call of duty. The losses on the field of battle and the commendation of superior officers attest to faithful service and duty well done, and not the least heritage the brave men of the command may proudly leave is that of having been members of

THE ONE HUNDRED AND FIFTY-NINTH NEW YORK.

THE 159TH REGIMENT INFANTRY,
NEW-YORK STATE VOLUNTEERS.

ERRATA.

Page 132: "was 197"—should be *was 196*.

Page 133: "(less apprehended, 19)"—should be *less apprehended, 18*.

Muster Out Rolls, page XLII: "Deserted, 32; returned, 6"—should be *Deserted, 31; returned, 5*.

Page XXXIX: Opposite "WENSTROM, CHARLES R."—*erase* "Deserted Jan. 8, 1865. Apprehended and ret'd, April 16, 1865." which correction is made by the following authority:

[COPY.]

WAR DEPARTMENT,
RECORD AND PENSION DIVISION,
WASHINGTON, Nov'r 24th, 1891.

It has this day been determined, from record evidence on file in this Department, that the charge of desertion referred to herein is erroneous, and a notation to that effect has been placed on the official record.

By authority of the Secretary of War:

(Signed) F. C. AINSWORTH,
Major and Surgeon U. S. Army.

MUSTER OUT ROLLS.

Copied from those on file in the *Adjutant-General's Office, Albany, New-York*, by permission of the Adjutant-General, State of New-York,—revised and corrected from BI-MONTHLY MUSTER AND PAY ROLLS in possession of the company commanders as far as obtainable.

THE 159TH REGIMENT INFANTRY, N. Y. S. V.—FIELD AND STAFF.

	Rank.	Age.	Date.	Place.	Joined.
Mustered Out with Regt.					
WILLIAM WALTERMIRE.	Lt.-Col.	30	Oct. 15, 1862.	Hudson.	Promoted from Capt. Co. E, to Major, Jan. 10, 1864. Promoted Lt.-Col., June 2, 1864. Commissioned Colonel.
CALEB C. BRIGGS.	Asst.-Surg.	36	" 30, "	Albany.	Commissioned Surgeon.
Resigned and Discharged.					
HOMER A. NELSON.	Colonel.		Oct. 31, 1862.	Hudson.	Nov. 25, 1862.
EDWARD L. MOLINEUX.	Colonel.	29	Aug. 28, "	Brooklyn.	Aug. 4, 1865. Promoted from Lt.-Col., Nov. 25, 1862. Commissioned Brevet Brig.-Gen. and Brevet Maj.-Gen.
CHAS. A. BURT.	Lt.-Col.		Nov. 25, "	New-York.	Jan. 7, 1864. Promoted from Capt. 91st N. Y. V., Nov. 25, 1862. Promoted Lt.-Col., April 14, 1863.
EDWARD L. GAUL.	Lt.-Col.	25	Sept. 18, "	Hudson.	June 2, 1864. Promoted from Capt. Co. A, to Major, April 14, 1863. Promoted Lt.-Col., Jan. 10, 1864.
CHARLES A. ROBERTSON.	Surgeon.		Aug. 30, "	Albany.	Nov. 2, 1863.
WILLIAM Y. PROVOST.	Surgeon.	25	Sept. 29, "	Brooklyn.	July 28, 1865. Promoted from 1st Asst. Surgeon, Dec. 2, 1863.
ISAAC L. KIPP.	Chaplain.		Nov. 10, "	New-York.	Sept. 9, 1863.
MARK D. WILBER.	Regt. Q. M.	33	Sept. 18, "	Hudson.	Dec. 5, 1863.
JOHN H. CHARLOTTE.	Regt. Q. M.	20	" 18, "	"	Aug. 22, 1865. Promoted Private Co. C. Promoted Q. M. Sgt. Nov. 2, 1862. Promoted 1st Lt. and R. Q. M., Jan. 25, 1864.
Died.					
GILBERT A. DRAPER.	Lt.-Col.	27	Aug. 28, 1862.	Brooklyn.	April 14, 1863. In action, Irish Bend, La. Promoted Major, Nov. 25, 1862.
ROBERT McD. HART.	Major.	22	Sept. 6, "	"	Oct. 19, 1864. In action, Cedar Creek, Va. Promoted from Capt. Co. F, June 2, 1864.
ROBERT D. LATHROP.	Adjutant.	22	" 17, "	Hudson.	April 14, 1863. In action, Irish Bend, La.
NON-COM. STAFF.					
Mustered Out with Regt.					
GUILEN, GILBERT S.	Sergt.-Maj.	21	Sept. 23, 1862.	Brooklyn.	Promoted from Sergt. Co. F, Aug. 16, 1865.
JAQUINS, WILLIAM A.	Q. M. Sergt.	26	" 26, "	Hudson.	Promoted from Corp. Co. C, Jan. 25, 1864. Commis'd 1st Lt.
BERGEN, THOMAS.	Com. Sergt.	29	Aug. 28, "	Brooklyn.	Promoted from 1st Sergt. Co. K, July 25, 1863. Com'd 1st Lt.
BAKER, EDWARD E.	Hosp. Stwd.	20	Sept. 25, "	"	Promoted from Private Co. B, Nov. 22, 1863. Absent sick.

111

THE 159TH REGIMENT INFANTRY, N. Y. S. V.—FIELD AND STAFF.—Continued.

	Rank.	Age.	Joined.		Place.	
			Date.			

Mustered Out with Regt.

MILLER, THOMAS B	1st Prl Mus.	15½	Sept. 13, 1862.		Livingston.	Promoted from Musician Co. A, Jan. 28, 1864.
DAYTON, GEORGE D	2d Prl Mus.	21	" 4, "		Brooklyn.	Promoted from 1st Sergt. Co. B, Nov. 2, 1862. Reduced Aug. 16, 1865. Reinstated Sept. 21, 1865.

Discharged.

TIEMANN, WILLIAM F	Sergt.-Maj.	18	Sept. 5, 1862.		Brooklyn.	Jan. 14, 1863, for promotion to 2d Lt. Co. A. Enrolled Sergt. Co. B, Promoted Nov. 2, 1862.
BRUCE, ALFRED H	Sergt.-Maj.	23	" 15, "		Kinderhook.	March 6, 1863, for promotion to 2d Lt. Co. F. Enrolled 1st Sergt. Co. G, Promoted Jan. 14, 1863.
SMITH, HERMAN	Sergt.-Maj.	18	" 3, "		Brooklyn.	June 10, 1863, for promotion to 2d Lt. Co. G. Enrolled Sergt. Co. H. Promoted March 6, 1863.
DUNHAM, MARSHALL A	Sergt.-Maj.	22	" 17, "		New Lebanon.	Mar. 19, 1864, for promotion U. S. C. T. Enrolled Private Co. A. Promoted June 10, 1863.
PALMER, WILLIAM E	Sergt.-Maj.	18	" 5, "		Brooklyn.	Aug. 7, 1865, for disability. Enrolled Corp. Co. D. Promoted April 9, 1864.
CHARLOTTE, JOHN H	Q. M. Sergt.	20	" 18, "		Hudson.	Jan. 25, 1864, for promotion to 1st Lt. and R. Q. M. Enrolled Private Co. C. Promoted Nov. 2, 1862.
MOORE, ALFRED H. S	Hosp. Stwd.	24	" 5, "		Brooklyn.	Nov. 10, 1863, for disability. Enrolled Private Co. H. Promoted Nov. 2, 1862.

Transferred.

MAMBERT, JOHN W	Princ'l Mus.	43	Sept. 20, 1862.		Taghkanic.	Jan. 28, 1864, reduced and returned to Co. G. Enrolled Musician Co. G. Promoted Nov. 2, 1862.
FRENCH, WILLIAM F	Com. Sergt.	19	" 18, "		Hudson.	Promoted Nov. 2, 1862. Enrolled Sergt. Co. G. (Not accounted for at muster out.) On Co. H roll.

	Officers.	Men.
Original Strength	8	
Gain by Appointment	2	
Total genuine members	10	
Gain { Promoted from Companies	3	15
Gain { Promoted from Non-com. Staff	1	
Total borne on Rolls	14	15

		Officers.	Men.	Officers.	Men.
Brought forward				14	15
	Discharged	9	7		
Loss {	Transferred		2		
	Died	3		12	9
Mustered Out on Roll				2	6
Absent sick at Muster Out					1
Present at Muster Out				2	5

IV

THE 159TH REGIMENT INFANTRY, N. Y. S. V.—COMPANY A.

	Rank.	Age.	Joined. Date.	Place.	
Mustered Out with Regt.					
WILLIAM F. TIEMANN	Captain.	18	Sept. 5, 1862.	Brooklyn.	Enrolled Sergt. Co. B. Promoted Sergt. Maj., Nov. 2, 1862; 2d Lt. Co. A, Jan. 14, 1863; 1st Lt. Co. A, Apr. 30, 1863; Capt. Co. A, Feb. 23, 1864. Commissioned Major.
Discharged.					
F. EDWIN ATWOOD	1st Lieut.	20	Sept. 18, 1862.	Hudson.	Jan. 19, 1863.
EDWARD DUFFY	1st Lieut.	32	Oct. 6, "	"	Aug. 30, 1865. Dishonorably dismissed. Enrolled Corp. Co. G. Promoted May 23, 1864.
Transferred.					
EDWARD L. GAUL	Captain.	25	Sept. 18, 1862.	Hudson.	April 14, 1863. Promoted Major.
WESLEY BRADLEY	2d Lieut.	32	" 18, "	"	Jan. 14, 1863. Promoted 1st Lt. Co. E.
Died.					
JOHN W. MANLEY, JR.	1st Lieut.	22	Sept. 24, 1862.	Brooklyn.	April 14, 1863. In action, Irish Bend, La. Promoted from 2d Lt. Co. D, Jan. 27, 1863.
Mustered Out with Regt.					
HARRINGTON, JOSHUA D.	1st Sergt.	24	Sept. 12, 1862.	Hudson.	Enrolled 4th Sergt. Promoted March 16, 1864. Reduced Aug. 16, 1865. Reinstated Sept. 9, 1865.
BERRIDGE, THOMAS	Sergeant.	22	" 6, "	Greenport.	Enrolled 5th Sergt. Red. Aug. 16, 1865. Reinstated Sept. 9, 1865.
OSBORN, HENRY A.	"	21	" 19, "	Claverack.	Enrolled Private. Promoted Corp, July 15, 1864. Reduced Aug. 16, 1865. Promoted Sept. 9, 1865.
MOSIER, RICHARD M.	"	22	" 12, "	Hudson.	Enrolled Private. Promoted Corp. July 15, 1864. Promoted Sept. 9, 1865.
GARDNER, ROBERT R.	Corporal.	23½	" 9, "	"	Mustered out on separate rolls Oct. 11, 1865.
HUESTED, ROSSMAN	"	25	" 5, "	"	
PARIS, SAMUEL	"	20½	" 11, "	Greenport.	Enrolled Private. Promoted Sept. 9, 1865.
BRENZEL, WILLIAM	"	22	" 20, "	Livingston.	Enrolled Private. Promoted Sept. 9, 1865.
SCOTT, WILLIAM H.	Musician.	18½	" 10, "	Hudson.	
AKINS, THOMAS	Private.	24	" 12, "	"	
CONTOIS, VICTOR	"	35	" 11, "	New Leb'n.	
FERRIS, JOSEPH	"	39	" 4, "	Greenport.	Absent. Sick in hospital.
FUNK, MORGAN	"	19	" 27, "	Livingston.	

THE 159TH REGIMENT INFANTRY, N. Y. S. V.—COMPANY A.—Continued.

	Rank.	Age.	Date.	Joined. Place.	
Mustered Out with Regt.					
Howes, George	Private.	18	Sept. 5, 1862.	Hudson.	
Hawver, William	"	18½	" 8, "	Livingston.	
Jones, Justus	"	32	" 15, "	Hudson.	
Jennings, Daniel	"	19	" 20, "	Greenport.	
Loucks, Henry H.	"	22½	" 8, "	Hudson.	
Leonard, John	"	45	" 5, "	"	
Morgan, John J.	"	33	" 4, "	"	Absent. In confinement by sentence Court-martial.
Maguire, John	"	38	" 11, "	"	Enrolled Private. Promoted Corp. Feb. 24, 1863. Reduced at his own request July 15, 1864.
Moore, James	"	33	" 8, "	"	
Reid, John	"	32¾	" 13, "	"	Enrolled Corp. Reduced Nov. 4, 1862.
Roraback, Amos	"	18	" 26, "	Claverack.	
Rupff, Christian M	"	28	" 26, "	Hudson.	
Shaver, Granville M	"	34	" 6, "	Stuyvesant.	Enrolled Wagoner. Reduced June 21, 1863.
Smith, Sloan	"	18	" 8, "	Greenport.	
Wheeler, Myron	"	23	" 17, "	Hudson.	
Winans, Edward V.	"	18½	" 12, "	"	
Birdlong, Washing'n	Cd. Cook.	46½	Jan. 1, 1864.	Thibodeaux, La.	Recruit.
Discharged.					
Tynan, Edward	1st Sergt.	20½	Sept. 5, 1862.	Hudson.	Mar. 16, 1864. Disability from wounds. Enrolled 2d Sergt. Promoted Nov. 4, 1862.
White, Laban A.	Sergeant.	36	" 5, "	"	Mar. 23, 1863. Enrolled 1st Sergt. Reduced at his own request Nov. 4, 1862.
Sagendorph, Jacob	Corporal.	31½	" 8, "	Claverack.	Aug. 24, 1863. Enrolled Private. Promoted March 23, 1863.
Tator, Silas	"	21	" 2, "	"	Aug. 24, 1863. Enrolled Private. Promoted Jan. 16, 1863.
Peary, Silas W	"	18	" 22, "	Germantown.	G. O. 77, A. G. O., W. D. Enrolled Private. From July 15, 1864.
Benneway, Jeremiah	Private.	44½	" 6, "	Greenport.	Dec. 3, 1862.
Clearwater, Joseph	"	25	" 26, "	Fishkill.	G. O. 77, A. G. O., W. D.
Paley, Thomas	"	31	" 17, "	Hudson.	Mar. 5, 1864. Disability.
Ford, John H.	"	18	" 25, "	Livingston.	June 30, 1863. Disability.

THE 159TH REGIMENT INFANTRY, N. Y. S. V.—COMPANY A.—Continued.

	Rank.	Age.	Date.	Place.	
Discharged.			*Joined.*		
KEEGAN, PATRICK	Private.	32	Sept. 29, 1862.	Hudson.	Disability.
KELLER, JACOB		45	Oct. 3, "	Livingston.	Disability.
KINZLER, THEODORE		40	Sept. 12, "	Hudson.	Disability.
LAWTON, CHARLES		32	" 8, "	Livingston.	Disability.
LINES, JOHN M.	"	28	" 27, "	"	Disability.
LOWN, JOHN S.	"	40	Jan. 15, 1864.	New Leb'n.	Recruit.
LOUCKS, RENSELLAER	"	22	Aug. 25, "	Po'keepsie.	G. O. 94, A. G. O., W. D. Recruit.
RAUKINS, CHARLES	"	18	Sept. 12, 1862.	Greenport.	Writ Habeas Corpus.
TEAVER, WILLIAM H.		44	" 4, "	Claverack.	Disability.
THOMPSON, HENRY	"	44	Oct. 20, "	Hudson.	Disability.
VAN HOESEN, GARRET S.	"	25½	Sept. 9, "	"	Disability.
VAUGHN, LEWIS	"	18	Oct. 10, "	Ghent.	Writ Habeas Corpus.
WINANS, CHARLES I.	"	18½	Sept. 8, "	Hudson.	Disability. Enrolled Private. Promoted Corp. Dec. 1862. Reduced Jan. 20, 1863.
WALLACE, PHILIP	"	44	" 9, "	Greenport.	June 1, 1863.
Transferred.					
MILLER, THOMAS B.	Musician.	15½	Sept. 13, 1862.	Livingston.	Jan. 28, 1864, to N. C. S. Promoted 2d Principal Musician.
COONEY, JAMES	Private.	35	" 7, "	Hudson.	Mar. 3, 1864, to Co. C. Returned as a Deserter. Not enrolled in Co. A.
DUNHAM, MARSHALL A.	"	22	" 17, "	New Leb'n.	June 19, 1863, to N. C. S. Promoted Sergeant-Major.
FINNEY, GEORGE	"	42½	" 10, "	Auxerlitz.	April 6, 1864, to V. R. C. Enrolled Corp. Reduced Feb. 24, 1863.
HOLLENBECK, WM. H.	"	30	" 18, "	Hudson.	Jan. 10, 1865, to V. R. C. Enrolled Corp. Reduced Dec. 1862.
HOLLENBECK, JACOB	"	40	" 6, "	"	Nov. 6, 1863, to Co. F. Not enrolled in Co. A. Ret'd as a Deserter.
HERBERT, THOMAS					
MAROS, FRANCIS	"	28	Sept. 8, "	Brooklyn.	Nov. 6, 1863, to Co. F. Not enrolled in Co. A. Returned as a Deserter.
MAURER, SOLOMON	"	34	" 16, "	Stockport.	April 6, 1864, to V. R. C. Enlisted in Co. K.
Died.					
HUGGINS, JOHN	Corporal.	18	Sept. 6, 1862.	Hudson.	May 18, 1863, of wounds in action, Irish Bend, La., April 14, 1863.

VII

THE 159TH REGIMENT INFANTRY, N. Y. S. V.—COMPANY A.—Continued.

	Rank.	Age.	Joined Date.	Joined Place.	
Died.					
RACE, JONATHAN J.	Corporal.	45	Sept. 13, 1862.	Greenport.	May 27, 1863. In action, Port Hudson, La. Enrolled Private. Promoted Nov. 4, 1862, Color Corporal.
NIVER, PETER P.	"	45	" 13, "	"	May 13, 1863. Disease. Enrolled Private. Promoted Dec. 1862.
TATOR, JOHN D.	"	33	" 4, "	Claverack.	Sept. 19, 1864. In action, Opequan, Va.
CONNERY, PATRICK	Private.	40	" 11, "	Hudson.	April 14, 1863. In action, Irish Bend, La.
DENNIS, JOHN	"	32	" 6, "	"	June 5, 1863. Disease.
KELLY, JOHN	"	44	" 11, "	"	April 14, 1863. In action, Irish Bend, La.
KIPP, ROBERT	"	18	" 22, "	Greenport.	April 14, 1863. In action, Irish Bend, La.
LAPE, ANDREW W.	"	30	" 6, "	Ghent.	July 25, 1861. Disease.
MILLER, PETER H.	"	25½	" 8, "	Livingston.	Aug. 1, 1863. Disease.
MORAN, LEWIS	"	40	" 7, "	New Leb'n.	Oct. 19, 1864. In action, Cedar Creek, Va.
RORABACK, FREDERICK	"	23	" 26, "	Hudson.	April 6, 1865. Disease.
REYNOLDS, JAMES	"	42	" 5, "	Livingston.	April 14, 1863. In action, Irish Bend, La.
SNYDER, JOSEPH	"	32½	" 3, "	Greenport.	April 14, 1863. In action, Irish Bend, La.
SMITH, JOSEPH	"	25	" 10, "	New Leb'n.	April 12, 1863. Disease.
VAN DEUSEN, DELBERT	"	18½	" 6, "	Greenport.	Sept. 19, 1864. In action, Opequan, Va.
WINSLOW, WARREN	"	26	" 15, "	"	April 27, 1863. Of wounds in action, Irish Bend, La., April 14, 1863.
WARD, THOMAS	"	44	" 22, "	Hudson.	Nov. 15, 1864. Prisoner of war, Salisbury, N. C.
Deserted.					
MADDER, GEORGE	Corporal.	22½	Sept. 5, 1862.	Hudson.	Nov. 4, 1863.
ALGER, EDMOND H.	Private.	20	" 4, "	Claverack.	Nov. 4, 1862.
AGEN, JAMES	"	24	" 5, "	Greenport.	Nov. 22, 1862.
BRADLEY, AVERY SMITH	"	21	" 12, "	Hudson.	Aug. 7, 1864. Enrolled Corp. Reduced Aug. 17, 1863.
BRADLEY, JOHN H	"	21	" 15, "	"	Nov. 14, 1862.
DOYLE, CHARLES	"	21	April 25, 1864.	Po'keepsie.	Aug. 7, 1864. Recruit.
GARDNER, CHARLES H.	"	21	Sept. 7, 1862.	Hudson.	May, 1863.
HERMANCE, ANDREW	"	22	April 25, 1864.	9th dist.N.Y.	June 20, 1864. Recruit.
HAWVER, JONAS	"	21	Sept. 8, 1862.	Hudson.	Nov. 14, 1862.
JUNES, THOMAS	"	23½	" 15, "	"	Nov. 12, 1862.
KNOWLES, JOSEPH	"	33	Oct. 17.	Ghent.	April 1, 1863.

VIII

THE 159TH REGIMENT INFANTRY, N. Y. S. V.—COMPANY A.—Continued.

	Rank.	Age.	Joined.		
			Date.	Place.	

Deserted.

STEWART, JAMES	Private.	40	Sept. 6, 1862.	Greenport.	Nov. 22, 1862.
STEVENS, GEORGE C.	"	35½	" 15, "	Hudson.	Sept. 13, 1863. Missing April 14, 1863. Reported in Parole Camp, St. Louis, Mo., Sept. 1863, from which he deserted.
TYNAN, JOHN	"	36	" 17, "	"	Nov. 2, 1862.
WALTERS, RICHARD	"	37	" 17, "	"	Nov. 11, 1862. Apprehended and returned June 22, 1864. Again deserted Nov. 30, 1864.

	Officers.	Men.
Original Strength	3	87
Gain by Recruits		5
Deserters returned		2
Total genuine members	3	94
Gain { Promoted from ranks other Companies	3	
Promoted from officers other Companies	2	
Transfers from other Companies	1	1
Total borne on Rolls	6	95

		Officers.	Men.	Officers.	Men.
Brought forward				6	95
Loss { Discharged		2	23		
Transferred		2	9		
Died		1	18		
Deserted			15		
				5	65
Mustered Out on Rolls				1	30
Absent at Muster Out					3
Present at Muster Out				1	27

THE 159TH REGIMENT INFANTRY, N. Y. S. V.—COMPANY B.

	Rank.	Age.	Date Joined.	Place Joined.	
Mustered Out with Regt.					
JOHN DAY	1st Lieut.	23	Aug. 23, 1862.	Brooklyn.	Enrolled Corporal Co. K. Promoted Sept. 2, 1864.
Discharged and Resigned.					
AUGUSTUS J. DAYTON	Captain.	33	Aug. 28, 1862.	Brooklyn.	Feb. 28, 1863.
JULIUS H. TIEMANN	1st Lieut.	22	Sept. 24, "	"	Dec. 24, 1863.
ALFRED GREENLEAF, Jr.	2d Lieut.	24	" 24, "	"	May 2, 1864.
Transferred.					
GEORGE W. HUSSEY	1st Lieut.	24	Oct. 4, 1862.	Brooklyn.	Sept. 3, 1864. Promoted Capt. Co. F. Promoted from 2d Lt. Co. F to 1st Lt. Co. G., March 6, 1863. Transferred March 12, 1864.
Mustered Out with Regt.					
GAVAN, FRANK P.	1st Sergt.	22	Sept. 5, 1862.	Brooklyn.	Absent. Detached.
HARK, AMOS	Sergeant.	19	Oct. 20, "	"	Enrolled Private. Promoted Aug. 27, 1863.
LEWIS, SMITH H.	"	21	Sept. 17, "	"	Enrolled Private. Prom. Corp. Sept. 17, 1863. Prom. April 1, 1864.
SMYTH, JAMES	"	30	" 12, "	"	Enrolled Corporal. Promoted Sept. 17, 1863.
HATFIELD, GEORGE W.	Corporal.	18	" 29, "	"	Enrolled Private. Promoted April 1, 1864.
SMALIX, MARTIN	"	35	" 10, "	"	Enrolled Private. Promoted May 14, 1864.
DUNHAM, HENRY C.	Musician.	20	" 10, "	"	
MAMBERT, JOHN W.	"	43	" 20, "	Taghkanic.	Transferred from Co. G March 12, 1864.
CAVANAGH, THOMAS	Private.	34	" 6, "	Brooklyn.	Absent. Sick in hospital.
CORSON, THOMAS	"	18	" 17, "	"	
DECKER, EPHRAIM P.	"	18	" 9, "	Stockport.	Transferred from Co. G March 12, 1864.
DREWETT, JAMES	"	44	" 17, "	Brooklyn.	
FOX, JOHN H	"	30	" 6, "	"	
GASS, ROBERT	"	18	" 15, "	Claverack.	Transferred from Co. G March 12, 1864.
GAULT, JOHN	"	28	" 26, "	Brooklyn.	
JOY, JOHN	"	21	" 16, "	"	
KEROS, JOHN	"	40	" 8, "	"	Absent. Sick in hospital.
LAWRENCE, FRED'K J.	"	18	" 11, "	"	Absent. Sick in hospital.
LOUGHLIN, STEPHEN	"	36	" 3, "	"	
MACK, PATRICK	"	40	" 18, "	"	
MCELRAVEY, HUGH	"	38	" 11, "	"	
MURRAY, MICHAEL	"	18	" 15, "	"	Deserted, Baton Rouge, La., Feb. 27, 1863. Returned Oct. 31, 1863.
O'NEILL, JAMES	"	30	" 18, "	"	Absent. Detached.
PITTS, WILLIAM	"	23	" 5, "	"	

Mustered Out with Regt.					
RICHMOND, SILAS W.	Private.	18	Sept. 28, 1862.	Kinderhook.	Transferred from Co. G March 12, 1864.
SIEGLER, FREDERICK	"	41	" 26, "	Brooklyn.	
TAYLOR, JOHN	"	18	" 10, "	"	Absent. In confinement by sentence G. C. M.
WURTZ, BALTHAZAR	"	28	" 18, "	"	Recruit.
WASHINGTON, GEORGE.	C'd Cook.	30	Jan. 1, 1864.	Thibodeaux, La.	
Discharged.					
LARKIN, PATRICK	Sergeant.	34	Sept. 12, 1862.	Brooklyn.	Aug. 24, 1863. Disability. Enrolled Corporal.
RANSOM, BARZILLAI	"	32	" 8, "	"	Feb. 23, 1864.
TIEMANN, J. ANTHONY	"	31	" 18, "	"	Aug. 24, 1864. for promotion to 1st Lt. Co. F.
BROWN, HORACE J.	Private.	18	" 8, "	"	July 18, 1865. Enrolled Musician.
COSTELLO, JAMES	"	43	" 10, "	"	Mar. 14, 1864. Disability.
COYLE, JOHN	"	43	" 17, "	"	May 17, 1865.
IRVING, ALEXANDER F.	"	27	" 6, "	"	Jan. 17, 1864. Disability. Enrolled Corporal. Reduced.
MCCAULEY, JOHN	"	21	" 5, "	"	July 29, 1863. Disability. Enrolled Corporal. Reduced.
SAHLER, JACOB	"	44	" 15, "	"	June 29, 1863. Disability.
SHERMAN, WILLIAM	"	19	Jan. 1, 1864.	Hudson.	June 28, 1865. Recruit.
SNYDER, CHARLES	"	18	Sept. 22, 1862.	Ghent.	July 21, 1865. Transferred from Co. G March 12, 1864.
TAPPAN, JOHN J.	"	27	" 17, "	Brooklyn.	June 7, 1863. Disability.
WOLFERT, NICHOLAS	"	44	" 29, "	"	Oct. 19, 1863. Disability.
Transferred.					
DAVTON, GEORGE D.	1st Sergt.	21	Sept. 4, 1862.	Brooklyn.	Nov. 2, 1862, to N. C. S. Promoted Principal Musician. Reduced to ranks Aug. 16, 1865. Reinstated Sept. 21, 1865.
TIEMANN, WILLIAM F.	Sergeant.	18	" 5, "	"	Nov. 2, 1862, to N. C. S. Promoted Sergeant-Major.
ROBERTS, WILLIAM H.	Corporal.	26	Oct. 10, "	"	April 6, 1864, to V. R. C.
BAKER, EDWARD E.	Private.	26	Sept. 25, "	"	Nov. 22, 1863, to V. R. C. Promoted Hospital Steward.
DOOLAN, WILLIAM	"	44	" 11, "	"	Jan. 10, 1865, to V. R. C.
FRENCH, STEPHEN	"	19	" 13, "	"	April 6, 1864, to V. R. C.
HART, SHERMAN	"	40	" 27, "	"	May 1, 1864, to Navy.
HENNESSY, JOHN	"	43	" 12, "	Kinderhook.	Jan. 15, 1865, to V. R. C. Transferred from Co. G, Mar. 12, 1864.
Died.					
DAILEY, JOHN	Private.	30	Sept. 22, 1862.	Kinderhook.	Nov. 12, 1864. Prisoner of war, Salisbury, N. C. Transferred from Co. G March 12, 1864.

xi

THE 159TH REGIMENT INFANTRY, N. Y. S. V.—COMPANY B.—Continued.

	Rank.	Age.	Joined Date.	Joined Place.			
Died.							
GAFFNEY, RICHARD	Private.	38	Oct. 11, 1862.	Brooklyn.	July 9, 1865.	Disease.	
HANLIN, JAMES	"	30	Sept. 5, "	"	Aug. 20, 1864.	Disease.	
LENFESTY, JAMES J.	"	18	" 24, "	"	Aug. 26, 1864.	Of wounds in action, Halltown, Va., Aug. 24, 1864.	
McCARTNEY, THOMAS	"	19	" 22, "	"	July 30, 1863.	Of wounds in action, Port Hudson, La., May 27, [1863.	
RIERDON, THOMAS	"	38	" 23, "	"	Aug. 18, 1864.	Delirium tremens.	
SCHNEFF, GOTTFRIED	"	36	" 11, "	"	Dec. 5, 1864.	Prisoner of war, Salisbury, N. C.	
TETLEY, DAVID R.	"	30	" 16, "	"			
Deserted.							
PRICE, JAMES	Corporal.	21	Sept. 22, 1862.	Brooklyn.	Nov. 1, 1862.		
STEELE, JOHN H.	"	40	" 30, "	"	Nov. 1, 1862.		
CARNEY, THOMAS	Private.	18	" 6, "	"	Nov. 1, 1862.		
CASSIDY, OWEN	"	44	" 8, "	"	Nov. 1, 1862.		
CHAPIS, CLARENCE	"	24	" 22, "	Kinderhook.	May, 1863.	Transferred from Co. G March 12, 1864. (Desertion not known until after transfer.)	
McCAULEY, THOMAS	"	18	" 10, "	Brooklyn.	Oct. 30, 1863.		
MULLEN, THOMAS	"	19	" 9, "	"	Nov. 6, 1862.		
Unaccount'd for at Muster Out.							
KIRCHNER, ADOLPH	Private.	27	Oct. 6, 1862.	Brooklyn.			
SHAW, THOMAS	"	23	" 6, "	"			
SHAW, HEZEKIAH	"	34	" 13, "	"			
VAN LOAN, HENRY	"	23	Sept. 22, "	"			

	Officers.	Men.
Original Strength	3	59
Gain by Recruits		2
Total genuine members	3	61
Promoted from ranks other Companies	1	
Transferred from other Companies	1	8
Total borne on Rolls	5	69

	Officers.	Men.	Officers.	Men.
Brought forward			5	69
Discharged	3	13		
Transferred	1	8		
Died, 8; deserted, 7; unaccounted for, 4		19	4	40
Mustered Out on Rolls			1	29
Absent at Muster Out				6
Present at Muster Out			1	23

XII

THE 159TH REGIMENT INFANTRY, N. Y. S. V.—COMPANY C.

	Rank.	Age	Joined.		Place.
			Date.		

Mustered Out with Regt.

	Rank.	Age	Date.	Place.	
BARZILLAI RANSOM	1st Lieut.	34	Oct. 1, 1864.	Cedar Creek, Va.	Appointed from civil life.

Discharged and Resigned.

ARIEL M. GAMWELL	Captain.	39	Sept. 28, 1862.	Hudson.	Feb. 11, 1863.
CRAWFORD WILLIAMS	1st Lieut.	27	Oct. 4, "	"	Feb. 12, 1864. Commissioned Captain.
EDGAR G. HUBBELL	2d Lieut.	20	Oct. 4, "	"	July 30, 1863.

Transferred.

| CHARLES LEWIS | Captain. | 31 | Oct. 14, 1862. | Hudson. | Jan. 15, 1864. Promoted Major 176th N. Y. S. V. Promoted from 1st Lt. Co. G, June 10, 1863. |

Died.

| HERMAN SMITH | 2d Lieut. | 18 | Sept. 3, 1862. | Brooklyn. | Oct. 4, 1864, of wounds in action, Opequan, Va., Sept. 19, 1864. Enrolled Sergt. Co. H. Promoted Sergt.-Maj. March 6, 1863. Prom. 2d Lt. Co. G June 10, 1863. Transferred Jan. 15, 1864. |

Mustered Out with Regt.

HOLLENBECK, EDGAR	1st Sergt.	17	Sept. 9, 1862.	Livingston.	Enrolled Private. Promoted Corp. Nov. 10, 1862 ; Sergt., Aug. 23, 1863 ; 1st Sergt., Sept. 19, 1864.
COONS, WILLIAM	Sergeant.	19	" 27, "	Taghkanic.	Enrolled Private. Promoted Corp. March 22, 1864 ; Sergt., Aug. 7, 1865.
PIERCE, HIRAM D	"	19	" 30, "	Copake.	Enrolled Private. Promoted Corp. Nov. 3, 1862 ; Sergt., April 24, 1864. Reduced Aug. 16, 1865. Reinstated Sept. 9, 1865.
WHEELER, JOHN	Corporal.	20	" 15, "	Taghkanic.	Enrolled Private. Promoted Aug. 7, 1865.
BEATTY, JACOB	"	20	" 27, "	"	Enrolled Private. Promoted Jan. 1, 1865. Reduced Aug. 16, 1865. Reinstated Sept. 9, 1865.
HART, LOUIS S	Musician.	16	" 13, "	Hudson.	Absent. Sick in hospital. Reduced from Corporal.
ANDREWS, WILLIAM H	Private.	27	" 29, "	"	Reduced from Corporal.
BINGHAM, EDWARD H	"	19	" 22, "	"	
COPPINS, LEWIS	"	40	Oct. 13, "		
COONEY, JAMES	"	35	Sept. 7, "		
CONNELLY, PATRICK	"	21	Oct 10, 1864.	Kingston.	Transferred from Co. A, March 3, 1864.
DUNTZ, ADAM	"	18	" 13, 1862.	Taghkanic.	Recruit.
EDWARDS, ALB. EUGENE	"	19	Sept. 20, "	Copake.	
FOX, LOUIS	"	19	" 25, "	Hudson.	
GARNER, MARTIN M	"	20	" 20, "	"	Reduced from Corporal.

XIII

THE 159TH REGIMENT INFANTRY, N. Y. S. V.—COMPANY C.—Continued.

Name	Rank	Age	Date Joined	Place Joined	Remarks
Mustered Out with Regt.					
HOGAN, MICHAEL	Private	19	Sept. 13, 1862.	Stuyvesant.	
HELLER, JOHN	"	22	Oct. 2, "	Taghkanic.	
HARROWS, EDWARD H	"	35	Dec. 29, 1863.	Hudson.	Recruit.
KEIST, ALEXANDER	"	24	Sept. 24, 1862.	Livingston.	Missing. [of Barracks, Augusta, Ga., Oct. 9, 1865. Supposed to have been burned to death at the burning
MILLER, GEORGE C	"	32	" 25, "	Hudson.	
MELIUS, JAMES M	"	22	" 30, "	"	
NASH, JARED M	"	19	Oct. 13, 1864.	Jamaica.	Recruit.
NICHOLS, WILLIAM	"	17	Sept. 16, 1862.	Hudson.	
OSTRANDER, ALBERT	"	35	Oct. 26, "	Copake.	
ROCKEFELLER, M'TIMER	"	18	Sept. 29, "	Taghkanic.	
SMITH, HENRY C	"	19	" 9, "	Stockport.	
SMITH, LEONARD	"	30	" 11, "	Taghkanic.	Absent. Detached
SCHNACK, CHRISTIAN	"	23	" 27, "	Hudson.	
SCHERMERHORN, JOHN	"	20	" 27, "	"	
VAN VALKENBURGH, CORNELIUS	"	18	Oct. 27, "	"	
BROWN, ANTHONY	Col Cook	30	Sept. 26, "	Stockport.	Recruit.
HARRISON, JAMES	"	35	Nov. 6, 1863.	Thit's, La.	Recruit.
Discharged.		22	" 6, "	"	
CAMERON, ROBERT V. L.	Sergeant.	19	Sept. 9, 1862.	Taghkanic.	Disability. Promoted from Corporal.
SPANBURGH, WM. H	"	22	" 12, "	Hudson.	Commissioned 2d Lt.
FITZGERALD, JAMES	"	23	" 10, "	"	
CONRON, WALTER R	Corporal.	20	" 9, "	Taghkanic.	Disability. Enrolled Private.
ALLEN, JOHN H	Musician.	35	" 4, "	Hudson.	Nov. 16, 1862. Writ Habeas Corpus.
DESASIA, ROBERT	Private.	15	" 4, "	"	Nov. 3, 1862. Writ Habeas Corpus.
ARMSTRONG, JAMES C	"	19	" 5, "		Disability.
ARTH, LUCAS	"	30	" 20, "	Brooklyn.	
BRADLEY, JOHN	"	35	" 25, 1864.	Po'keepsie.	May 9, 1865. G. O. 77, A. G. O., W. D. Recruit.
BARLOW, FAYETTE W	"	18	" 19, "	Taghkanic.	May 9, 1865. G. O. 77, A. G. O., W. D. Recruit.
COONS, HOWARD	"	23	" 25, 1862.	"	Disability.
COONS, SAMUEL	"	35	" 25, "	"	Disability.
GAILOR, AUSTIN	"	19	Mar. 11, 1863.	Kingston.	Disability. Recruit.

THE 159TH REGIMENT INFANTRY, N. Y. S. V.—COMPANY C.—Continued.

	Rank.	Age.	Date.	Joined. Place.		
Discharged.						
HART, JOHN	Private.	21	Sept. 19, 1864.	Jamaica.	May 9, 1865.	G. O. 77, A. G. O., W. D. Recruit.
MOREY, STEPHEN	"	25	" 5, 1862.	Stuyvesant.	Sept. 2, 1865.	Disability.
OTTIS, THOMAS	"	30	" 28, 1864.	Kingston.	May 9, 1865.	G. O. 77, A. G. O., W. D. Recruit.
PATTERSON, JOSEPH	"	28	" 13, 1862.	Hudson.	April 1864.	Disability.
STICKLES, EPHRAIM	"	35	" 19, "	Taghkanic.	Aug. 25, 1865.	Disability.
STAATS, MYRON	"	25	" 15, "	Stockport.		Disability.
SCRIVER, HIRAM	"	25	" 3, "	Hudson.		
SMITH, JOHN	"	21	Aug. 19, 1864.	Po'keepsie.	May 9, 1865.	G. O. 77, A. G. O., W. D. Recruit.
TATOR, WILLIAM	"	51	Oct. 13, 1862.	Taghkanic.	Aug. 25, 1865.	Disability.
WHEELER, FREELAND	"	18	Sept. 9, "	Hudson.		Deafness.
WINANS, CHARLES I.	"	19	" 12, 1864.	Albany.	May 9, 1865.	G. O. 77, A. G. O., W. D. Recruit.
Transferred.						
NORMAN, SAMUEL A.	Sergeant.	40	Sept. 12, 1862.	Stockport.	June 7, 1864.	to V. R. C. Enrolled Private.
KELLERHOUSE, JONAS A.	"	25	Oct. 26, "	Copake.	May 3, 1865.	to V. R. C.
HOLLENBECK, TUNIS	Wagoner.	35	Sept. 13, "	Hudson.		to V. R. C.
CHARLOTTE, JOHN H.	Private.	20	" 18, "	"	Nov. 2, 1862.	to Cavalry Corps. Promoted Q. M. Sergt.
MAYOT, ALEXANDER I.	"	18	" 10, "	"	Nov. 4, 1862.	to Cavalry Corps.
JAQUINS, WILLIAM A.	"	26	" 26, "	"	Jan. 25, 1864.	to N. C. S. Promoted Q. M. Sergt.
WILKINSON, HENRY A.	"	21	" 8, "	"		to Signal Corps.
Died.						
WENDT, AUGUSTUS W.	1st Sergt.	26	Sept. 16, 1862.	Hudson.	Sept. 19, 1864.	In action, Opequan, Va.
WHITBECK, JOHN	Sergeant.	19	" 30, "	Copake.	June 1863.	Typhoid.
MICHAEL, LEONARD	Corporal.	24	Oct. 27, "	"	Sept. 19, 1865.	Enrolled Corporal.
ALLEN, WILLIAM P.	"	30	Sept. 17, "	Taghkanic.	May 1863.	Compound fracture skull.
CRUMBIE, HIRAM	Private.	27	" 6, "	Hudson.	Mar. 10, 1863.	
COON, AMBROSE	"	34	" 27, "	"	Sept. 16, 1863.	
CALKINS, WILLIAM	"	10	" 27, "	Taghkanic.	Aug. 1863.	
DEWITT, DORR	"	28	" 26, "	"	May 1863.	Of wounds in action, Irish Bend, La., Apr. 14, 1863.
FINKLE, WILLIAM H.	"	19	Oct. 5, "	Stuyvesant.	Oct. 5, 1864.	Prisoner of war, Richmond, Va.
GABRIZ, JOHN	"	23	Sept. 17, "	Taghkanic.	May 1863.	
HOUGHTALING, WM.	"	45	Oct. 4, "	Stockport.	June 2, 1863.	
HOUGHTALING, WM.	"	20	Sept. 14, "	Hudson.	June 1863.	

xv

THE 159TH REGIMENT INFANTRY, N. Y. S. V.—COMPANY C.—Continued.

	Rank.	Age.	Joined.		Place.		
			Date.				
Died.							
HOUGHTALING, JAMES	Private.	17	Sept. 25,	1862.	Hudson.	April 14, 1863.	In action, Irish Bend, La.
MORRISON, JAMES	"	20	" 13,	"	"	April 14, 1863.	In action, Irish Bend, La. Transferred from Co. D.
OLDS, NEWELL H	"	48	" 14,	"	Chatham.	June 16, 1863.	
PULVER, JOHN W	"	19	" 30,	"	Copake.	Feb. 1863.	
RILSING, JOHN	"	35	Oct. 21,	"	Hudson.	Oct. "	Of wounds in action, Irish Bend, La. April 14, 1863.
RILEY, DANIEL	"	20	Sept. 16,	"	"	April 14, 1863.	In action, Irish Bend, La.
SMCFELDT, WILLIAM J.	"	34	" 17,	"	Germanto'n.	Oct. 14, 1864.	Of wounds in action, Opequan, Va., Sept. 19, 1864.
WHEELER, STEPHEN	"	19	" 21,	"	Taghkanic.	June 12, 1863.	
Deserted.							
BENEDICT, NEWTON R	Private.	19	Sept. 10,	1862.	Hudson.	Nov. 1862.	
CLEVEND, HARVEY	"	21	" 24,	1864.	Kingston.	Jan. 27, 1865.	Recruit.
DUNTZ, JEREMIAH	"	30	" 20,	1862.	Taghkanic.	Nov. 1862.	
HELLER, GEORGE	"	34	Oct. 8,	"	Hudson.	Nov. "	
MILLER, OBEDIAH	"	38	Sept. 24,	"	Taghkanic.	Nov. "	
NICHOLS, JOHN	"	32	" 10,	"	Stockport.		
STICKLES, EZRA	"	30	" 25,	"	Taghkanic.		
SIMPSON, ROBERT	"	21	"	"	Hudson.		
Unacc'd for at Muster Out.							
RAGGITT, CHARLES	Private.	24	Oct. 30,	1862.	Hudson.		
SMITH, DEDRICK	"	19	Sept. 16,	"	Taghkanic.		
TEN EYCK, JACOB	"	43	Oct. 29,	"	Germanto n.		

	Officers.	Men.
Original Strength	3	80
Gain by Appointment and Recruits	1	13
Total genuine members	4	93
Promoted from Officers other Company	1	
Transferred from other Companies	1	2
Total borne on Rolls	6	95

		Officers.	Men.
Brought forward		6	95
Discharged	3	24	
Transferred	1	7	
Died	1	20	
Deserted, 8 ; unaccounted for, 3		11	
		5	62
Mustered Out on Rolls		1	33
Absent at Muster Out			3
Present at Muster Out		1	30

XVI

THE 159TH REGIMENT INFANTRY, N. Y. S. V.—COMPANY D.

	Rank.	Age.	Date.	Place.	
Mustered Out with Regt.					
E. Parmly Brown	1st Lieut.	19	Nov. 20, 1863.	Brooklyn.	Recruit. Enrolled Private Co. I. Promoted June 22, 1865.
Discharged and Resigned.					
Joseph A. Hayek	Captain.	32	Sept. 24, 1862.	Brooklyn.	Nov. 16, 1863. Dishonorably dismissed by sentence G. C. M.
Charles A. Lorenz	1st Lieut.	22	" 24, "	"	April 3, 1863. Disability.
Henry M. Howard	1st Lieut.	20	" 6, "	"	Dec. 29, 1864. Disability. Enrolled Sergt. Promoted 2d Lieut. Jan. 27, 1863. Promoted 1st Lieut. Co. F, June 10, 1863. Transferred Aug. 25, 1863.
Transferred.					
John W. Manley, Jr.	2d Lieut.	22	Sept. 21, 1862.	Brooklyn.	Jan. 27, 1863. Promoted 1st Lieut. Co. A.
Mustered Out with Regt.					
Jennings, John T	1st Sergt.	32	Sept. 17, 1862.	Brooklyn.	Enrolled Corp. Promoted Sergt. Jan. 27, 1863; 1st Sergt. Sept. 1, 1864.
Marozzi, Americus	Sergeant	27	Mar. 11, 1863.	N. Orl's, La.	Enrolled Private. Promoted Corp. April 12, 1864; Sergt. May 1, 1864. Recruit.
Peaslee, Alanson	Corporal.	30	Sept. 8, 1862.	Brooklyn.	Enrolled Private. Promoted Jan. 27, 1863.
Mayo, Reuben		31	" 6, "	"	
Ricci, Joseph W.	Musician.	16	" 4, "	"	
Velsor, Henry C.		16	" 4, "	"	
Becker, Philip B	Private.	22	" 5, "	"	
Clapp, James		18	" 6, "	"	Enrolled Corp. Promoted Sergt. June 15, 1864. Reduced Sept. 1, 1864.
Connors, James		18	" 12, "	"	Absent. Sick in hospital.
Doremus, Frank H		18	" 12, "	"	
Grinser, Lawrence		21	" 11, "	"	
Howe, James		44	" 24, "	"	Transferred from Co. G, March 12, 1864.
Hobee, Patrick		19	" 15, 1863.	Kinderhook.	Recruit.
Kisters, Frank W		42	Mar. 11, 1863.	N. Orl's, La.	Deserted. Apprehended and returned.
Messensole, Lewis		18	Sept. 13, 1862.	Brooklyn.	
McCanty, John		25	" 22, "	"	

XVII

THE 159TH REGIMENT INFANTRY, N. Y. S. V.—COMPANY D.—Continued.

	Rank.	Age.	Date.	Joined. Place.	
Mustered Out with Reg't.					
MARTIN, GEORGE	Private.	18	Oct. 7, 1862.	Chatham.	Transferred from Co. G, March 12, 1864.
MARTIN, JOHN	"	19	" 7, "	"	Transferred from Co. G, March 12, 1864.
MILLER, GEORGE D	"	20	" 1, "	Brooklyn.	Deserted. Apprehended and returned.
MORRIS, ISAAC	"	42	Aug. 22, 1864.	Schenectady.	Absent. Sick in hospital. Recruit.
NEVISS, THOMAS	"	42	Sept. 18, 1862.	Brooklyn.	
POWELL, WILLIAM C	"	43	Oct. 1, "	"	Absent. Sick in hospital.
PIERRE, LOUIS	"	24	Nov. 24, 1863.	New York.	Recruit.
PENDERGAST, JOHN	"	32	Sept. 16, 1862.	Brooklyn.	
ROBERTS, JOHN C	"	18	" 5, "	"	
ROSE, ISAAC L	"	19	" 8, "	"	Enrolled Corp. Promoted Sergt. Jan. 27, 1863. Reduced Aug. 16, 1865.
VORNESS, MICHAEL	"	21	Oct. 1, "	Fishkill.	
WILLIAMS, JAMES B	"	20	Sept. 29, "	Claverack.	Transferred from Co. G, March 12, 1864.
WILLIAMS, TITUS	"	19	" 15, "	Brooklyn.	Transferred from Co. G, March 12, 1864.
WHITE, WILLIAM H	"	19	" 15, "	"	
Discharged.					
HOWARD, HENRY M	Sergeant	20	Sept. 6, 1862.	Brooklyn.	Jan. 26, 1863. For promotion to 2d Lt.
BOWDISH, LUKE	Corporal.	43	" 4, "	"	Aug. 27, 1863. Disability.
SHERMAN, JOHN W, JR	"	21	" 12, "	"	Mar. 22, 1863. Disability. Enrolled Sergt. Reduced Nov. 1, 1862.
ACKEN, JOSEPH	Private.	40	" 15, "	"	Mar. 22, 1863. Disability.
DOTY, ALFRED	"	35	Oct. 22, "	"	June 27, 1863. Disability.
FEISLER, MICHAEL	"	21	Sept. 1, "	"	Aug. 30, 1863. Disability.
FARRELL, THOMAS	"	44	" 19, "	"	June 22, 1864. Disability.
HARRISON, THOMAS B	"	18	April 3, 1863.	N. Orl's, La.	April 13, 1864. Commissioned 2d Lt. 7th U. S. C. T., H. A.
MCKINLEY, DAVID	"	25	Sept. 9, 1862.	Brooklyn.	Mar. 7, 1864. Disability.
PORTER, ISAIAH	"	27	Nov. 11, 1863.	Thod'x, La.	Aug. 11, 1864. Expiration term of service. Recruit.
SLAVAN, MARK	"	44	Sept. 8, 1862.	Brooklyn.	Aug. 24, 1863. Disability.
SMITH, CONRAD	"	22	" 18, "	"	July 24, 1865. Disability.
YOUNGS, SAMUEL	"	37	Nov. 11, 1863.	Thibodeaux, La.	Aug. 11, 1864. Expiration term of service. Recruit.

XVIII

THE 159TH REGIMENT INFANTRY, N. Y. S. V.—COMPANY D.—Continued.

	Rank.	Age.	Joined.		
			Date.	Place.	

Name	Rank	Age	Date	Place	Remarks
Transferred.					
PALMER, WM. E., JR.	Sergeant.	18	Sept. 5, 1862.	Brooklyn.	April 9, 1864, to N. C. S. Promoted Sergt.-Maj. Enrolled Corp. Promoted May 24, 1863.
KREUTSCHER, PHILIP, JR.	Private.	18	" 11, "	"	Aug. 10, 1864, to V. R. C.
SCHREIBER, JOHN A.	"	44	" 2, "	"	June 22, 1864, to V. R. C. Enrolled Sergt. Reduced Jan. 27, 1863.
SCHUCK, ADAM	"	44	" 2, "	"	April 10, 1864, to V. R. C.
VOLKINER, PETER	"	21	" 8, "	"	Aug. 10, 1864, to V. R. C. Deserted. Apprehended and returned.
Died.					
CALDICOTT, CHAS. H.	1st Sergt.	32	Sept. 5, 1862.	Brooklyn.	April 9, 1863. Dropsy.
RACKETT, APPLETON W.	Corporal.	26	" 8, "	"	April 17, 1863. Vermilion Bayou, La. Shot by the rebels while drawing water.
BENNETT, JAMES		39	" 9, "	"	Dec. 5, 1862.
NEWMAN, HENRY	Wagoner.	41	" 4, "	"	July 3, 1864.
BROWN, JOHN J.	Private.	21	" 22, "	"	Oct. 27, 1864. Of wounds in action, Cedar Cr'k, Va., Oct. 19, 1864.
DORGAN, JAMES	"	37	" 10, "	"	Dec. 24, 1864. Typhoid fever.
FITZGERALD, PATRICK	"	32	Oct. 21, "	Ghent.	Sept. 19, 1864. In action, Opequan, Va. Transferred from Co. G, March 12, 1864.
HALUCS, CHARLES	"	21	Sept. 22, "	Brooklyn.	April 14, 1863. In action, Irish Bend, La.
HASSKOFF, JOHN	"	40	" 19, "	"	June 9, 1863. Of wounds in action, Port Hudson, La., May 27, 1863.
HAWKS, GEORGE	"	44	" 5, "	"	Nov. 6, 1863.
KLISSING, JOHN A	"	39	" 6, "	Claverack.	July 22, 1864. Transferred from Co. G, March 12, 1864.
MCEVOY, THOMAS	"	37	" 6, "	Brooklyn.	Oct. 6, 1863.
STAUNTON, ABNER	"	34	Oct. 10, "	Po'keepsie.	Oct. 28, 1864. Prisoner of war, Camp Tyler, Texas. Transferred from Co. G, March 12, 1864.
TREITLEIN, JOSEPH		19	" 4, "	Brooklyn.	Jan. 1, 1865. Prisoner of war, Salisbury, N. C.
WEBBER, MICHAEL	"	29	Sept. 12, "	"	Sept. 30, 1863.
Deserted.					
GABRIEL, JACOB	Sergeant.	21	Sept. 4, 1862.	Brooklyn.	Nov. 10, 1862.
SANFORD, SAMUEL	Corporal.	21	" 26, "	"	Nov. 10, 1862.
DONAVAN, THOMAS	Private.	19	" 9, "	"	Oct. 1, 1865.

THE 159TH REGIMENT INFANTRY, N. Y. S. V.—COMPANY D.—Continued.

	Rank.	Age.	Joined. Date.	Place.	
Deserted.					
GABRIEL, FRANK	Private.	18	Sept. 18, 1862.	Brooklyn.	Nov. 10, 1862.
KRIPE, JOHN	"	21	" 9.	"	Nov. 10, 1862.
MESSENSOLE, LEWIS	"	18	" 13.	"	July, 1863. Apprehended and returned.
MURPHY, JOHN	"	18	" 9.	"	Nov. 10, 1862.
MOST, JOHN	"	33	" 4.	"	Nov. 10, 1862.
PLUNKETT, PATRICK	"	44	" 13.	"	Nov. 10, 1862.
SCHMITT, MICHAEL	"	39	" 4.	"	Nov. 10, 1862.
THOMAS, WILLIAM	"	21	" 11.	"	Nov. 10, 1862.
VOLKINGR, PETER	"	21	" 8.	"	April 14, 1863. Apprehended and returned.
VOGHINER, LEWIS	"	20	Nov. 24, 1863.	New York.	July 1, 1864. Recruit.
VAN NOSDALL, JOHN S	"	17	Oct. 1, 1862.	Fishkill.	July 24, 1865. Transferred from Co. G, March 12, 1865.
WARD, MARTIN	"	27	Sept. 8, "	Brooklyn.	Nov. 10, 1862.
CAREY, EDWARD	C'd Cook.	20	Oct. 28, 1863.	Thibodeaux La.	July 31, 1864. Recruit.
Unac'd for at Muster Out.					
ARCHIBALD, CHARLES	Private.	32	Sept. 18, 1862.	Brooklyn.	
ANDERSON, JAMES	"	21	" 17.	"	
CHAPIN, CLARENCE	"	24	Aug. 14.	Kinderhook.	Transferred to Co. G.
COONS, JONAS	"	25	Oct. 1.	Livingston.	Transferred to Co. E.
DOXIE, WILLIAM A	"	18	Nov. 1.	Fishkill.	Transferred to Co. E.
DELANCY, ARCHIBALD	"	32	Nov. 1.	New York.	Transferred to Co. G.
FITZGERALD, THOMAS	"	21	Sept. 9.	Brooklyn.	
GABRIEL, JOHN	"	21	Sept. 4.	"	
HOWARD, CHARLES	"	22	Oct. 13.	"	
HAWVER, CHARLES N	"	18	Sept. 18.	Ghent.	Transferred to Co. E.
IRISH, WILLIAM I	"	20	" 25.	Brooklyn.	
KONIG, MICHAEL	"	21	" 29.	"	
KEESLER, JOHN W	"	22	" 26.	Hudson.	
MARTIN, JOHN	"	19	Oct. 7.	Chatham.	Transferred to Co. G.
MORRISON, JAMES	"	20	Sept. 13.	Hudson.	Transferred to Co. C.
NURBER, FREDERICK	"	31	" 10.	Brooklyn.	

Rank.	Age.	Date.	Joined Place.		

Unacc'd for at Muster Out.

Perkins, James T.	Private.	18	Sept. 26, 1862.	Hudson.	Transferred to Co. E.
Smith, William H.	"	18	Oct. 1, "	Fishkill.	Transferred to Co. E.
Sweeny, John	"	23	Sept. 9, "	Brooklyn.	
Tober, John	"	39	" 3, "	"	
Thrust, Victor.	"	36	" 23, "	"	
Wolf, Henry D.	"	45	" 11, "	Ghent.	Transferred to Co. E.

	Officers.	Men.
Original Strength	3	81
Gain by Recruits		9
Total genuine members	3	90
Promoted from ranks this Company	1	
Promoted from ranks other Companies	1	
Transferred from other Companies	1	9
Total borne on Rolls	6	99

	Officers.	Men.	Officers.	Men.
Brought forward			6	99
Discharged	3	13		
Transferred	2	15		
Died		15		
Deserted		14		
Unaccounted for at Muster Out		22		
Less found Transferred		10	12	
Mustered Out on Rolls			5	69
Absent at Muster Out			1	30
				3
Present at Muster Out			1	27

THE 159TH REGIMENT INFANTRY, N. Y. S. V.—COMPANY E.

	Rank.	Age	Joined. Date.	Place.	
Mustered Out with Regt.					
ANDREW RIFENBURGH	1st Lieut.	32	Aug. 20, 1862.	Hudson.	Enrolled Corp. Co. G. Promoted Sergt. Promoted 2d Lt. Feb. 25, 1864. Transferred from Co. G, March 12, 1864. Promoted June 10, 1864. Commissioned Captain.
Discharged.					
NATHAN S. POST	1st Lieut.	34	Oct. 7, 1862.	Hudson.	Jan. 14, 1863. Disability.
ROBERT H. TRAVER	2d Lieut.	27	" 7, "	"	Aug. 25, 1863.
Transferred.					
WILLIAM WALTERMIRE	Captain.	30	Oct. 15, 1862.	Hudson.	Feb. 25, 1864. Promoted Major.
Died.					
WESLEY BRADLEY	1st Lieut.	32	Sept. 18, 1862.	Hudson.	May 10, 1863. Typhoid fever. Promoted from 2d Lt. Co. A, Jan. 14, 1863.
Mustered Out with Regt.					
PHILLIPS, JOHN W.	1st Sergt.	19	Sept. 10, 1862.	Ghent.	Enrolled Corp. Promoted May 3, 1865.
FREEMAN, NICHOLAS	Sergeant.	20	" 10, "	"	Enrolled Private. Promoted Corp. Nov. 1, 1862. Promoted July 11, 1865.
COOK, JONAS		25	Aug. 14, "	Livingston.	Enrolled Private. Trans. from Co. D. From Sept. 13, 1863.
BUNT, RUTSON		28	Oct. 1, "	Claverack.	Absent. Detached.
WALTERMIRE, DAVID E.	Corporal.	19	Sept. 10, "	Ghent.	
HAMLIN, FREDERICK	Musician	17	" 22, "	Hudson.	
BRISTOL, JOHN F.	Private.	18	" 11, "	Ghent.	Absent. Detached.
BOWDY, JAMES, No. 1		18	" 18, "	Claverack.	
BOWDY, JAMES, No. 2		26	Oct. 4, "	Gallatin.	Absent. In confinement by sentence G. C. M.
BENZIE, GEORGE A.		18	Sept. 20, "	Hudson.	
CLAPP, EDWARD W.		18	Oct. 1, "	Stuyvesant	Absent. Sick in hospital.
CLARK, ALBERT H		44	" 4, "	Copake.	Absent. Sick in hospital.
DECKER, JAMES		18	Sept. 25, "	Claverack.	
EPPSER, SEBASTIAN		35	" 3, "	Hillsdale.	Enrolled Corp. Reduced March 20, 1864.
GUYON, FREDERICK		18	" 22, "	Claverack.	Trans. from Co. D.
HAWVER, CHARLES N		18	" 18, "	Greenport.	
HART, WILLIAM H		18	Aug. 9, "		

XXII

THE 159TH REGIMENT INFANTRY, N. Y. S. V.—COMPANY E.—Continued.

	Rank.	Age.	Joined.		Place.	
			Date.			
Mustered Out with Regt.						
HAWVER, EDWARD H	Private.	23	Sept. 11,	1862	Claverack.	Enrolled Sergt. Reduced Nov. 16, 1863.
HAMILTON, CHARLES	"	19	" 17,	"	Ghent.	Absent. Prisoner of war.
KRAUSE, JOHN	"	21	" 22,	"	Livingston.	
LAFEOUS, STEPHEN	"	27	" 20,	"	Claverack.	
MAXWELL, ANTHONY	"	18	" 20,	"	Ghent.	
MYERS, JOHN W	"	24	" 27,	"	Fishkill.	
MILLS, ALONZO	"	33	" 19,	"	Taghkanic.	
MACY, SOLON	"	43	" 19,	"	Hillsdale.	
MILLER, ORSON A	"	18	" 18,	"	Claverack.	
PROPER, GEORGE	"	19	" 7,	"	Ghent.	
POUCHER, JOHN J	"	38	" 17,	"	Hudson.	
ROTE, EDWARD	"	19	Oct. 11,	"	Ghent.	
SYRE, FRANCIS R	"	28	Sept. 20,	"	Hillsdale.	
THORP, JOHN	"	18	Oct. 14,	"		
WEBSTER, EGBERT	"	36	Jan. 1,	1864	Thibo'x, La.	Recruit.
BALTHES, JOHN	C'd Cook.	19	" 1,	"		Recruit.
ELIE, FRANK	"	20				
Discharged.						
MACY, SAMUEL B	1st Sergt.	29	Oct. 13,	1862.	Ghent.	May 3, 1865.
OSTRANDER, JAMES M	Sergeant.	24	Sept. 10,	"		July 11, 1865. Enrolled Private. Promoted.
MCNEILL, DEWITT C	"	18	" 23,	"	Copake.	Aug. 4, 1865. Writ Habeas Corpus.
PLATNER, MARTIN	Corpor'l.	18	" 27,	"	Claverack.	Nov. 16, 1862.
SAGENDORF, HIRAM P	"	24	" 20,	"	Ghent.	Sept. 17, 1863. Commissioned 1st Lt. U. S. C. T.
ALLEN, PETER H	Private.	44	" 30,	"	Claverack.	Nov. 24, 1863. Disability.
ALMSTEAD, JOHN W	"	17	" 11,	"	Ghent.	June 7, 1865.
BRUSH, ANDREW	"	44	" 20,	"	Claverack.	July 9, 1864.
COVENTRY, FRANK	"	28	" 25,	"	Kinderhook.	July 20, 1864. Disability.
DECKER, HENRY	"	33	" 20,	"	Livingston.	Dec. 22, 1862. Disability.
HENRY, MARTIN	"	44	" 20,	"	Ghent.	Dec. 2, 1862. Disability.
MILLER, JESSE	"	18	" 10,	"	Claverack.	Sept. 27, 1863. Wounds in action, Irish Bend, La., Apr. 14, 1863.

THE 159TH REGIMENT INFANTRY, N. Y. S. V.—COMPANY E.—Continued.

Name	Rank	Age	Date	Place		
Discharged.						
McCracken, Robert	Private.	28	Sept. 29, 1862.	Hillsdale.	Aug. 31, 1863.	Disability.
O'Brien, Patrick	"	34	" 24, "	Ghent.	Oct. 19, 1863.	Disability.
Rouse, Aaron	"	18	Oct. 6, "	"	Nov. 10, 1862.	Writ Habeas Corpus.
Reckett, Thomas	"	39	" 3, "	Ghent.	Aug. 16, 1863.	Disability.
Smith, Francis	"	23	Sept. 19, "	Claverack.	Dec. 2, 1862.	Disability.
Shuragar, Rachaff	"	44	" 18, "	Livingston.	May 21, 1863.	Disability.
Wheeler, Albert	"	28	" 20, "	Claverack.	May 29, 1863.	Disability.
Transferred.						
Shufelt, Philip D.	Corporal.	34	Sept. 25, 1862.	Ghent.	April 6, 1864.	to V. R. C.
Hamlin, James	Musician.	19	Oct. 6, "	Hudson.	July 17, 1864.	to V. R. C.
Coyles, William H.	Private.	26	Sept. 12, "	Copake.	May 12, 1865.	to V. R. C.
Peterson, Charles H.	"	26	" 1, "	Ghent.	May 1, 1864.	to Navy.
Died.						
Smith, John	Corporal.	19	Sept. 4, 1862.	Claverack.	Aug. 18, 1864.	Disease.
Benzie, George W.	Wagoner.	45	Oct. 20, "	Hudson.	Aug. 14, 1863.	Of wounds in action, Irish Bend, La., April 14, 1863.
Burnes, James	Private.	18	Sept. 20, "	Copake.	May 15, 1863.	
Boice, Leonard	"	21	" 29, "	Claverack.	Feb. 11, 1863.	Disease.
Boice, Richard	"	23	" 27, "	"	April 14, 1863.	In action, Irish Bend, La.
Citty, Edward	"	28	" 27, "	Ghent.	Feb. 16, 1865.	Disease.
Christman, Jacob H.	"	20	" 12, "	"	May 27, 1863.	In action, Port Hudson, La.
Decker, Edmond	"	19	Oct. 16, "	Claverack.	Feb. 21, 1863.	Disease.
Doran, James	"	45	" 22, "	Ghent.	April 25, 1863.	Of wounds in action, Irish Bend, La., Apr. 14, [1863.]
Doxey, William A.	"	18	Sept. 19, "	Fishkill.	Mar. 20, 1863.	Disease. Transferred from Co. D.
Hawver, Henry F.	"	45	" 20, "	Ghent.	July 27, 1863.	Disease.
Kells, Alexander	"	28	" 6, "	Claverack.	Feb. 2, 1863.	Disease.
Ludlow, Owen	"	42	" 18, "	Ghent.	Sept. 2, 1863.	Disease.
Maxwell, John	"	43	Oct. 7, "	Claverack.	May 27, 1863.	In action, Port Hudson, La.
McLean, Edward	"	24	Sept. 14, "	"	Oct. 7, 1863.	Disease.
Proper, William H.	"	22	Oct. 22, "	Taghkanic.	May 27, 1863.	In action, Port Hudson, La.

THE 159TH REGIMENT INFANTRY, N. Y. S. V.—COMPANY E.—Continued.

	Rank.	Age.	Date.	Joined. Place.	
Died.					
PUGH, WILLIAM	Private.	17	Sept. 17, 1862.	Ghent.	In action, Port Hudson, La. May 27, 1863.
PERKINS, JAMES T.	"	18	Oct. 20, "	Hudson.	In action, Cedar Creek, Va. Trans. from Co. D. Oct. 19, 1864. Enroll'd Private. Prom. Sergt. Rec'd Mar 4, 1864. Com'd [2d Lt.
RACE, ROBERT	"	18	Sept. 24, "	Greenport.	Disease. June 18, 1864.
ROCKEFELLER, OBADIAH	"	40	" 22, "	Hudson.	Disease. May 20, 1863.
SPADES, HIRAM	"	44	Oct. 10, "	Copake.	Disease. July 2, 1863.
SMITH, WILLIAM H	"	18	Sept. 16, "	Fishkill.	Disease. Transferred from Co. D. Mar. 25, 1863.
SILVERNAIL, PETER	"	18	Oct. 21, "	Ghent.	In action, Irish Bend, La. April 14, 1863.
SHERWOOD, JOHN T	"	19	" 8, "	Hillsdale.	Disease. Feb. 25, 1863.
WARNER, JOHN F	"	43	" 2, "	Claverack.	Disease. Aug. 10, 1863.
WOLF, HENRY D.	"	45	Sept. 11, "	Ghent.	In action, Irish Bend, La. Trans. from Co. D. April 14, 1863.
Deserted.					
WINCHELL, BENTON S.	Corporal.	20	Sept. 29, 1862.	Claverack.	Nov. 14, 1862.
CHAPMAN, LESTER J	Private.	19	Oct. 20, "	Ghent.	Nov. 3, 1863.
HAGERDORN, PETER	"	35	Sept. 16, "	Claverack.	Jan. 25, 1863.
MATT, CASPAR	"	22	" 27, "		Sept. 27, 1864.
ROCKEFELLER, REUBEN	"	22	" 27, "	Ghent.	Nov. 14, 1862.
ROAT, REUBEN	"	23	" 26, "	Taghkanic.	Nov. 14, 1862.
RAUGHT, RICHARD	"	40	" 13, "	Claverack.	Jan. 25, 1863.

	Officers.	Men.
Original Strength	3	83
Gain by Recruits		2
Total genuine members	3	85
Promoted from Officers other Companies	1	
Transfers from other Companies	1	6
Total borne on Rolls	5	91

		Officers.	Men.
Brought forward		5	91
Discharged		2	19
Transferred		1	4
Died		1	26
Deserted			7
		4	56
Mustered Out on Rolls		1	35
Absent at Muster Out			6
Present at Muster Out		1	29

XXV

THE 159TH REGIMENT INFANTRY, N. Y. S. V.—COMPANY F.

	Rank.	Age.	Joined. Date.	Place.	
Mustered Out with Reg't.					
GEORGE W. HUSSEY	Captain.	24	Oct. 4, 1862.	Brooklyn.	Enrolled 2d. Lieut. Promoted 1st Lieut. Co. G, March 6, 1863. Transferred to Co. B, March 12, 1864. Prom. Sept. 3, 1864.
Discharged.					
WILLIAM BURTIS	1st Lieut.	22	Oct. 4, 1862.	Brooklyn.	Nov. 1862.
CHRISTOPHER BRANCH	1st Lieut.	22	Sept. 27, "	Oyster Bay.	May 7, 1864. Enrolled Private. Promoted 1st Sergt. Promoted April 18, 1864.
J. ANTHONY TIEMANN	1st Lieut.	31	" 18, "	Brooklyn.	Jan. 4, 1865. Enrolled Sergt. Co. B. Promoted Aug. 25, 1864.
Transferred.					
ROBERT McD. HART	Captain.	22	Sept. 6, 1862.	Brooklyn.	June 2, 1864. Promoted Major.
HENRY M. HOWARD	1st Lieut.	20	" 6, "	"	Aug. 25, 1863, to Co. D. Enrolled Sergt. Co. D. Promoted 2d Ld. Co. D, Jan. 27, 1863. Promoted June 10, 1863.
ALFRED H. BRUCE	2d Lieut.	23	" 15, "	Kinderhook.	April 30, 1863. Prom. 1st Ld. Co. K. Enr'd 1st Sergt. Co. G. Prom. Sergt.-Maj. Jan. 14, 1863. From. Mar. 6, 1863.
Mustered Out with Reg't.					
McCORMICK, PHILIP	1st Sergt.	30	Oct. 28, 1862.	Brooklyn.	Promoted Sept. 1, 1864. Enrolled Private. Promoted Sergt.
CORBOY, DANIEL	Corporal.	22	Sept. 15, "	"	Promoted July 15, 1864. Enrolled Private.
ELIAS, AUGUSTINE	Musician.	17	Oct. 4, "	"	Enrolled Corp.
BROWN, WILLIAM J	Private.	26	Sept. 24	"	Absent. Sick in hospital. Wounded, Vermilion Bayou, La., April 17, 1863. Enrolled Sergt. Reduced.
BLACKLEDGE, OLIVER	"	30	" 15,	Po'keepsie.	Transferred from Co. G, March 12, 1864.
BOLLINGER, JOHN C	"	18	" 6,	Brooklyn.	
CARROLL, BENJAMIN	"	28	Oct. 23,	"	
DULLOS, EDWARD	"	43	Sept. 17,	"	Absent. Sick in hospital.
HUESTON, JOHN B	"	29	Nov. 7,	"	Substitute for Josiah Gittens. Deserted, apprehended and ret.
HARRISON, ISIDORE J	"	19	Sept. 10,	"	Enrolled Corp. Promoted Sergt. Reduced Aug. 16, 1865.
MATTOON, BENJAMIN F	"	18	" 22,	Canaan.	Transferred from Co. G, March 12, 1864.
McGUIRN, RICHARD	"	18	" 22,	"	
MACKAY, TERENCE	"	18	" 17,	Brooklyn.	Transferred from Co. G, March 12, 1864.
MORRIS, EDWARD	"	18	" 20,	"	
McKERNEY, WILLIAM	"	32	" 6,	"	
MACKAY, EDWARD J	"	20	" 13,	"	Promoted Sergt., Feb. 1, 1864. Reduced April 2, 1864.

Mustered Out with Regt.

NOE, SMITH J	Private.	21	Oct. 11, 1862.	Brookhaven.	
O'MARA, JOHN	"	18	Sept. 8, "	Brooklyn.	
SMITH, LEONARD	"	18	" 20, "	Claverack.	
SCHELL, FREDERICK L	"	29	" 6, "	Islip.	Transferred from Co. G, March 12, 1864.
STILWELL, ISAAC D	"	22	" 12, "	Brooklyn.	
TERRY, BREWSTER	"	31	" 26, "	Brookhaven.	
TAYLOR, OLIVER	"	20	Feb. 23, 1865.	Brooklyn.	Recruit.

Discharged.

BRANCH, CHRISTOPHER	1st Sergt.	22	Sept. 27, 1862.	Oyster Bay.	April 18, 1864. Promoted 1st Lt. Enrolled Private.
TOMPKINS, SAMUEL C	Sergeant.	24	" 4, "	Brooklyn.	Aug. 5, 1863. Disability from wounds in action, Port Hudson, La., May 27, 1863. Enrolled Private.
CALLAGHAN, WILLIAM	Corporal.	32	" 10, "	"	July 19, 1865. Disability. Enrolled Corp.
BARNES, HENRY A	Private.	19	" 17, "	"	Mar. 5, 1864. Disability.
DOYLE, JOHN	"	18	" 17, "	"	Mar. " 1864. Substitute furnished.
GITTENS, JOSIAH	"	35	" 24, "	"	Nov. 7, 1862. Disability.
HILL, JAMES	"	44	" 5, "	"	July 27, 1863. Disability.
HERBERT, THOMAS	"	42	Oct. 1, "	"	Mar. 27, 1865. Transferred from Co. A, Nov. 6, 1863.
HUNTINGTON, JOSEPH V. R	"	30	Sept. 8, "	"	May 24, 1863. Disability.
KELLY, JOHN	"	30	" 8, "	Brookhaven.	June 30, 1863. Disability.
MOTT, DAVID	"	33	" 8, "	"	May 24, 1863. Disability.
MOTT, CHARLES W	"	44	" 6, "	Brooklyn.	May 15, 1865. Disability.
MILLER, AARON	"	42	" 13, "	"	Oct. 17, 1864. Disability.
PARMENTER, DAVID	"	40	" 19, "	"	June 1, 1863. Disability.
REILLY, FRANCIS	"	44	" 22, "	Brookhaven.	June 6, 1863. Disability.
SMITH, WILLIAM H	"	27	" 15, "	"	Oct. 10, 1863. Disability.
WICKS, SAMUEL C					Aug. 11, 1863. Disability.

Transferred.

GULLEN, GILBERT S	Sergeant.	21	Sept. 23, 1862.	Brooklyn.	Aug. 16, 1865, to N. C. S. Promoted Sergt.-Major.
FERGUSON, JOHN H	Corporal.	18	" 19, "	"	June 24, 1864, to V. R. C. Enrolled Private.
LAWS, AMOS B		29	Oct. 9, "	Brookhaven.	May 1, 1864, to Navy.

THE 159TH REGIMENT INFANTRY, N. Y. S. V.—COMPANY F.—Continued.

	Rank.	Age.	Date.	Place.		
Transferred.						
ROWLAND, MANLEY S.	Musician.	18	Oct. 9, 1862.	Brooklyn.	June 30, 1865, to V. R. C.	
BARRETT, THOMAS	Private.	35	" 3, "	"	Mar. 10, 1863, to Co. H.	Enrolled Corp.
SMITH, ROBERT A		21	Sept. 6, "	Brookhaven.	May 1, 1864, to Navy.	
WELLS, WILLIAM T		21	" 6, "	"	May 1, 1864, to Navy.	
WHITE, THOMAS		19	" 20, "	Brooklyn.		to V. R. C.
Died.						
DOSER, BARTHOLOMEW	Corporal.	32	Sept. 16, 1862.	Brooklyn.	Nov. 5, 1864. Prisoner of war, Salisbury, N. C. Enrolled Private. Promoted July 15, 1864.	
LAWS, JOHN G		18	Oct. 9, "	Brookhaven.	April 14, 1863. In action, Irish Bend, La.	
SMOCK, BYRON L.	Musician.	18	Sept. 8, "	"	Jan. 19, 1863. Typhoid fever.	
BROKEE, JOHN R	Private.	19	" 6, "	Brooklyn.	Nov. " 1863. Of wounds in action, Port Hudson, La.	
COLGAN, WILLIAM		20	Oct. 1, "		Sept. 30, 1864. Of wounds in action, Opequan, Va., Sept. 19, [1864].	
EATON, HENRY		28	Sept. 8, "		April 14, 1863. In action, Irish Bend, La.	
FLOWERS, ZEBULON V		16	" 9, "		April 14, 1863. In action, Irish Bend, La.	
HAWKINS, AZARIAH T		33	" 26, "	Brookhaven.	Dec. 5, 1864. Disease.	
KEROX, RICHARD		44	" 6, "	Brooklyn.	April 2, 1865.	
KENNEY, THOMAS		19	" 13, "	"	Aug. 27, 1863.	
McCAULEY, JOHN		42	" 6, "		May 23, 1865. In action, Port Hudson, La.	
McDONALD, JEROME		35	" 17, "	Claverack.	May 23, 1865. Transferred from Co. G, March 12, 1864.	
MARTIN, LAWRENCE		25	" 13, "	Brooklyn.	June 23, 1863. In action, Brashear City, La.	
NICHOLS, FLOYD C		18	" 15, "	Brookhaven.	Oct. 5, 1864. Of wounds in action, Opeq'n, Va., Sept. 19, 1864.	
STUMPF, PHILIP		44	" 26, "	New Lebanon.	June 18, 18–3. Disease. Transferred from Co. G, March 12, 1864, notice of death not having been received.	
Deserted.						
SMITH, ROBERT T	Sergeant.	42	Oct. 22, 1862.	Brookhaven.	Nov. 6, 1862.	
DILLON, JOHN	Musician.			Brooklyn.	May 5, 1864, enroute to Regiment as an apprehended deserter. Not enlisted in this Co.	
BOND, EPHRAIM L.	Private.	28	Sept. 18, "	Brookhaven.	Nov. 8, 1862. Enrolled Teamster.	
BARRETT, FREDERICK		21	Oct. 1, "	Brooklyn.	Nov. 9, 1862.	
BOWERS, WILLIAM H.		27	Sept. 6, "	Brookhaven.	Nov. 10, 1862. Enrolled Corporal.	
COYNE, JAMES		21	" 12, "	Brooklyn.	Nov. 2, 1862.	

XXVIII

THE 159TH REGIMENT INFANTRY, N. Y. S. V.—COMPANY F.—Continued.

	Rank.	Age.	Joined.		
			Date.	Place.	
Deserted.					
DURIE, JOHN	Private.	21	Sept. 29, 1862	Brooklyn.	Sept. 13, 1863. Missing in action, April 14, 1863. Deserted from Camp Parole, St. Louis, Mo.
DOWNS, ISAAC S.	"	22	" 6, "	Brookhaven.	Nov. 9, 1862.
GRIFFITH, WILLIAM	"	37	" 13, "	Brooklyn.	Nov. 2, 1862.
GAMMAGE, THOMAS W.	"	40	" 10, "	"	Dec. 3, 1862.
HALL, HENRY	"	30	Oct. 30, "	"	Nov. 2, 1862.
McMAHON, MICHAEL	"	35	Sept. 16, "	"	April 14, 1863. In action, Irish Bend, La.
MOTT, EDWARD F.	"	21	" 30, "	"	Nov. 10, 1862.
MARSH, SAMUEL H.	"	21	" 23, "	"	Nov. 18, 1862.
MAHON, FRANCIS	"	28	" 12, "	"	June 27, 1865, en route to Regiment as an apprehended deserter.
					Transferred from Co. A, Nov. 6, 1863.
OVERLANDER, HENRY	"	39	" 22, "	"	Nov. 17, 1862. Apprehended and again deserted, Sept. 30, 1864, en route to Regiment.
RUSSELL, JAMES S.	"	32	" 6, "	Brookhaven.	Nov. 2, 1862.
SHAW, GEORGE N.	"	21	" 29, "	Brooklyn.	Sept. 20, 1863.
SHEEHAN, DANIEL	"	39	" 6, "	"	Nov. 2, 1862.
TERRY, JAMES A.	"	32	" 15, "	Brookhaven.	Nov. 10, 1862.
VAN ROSPATCH, CHARLES	"	40	" 29, "	"	Nov. 2, 1862.
WHELAN, JAMES	"	42	" 8, "	Brooklyn.	Dec. 3, 1862.

	Officers.	Men.
Original Strength	3	75
Gain by Recruits		1
Deserters returned to Co., not original		1
Total genuine members	3	77
Promoted from Officers other Companies	3	
Promoted from Ranks other Companies	2	
Promoted from Ranks this Company	1	
Transferred from other Companies		8
Total borne on Rolls	8	85

	Officers.	Men.
Brought forward	8	85
Discharged	3	17
Transferred	4	8
Died		15
Deserted		22
Mustered Out on Rolls	7	62
Absent at Muster Out	1	23
		2
Present at Muster Out	1	21

XXIX

THE 159TH REGIMENT INFANTRY, N. Y. S. V.—OLD COMPANY G.

	Rank.	Age.	Date.	Joined. Place.	
Discharged.					
WILLIAM H. SLATER	Captain.	26	Oct. 4, 1862.	Hudson.	July 30, 1863.
Transferred.					
CHARLES LEWIS	1st Lieut.	31	Oct. 14, 1862.	Hudson.	Mar. 6, 1863. Promoted Capt. Co. C.
GEORGE W. HUSSEY	1st Lieut.	24	" 4, "	Brooklyn.	Mar. 12, 1864, to Co. B. Promoted from 2d Lt. Co. F, March 6, 1863.
HERMAN SMITH	2d Lieut.	18	Sept. 3, "		Jan. 15, 1864, to Co. C. Prom. from Sgt.-Maj., June 10, 1863.
ANDREW RIFENBURGH	2d Lieut.	32	Aug. 20, "	Hudson.	Mar. 12, 1864, to Co. E. Enrolled Corp. Promoted Sergt. Promoted Feb. 25, 1864.
Died.					
BYRON LOCKWOOD	2d Lieut.	25	Oct. 14, 1862.	Hudson.	April 14, 1863. In action, Irish Bend, La.
Discharged.					
RIFENBURGH, ANDREW	Sergeant.	32	Aug. 20, 1862.	Hudson.	Feb. 25, 1864, for promotion. Prom. 2d Lt. Enrolled Corp.
DINGMAN, LAMBERT	Corporal.	23	Sept. 4, "	Kinderhook.	Mar. 1, 1863, for promotion. Prom. 2d Lt. Co. I, Jan. 27, 1863.
HORTON, FRANK		20	" 5, "	Claverack.	Aug. 25, 1863. Disability.
MESICK, CYRUS		24	" 2, "	Fishkill.	Disability. Enrolled Private. Promoted.
WHITNEY, OLIVER B	Musician.	20	" 6, "	German'n.	Disability.
MILLER, ELI		45	Oct. 3, "	Hillsdale.	Disability.
PRYOR, CHARLES	Private.	28	" 29, "	Taghkanic.	Disability.
BEST, MARTIN	"	41	Sept. 19, "	Kinderhook.	Nov. 19, 1862. Writ Habeas Corpus.
BAKER, LEWIS	"	43	" 15, "	Ghent.	Mar. 22, 1863. Disability.
DARLING, HENRY	"	39	" 18, "	Chatham.	Aug. 25, 1863. Disability.
FITZGERALD, WILLIAM	"	43	Oct. 3, "	Hudson.	Nov. 5, 1862. Writ Habeas Corpus.
HOUGHTALING, CHARLES	"	14	Sept. 17, "	Ghent.	Jan. 16, 1864. Disability.
ROMANZOFF, CHARLES G	"	28	" 25, "	Stockport.	Disability.
WHITLOCK, GEORGE	"	18	Oct. 14, "	Hudson.	Nov. 24, 1863. Disability.
WARNER, WILLIAM J	"	43	" 16, "		
Transferred.					
BRUCE, ALFRED H	1st Sergt.	23	Sept. 15, 1862.	Kinderhook.	Jan. 14, 1863, to N. C. S. Promoted Sergt.-Maj.

xxx

Transferred.

FRENCH, WILLIAM F	Sergeant.	19	Sept. 18, 1862.	Hudson.	March 12, 1864, to Co. H.	Promoted Com.-Sergt. Nov. 2, 1862
DUFFY, EDWARD	Corporal.	32	Oct. 6, "	"	" 12, " " L.	
TRAVER, MARTIN	"	22	Sept. 23, "	Kinderhook.	" 12, " " H.	
VAN ALSTYNE, GEORGE H.	"	25	" 19, "	"	" 12, " " K.	
SUYDAM, CLARK B	"	18	" 30, "	Fishkill.	" 12, " " K.	Reduced.
KLANSING, JOHN A	"	39	" 6, "	Claverack.	" 12, " " D.	
WORTMAN, WILLIAM H	Wagoner.	45	Oct. 1, "	Hudson.	" 12, " " H.	
ABBOTT, JOHN A	Private.	39	Sept. 14, "	Kinderhook.	" 12, " " H.	
BROPHY, EDWARD	"	18	" 6, "	"	" 12, " " K.	
BOLLINGER, JOHN C	"	24	" 22, "	Po'keepsie.	" 12, " " F.	Transferred from Co. F.
CHAPIN, CLARENCE	"	44	" 17, "	Kinderhook.	" 12, " " B.	
DREWETT, JAMES	"	30	" 22, "	Stockport.	" 12, " " R.	
DAILEY, JOHN	"	18	" 17, "	Kinderhook.	" 12, " " B.	
DEVLIN, JOHN	"	28	Oct. 20, "	Ghent.	" 12, " " L.	
DOOLIN, BERNARD	"	32	" 30, "	Fishkill.	" 12, " " K.	
FARRINGTON, WILLIAM	"	32	" 21, "	Ghent.	" 12, " " L.	
FITZGERALD, PATRICK	"	29	Sept. 30, "	Chatham.	" 12, " " D.	
GOSHA, ANDREW	"	28	" 26, "	Claverack.	" 12, " " K.	
GAULT, JOHN	"	43	" 12, "	Kinderhook.	" 12, " " B.	
HENNESSY, JOHN	"	19	" 15, "	Hudson.	" 12, " " B.	
HOBE, PATRICK	"	33	Oct. 16, "	Claverack.	" 12, " " D.	
HAVERTY, PATRICK	"	20	Sept. 25, "	Ghent.	" 12, " " K.	
HOFFMAN, GEORGE A	"	20	" 20, "	Canaan.	" 12, " " L.	Enrolled Private. Promoted Corp.
LYNCH, JOHN	"	18	" 22, "	New Lebn'n.	" 12, " " H.	Enrolled Private. Ap'd Musician.
LYNCH, WILLIAM	"	18	" 26, "	Chatham.	" 12, " " F.	
MATTOON, BENJAMIN F	"	25	" 7, "	Taghkanic.	" 12, " " H.	
MILLOTT, GEORGE	"	18	" 20, "		" 12, " " D.	
MARTIN, GEORGE	"	43			" 12, " " B.	Enrolled Musician. Promoted Principal Musician Nov. 2, 1862. Reduced Jan. 28, 1864.
MAMBERT, JOHN W	"	18	" 22, "	Canaan.	March 12, 1864, to Co. F.	
MCGURN, RICHARD						

XXXI

THE 159TH REGIMENT INFANTRY, N. Y. S. V.—OLD COMPANY G.—Continued.

	Rank.	Age.	Date.	Joined. Place.	
Transferred.					
McCormick, Thomas	Private.	28	Sept. 23, 1862.	Hudson.	March 12, 1864, to Co. K.
McDonald, Jerome	"	35	" 17, "	Claverack.	" " F.
Martin, John	"	19	Oct. 7, "	Chatham.	Transferred from Co. D.
Nevals, Austin	"	22	" 7, "	Ghent.	" " K.
Richmond, Silas W.	"	18	Sept. 23, "	Kinderhook.	" " B. Promoted Corp.
Shea, Thomas	"	24	Oct. 13, "	Po'keepsie.	" " K.
Staunton, Abner	"	34	" 10, "	Ghent.	" " D.
Snyder, Charles	"	18	Sept. 22, "	Ghent.	" " R.
Stickle, Henry S.	"	36	" 29, "	Kinderhook.	" " K.
Smith, Leonard	"	18	" 20, "	Claverack.	" " F.
Stickles, Cornelius	"	21	Oct. 7, "	Greenport.	" " H.
Stumpp, Philip	"	44	Sept. 26, "	New Lebanon	" " K.
Tanner, William B	"	36	Oct. 24, "	Kinderhook.	" " E.
Van Nospail, John S	"	17	" 1, "	Fishkill.	" " D.
Van Dewater, Benjamin	"	41	" 1, "		" " H.
Van Hoesen, Francis	"	28	Sept. 22, "	Ghent.	" " D.
Williams, Titus	"	19	" 29, "	Claverack.	" " D.
Williams, James B	"	20	Oct. 1, "	Fishkill.	" " D.
Died.					
Bean, David C	Private.	45	Sept. 26, 1862.	Livingston.	June 25, 1863.
De Groff, Platt	"	45	" 27, "	Hudson.	Mar. 29, 1863.
Gallagher, John	"	24	" 23, "	Chatham.	May 27, 1863. In action, Port Hudson, La.
Murphy, John	"	27	Oct. 12, "		April 14, 1863. In action, Irish Bend, La.
Morgan, John	"	42	Sept. 20, "	Claverack.	June 13, 1863.
Pultz, Harvey G	"	18	" 20, "	Ghent.	May 27, 1863. In action, Port Hudson, La.
Sharon, James W	"	37	Oct. 6, "	Ghent.	April 14, 1863. In action, Irish Bend, La.
Tanner, Wesley	"	28	" 6, "	Chatham.	June 30, 1863. Of wounds in action, Irish Bend, La. April 14.
Williams, George	"	18	Sept. 29, "	Ghent.	June 9, 1863. [1863.
Deserted.					
Shannon, Edward	Sergeant.	27	Sept. 23, 1862.	Chatham.	Nov. 23, 1862.

XXXII

THE 159TH REGIMENT INFANTRY, N. Y. S. V.—OLD COMPANY G.—*Continued.*

	Rank.	Age	Joined.		Place.	
			Date.			
Deserted.						
BOYCE, ABRAM F.	Corporal.	35	Sept. 30, 1862.		Stuyvesant.	
BANNON, THOMAS	Private.	18	" 25, "		Kinderhook.	
BREZEL, AMBROSE	"	26	" 22, "		Stockport.	
COON, CONRAD L.	"	22	" 25, "		Ghent.	
DE LANCEY, ARCHIBALD	"	32	Nov. 1, "		New-York.	
FORTIN, MICHAEL	"	24	Sept. 12, "		Ghent.	
HAIGHT, JOHN I.	"	39	Oct. 7, "	Aug. 15, 1863.	Pleas. Val'y.	Carrollton, La. Transferred from Co. D.
HACKER, DAVID P.	"	39	Sept. 29, "	Oct. 16, 1863.	Stockport.	
KNICKERBOCKER, PLATT	"		" 17, "	Nov. 2, 1862.	Hudson.	
McENNESSY, FRANK	"	27	Oct. 28, "	Dec. 2, 1862.	Chatham.	
SCHERMERHORN, ISAAC C.	"	23	" 13, "	Nov. 2, 1862.	Claverack.	
WILSON, JAMES	"	20	" 29, "	Nov. 22, 1862.	Chatham.	
Unaccounted for at Muster-Out.				Nov. 3, 1862.		
REYNOLDS, ALFRED	Private.	18	Sept. 12, 1862.		Kinderhook.	

	Officers.	Men.
Original Strength	3	84
Total genuine members	3	84
Promoted from Officers other Companies	3	
Promoted from Ranks other Companies	1	
Promoted from Ranks this Company	1	
Transferred from other Companies		3
Total borne on Rolls	6	87

	Officers.	Men.
Brought forward	6	87
Discharged	1	15
Transferred	4	49
Died	1	9
Deserted		13
Unaccounted for		1
	6	87

XXXIII

THE 159TH REGIMENT INFANTRY, N. Y. S. V.—NEW COMPANY G—RECRUITS.

	Rank.	Age.	Joined. Date.	Place.	
Mustered Out with Reg't.					
JAMES S. REYNOLDS	Captain.	38	Dec. 22, 1863.	Albany.	Promoted from 2d Lt. Feb. 8, 1864.
E. SPENCER ELMER	1st Lieut.	25	Feb. 8, 1864.	Po'keepsie.	Commissioned Captain.
Discharged.					
PETER VAN DEUSEN	2d Lieut.	44	Feb. 8, 1864.	Po'keepsie.	July 17, 1864.
Mustered Out with Reg't.					
COVEY, EGBERT E.	1st Sergt.	28	Dec. 30, 1863	Hudson.	Veteran.
COVEY, JENNINGS J.	Sergeant.	23	Jan. 4, 1864.	"	Veteran. Reduced Aug. 16, 1865. Promoted Sept. 9, 1865.
MESICK, WILLIAM H.	"	21	" 25, "	"	Enrolled Private. Promoted Corp. May 31, 1864. Promoted Veteran.
DAY, MARTIN	"	25	" 26, "	"	Veteran. June 30, 1865.
POST, DAVID	Corporal.	23	" 25, "	"	Absent. Sick in hospital. Veteran.
SHULTIS, NICHOLAS R.	"	24	" 25, "	"	Veteran.
MICHAEL, CHARLES N.	"	21	Feb. 3, "	Po'keepsie.	Veteran. Reduced May 31, 1864. Promoted Sept. 1, 1865.
RETTIG, GEORGE	"	40	Jan. 4, "	Hudson.	Enrolled Private. Promoted Sept. 1, 1865.
LEWIS, OSCAR	"	18	" 25, "	"	Recruit.
TRYON, EDWARD	Musician.	18	" 23, "	12th District.	Veteran. Enrolled Sergt. Reduced March 1, 1864. Promoted Corp. Sept. 3, 1864. Reduced Sept 25, 1865.
BRISTOL, GEORGE W.	Private.	23	" 1, "	Hudson.	
BUNT, ABRAM	"	18	" 4, "	"	
BUTTS, ROBERT R.	"	18	Dec. 30, 1863	"	
BROOKS, ROWLAND	"	18	Jan. 26, 1864.	"	
CALLIGAN, DENNIS	"	19	" 25, "	"	
DOYSON, THOMAS	"	29	" 21, "	"	Absent. Sick in hospital.
DARKINS, JOHN W.	"	18	" 25, "	"	
DAY, ALEXANDER	"	18	" 26, "	"	Absent without leave. Recruit.
ELLISON, ALEXANDER	"	22	" 6, "	12th District.	Veteran. Enrolled Corp. Reduced July 10, 1864.
FULLER, LOTAN	"	27	" 4, "	Hudson.	
FITZGERALD, EDWARD	"	22	Feb. 1, "	"	
GUILFOIL, PATRICK	"	35	Jan. 30, "	"	

THE 159TH REGIMENT INFANTRY, N. Y. S. V.—NEW CO. G.—RECRUITS.—Continued.

	Rank.	Age.	Joined. Date.	Place.	
Mustered Out with Regt.					
Groat, Jacon H.	Private.	26	Feb. 22, 1865.	Aneram.	Veteran. Recruit.
Hallenbeck, Jacob	"	28	Jan. 28, 1864.	Hudson.	Enrolled Private. Promoted Corp. May 1, 1864. Reduced Dec. 31, 1864.
Hermance, Lewis H.	"	27	Dec. 26, 1863.	"	Deserted Feb. 8, 1865. Apprehended and ret'd, June 30, 1865.
Howes, Charles H.	"	21	" 30, "	"	Absent. Sick in hospital.
Helmes, Spencer	"	18	" 30, "	"	
Kitchell, Lodi	"	36	Jan. 6, 1864.	"	
Lane, Daniel	"	24	" 29, "	Copake.	
Morris, Simeon	"	21	" 25, "	Hudson.	
Melie's, Jacon B.	"	18	Feb. 3, "	11th District.	Recruit.
Michael, Anthony M.	"	18	" 16, "	Hudson.	Recruit.
Miller, Warren H.	"	20	Jan. 27, "	"	
Perry, Franklin	"	18	" 26, "	Po'keepsie.	Recruit.
Plumb, Joshua	"	18	Mar. 21, 1865.	Hudson.	Enrolled Corp. Reduced Oct. 1, 1864.
Root, Charles	"	37	Jan. 7, 1864.	"	Absent. Sick in hospital.
Rowlinson, Elliot	"	22	" 23, "	12th District.	Recruit.
Simpson, Henry M.	"	21	Mar. 22, "	Hudson.	Veteran. Prom. Corp. Dec. 31, 1864. Reduced Aug. 16, 1865.
Shultis, William H.	"	23	Jan. 25, "	"	Promoted Corp. Sept. 30, 1864. Reduced Dec. 31, 1864.
Shults, Charles E.	"	18	" 25, "	"	Enrolled Corp. Reduced May 31, 1864.
Shults, Jordan.	"	25	Dec. 30, 1863.	"	
Shaughnessy, John, 1st	"	28	Jan. 11, 1864.	"	
Steel, Henry H.	"	30	" 20, "	"	Veteran. Enrolled Corp. Reduced Feb. 3, 1865.
Van Deusen, Henry C.	"	20	" 20, "	"	Promoted Corp. Oct. 1, 1864. Reduced Dec. 31, 1864.
Van Deusen, Russell	"	17	" 18, "	"	
Van Valkenburgh, Ch's E.	"	18	" 25, "	"	
Van Deusen, Elias	"	25	Dec. 30, 1863.	"	
Wise, Fidelie	"	18	Jan. 6, 1864.	"	
Moore, Benjamin	C'd Cook.	30	" 1, "	Thibo's, La.	Recruit.
Bird, Levi	"	18	" 1, "	"	Recruit.
Discharged.					
Stewart, Luzerne	Musician.	18	Jan. 26, 1864.	Hudson.	July 22, 1864. Disability.

XXXV

THE 159TH REGIMENT INFANTRY, N. Y. S. V.—NEW CO. G—RECRUITS.—Continued.

	Rank.	Age	Joined.		
			Date.	Place.	
Discharged.					
LOOMIS, GEORGE W	Musician.	17	Dec. 30, 1863	Hudson.	May 18, 1865. Disability.
BRADY, CALEB	Private.	19	Jan. 29, 1864	"	Aug. 4, 1865. Disability.
COE, JAMES H	"	18	" 11, "	"	May 13, 1865. Recruit.
CULLEN, HEZEKIAH	"	23	Aug. 24, "	Goshen.	Aug. 4, 1865. Disability.
LEURIE, LEWIS M	"	30	Jan. 13, "	Hudson.	Mar. 31, 1865. Disability.
MCBAIN, GEORGE	"	21	" 25, "	"	Aug. 4, 1865. Recruit.
MEAGHER, JEREMIAH	"	18	" 21, "	"	Aug. 4, 1865. Recruit.
MORRIS, JOHN	"	25	Aug. 22, "	Goshen.	Aug. 4, 1865. Recruit.
OSBORN, DANIEL D	"	20	Jan. 11, "	Hudson.	May 22, 1865. Disability. Deserted Feb. 27, 1864. Returned, June 9, 1864.
PLASS, JOHN J	"	18	Sept. 5, "	Po'keepsie.	Aug. 4, 1865. Recruit.
REYNOLDS, PETER W	"	18	Jan. 1, "	Hudson.	July 2, 1865.
SHEEHAN, DENNIS	"	39	" 13, "	"	Jan. 17, 1865. Disability.
SMITH, SILAS	"	30	Dec. 30, 1863	Philmont.	June 21, 1865. Recruit.
SHERMAN, JACOB	"	18	Feb. 18, 1865	Hudson.	July 13, 1865. By telegraphic order from W. D., A. G. O., May [3, 1865.
SPAULDING, SAMOR S	"	17	Jan. 16, 1864	"	July 11, 1865.
SHAUGHNESSY, JOHN, 2d	"	39	" 26, "	"	Aug. 11, 1865.
TOOMEY, JOHN	"	22	" 21, "	Po'keepsie.	June 2, 1865.
Died.					
KERTZ, FRANK A	Sergeant.	21	Jan. 2, 1864	Hudson.	April 28, 1865. Of wounds in action, Halltown, Va., Aug. 24, 1864. Veteran.
ELDRIDGE, JOSEPH	Private.	25	" 23, "	"	July 19, 1864. Disability.
KARCHER, HENRY	"	28	" 4, "	"	Sept. 4, 1864. In action near Berryville, Va.
MILLER, FRANKLIN	"	20	" 6, "	"	Sept. 26, 1865. Of wounds at hands of a comrade.
PERRIGO, HENRY A	"	23	Dec. 30, 1863	"	Sept. 16, 1864. Consumption. Veteran.
SYSEN, HENRY	"	18	Jan. 6, 1864	"	June 28, 1864. Dysentery.
STICKLES, WILLIAM A	"	49	" 7, "	"	July 2, 1864. Chronic diarrhea.
SHERMAN, HENRY	"	20	" 7, "	"	Dec. 16, 1864. Prisoner of war, Salisbury, N. C.
WEAVER, MILTON	"	18	Dec. 30, 1863	"	July 30, 1864. Congestion of lungs.

THE 159TH REGIMENT INFANTRY, N. Y. S. V.—NEW CO. G—RECRUITS.—Continued.

	Rank.	Age	Joined.				
			Date.	Place.			
Deserted.							
Bruce, Robert C	Sergeant.	35	Jan. 11, 1864.	Hudson.	Sept. 26, 1865.	Veteran.	
Helmes, George	Musician.	14	Dec. 30, 1863	"	Feb. 27, 1864.		Enrolled Corp. From Mar. 1, 1864.
Allen, Bernard	Private.	20	Feb. 4, 1864	Po'keepsie.	Feb. 16, 1864.		
Abby, Thomas	"	21	" 1, "	Hudson.	Feb. 16, 1864.		
Bishop, John S	"	30	Jan. 2, "	"	Feb. 9, 1864.		
Burke, John	"	20	" 30, "	"	Feb. 16, 1864.		
Bennett, Charles	"	22	" 22, "	"	Feb. 16, 1864.		
Hogan, Martin	"	25	" 25, "	"	Feb. 9, 1864.		
Kirby, Michael	"	21	" 30, "	"	Feb. 16, 1864.		
Kenelly, William	"	24	" 12, "	"	Feb. 27, 1864.		
Lee, Patrick	"	18	" 22, "	"	Feb. 16, 1864.		
Mcknas, Thomas	"	20	" 30, "	"	Feb. 16, 1864.		
Moore, William	"	19	Feb. 4, "	Po'keepsie.	Feb. 16, 1864.		
Martin, William	"	28	" 5, "	"	Feb. 16, 1864.		
Murphy, Peter	"	20	" 4, "	"	Feb. 9, 1864.		
Pitts, James	"	21	" 1, "	Hudson.	Feb. 16, 1864.		
Smith, David C	"						

	Officers.	Men.
Original Strength	3	80
Gain by Recruits		13
Gain from Deserter returned		1
Total genuine members	3	94
Total borne on Rolls	3	94

		Officers.	Men.
Brought forward		3	94
	Officers.	Men.	
Discharged	1	18	
Died		9	
Deserted, 16; returned, 1		17	44
Mustered Out on Rolls		1	50
Absent at Muster Out		2	5
Present at Muster Out			45

XXXVII

THE 159TH REGIMENT INFANTRY, N. Y. S. V.—COMPANY H.

	Rank.	Age	Joined Date.	Place.	
Mustered Out with Regt.					
WELLS O. PETTIT	Captain	45	Sept. 10, 1862.	Brooklyn.	Commissioned Major and Lieut.-Colonel.
GEORGE B. STAYLEY	1st Lieut.	26	Aug. 8, 1864.	Charlestown Va.	Promoted from 1st Sergt. 48th N. Y. S. V. Commissioned Capt.
Discharged.					
GEORGE R. HERBERT	2d Lieut.	21	Sept. 1, 1862.	Brooklyn.	May 7, 1865. Detached to Signal Corps, Nov. 13, 1862.
Transferred.					
CHARLES C. BAKER	1st Lieut.	21	Sept. 1, 1862.	Brooklyn.	Jan. 27, 1863. Promoted Capt. Co. I.
DUNCAN RICHMOND	"	"	Nov. 3, "	"	Feb. 20, 1864. Promoted Captain Co. K. Promoted from 2d Lieut. Co. K, Jan. 27, 1863.
Mustered Out with Regt.					
KENNEDY, WILLIAM J.	1st Sergt.	24	Sept. 5, 1862.	Brooklyn.	Enrolled Sergt. Promoted 1st Sergt. Reduced Aug. 16, 1865. Promoted Sept. 9, 1865.
FRENCH, WILLIAM F.	Sergeant.	19	" 18, "	Hudson.	Absent. Detached. Transferred from Co. G, Mar. 12, 1864.
TRAVER, MARTIN	"	22	" 23, "	Kinderhook.	Enrolled Corp. Promoted June 13, 1864. Transferred from Co. G, Mar. 12, 1864.
CANONIER, ANDREW	Corporal	19	" 11, "	Brooklyn.	Enrolled Private. Promoted Sept. 1, 1863. Reduced Aug. 16, 1865. Promoted Sept. 9, 1865.
ABBOTT, JOHN P.	"	39	Oct. 16, "	Kinderhook.	Absent. Sick in hospital. Enrolled Private. Promoted May 3, 1864. Transferred from Co. G, Mar. 12, 1864.
CHURCHWARD, WILLIAM F.	Private.	20	Aug. 25, "	Brooklyn.	
ESSER, HERMAN	"	18	Sept. 11, "	"	
GRAHAM, JAMES	"	25	" 17, "	"	
GRAHAM, THOMAS	"	40	Oct. 21, "	"	
HANDY, WILLIAM C	"	44	Sept. 5, "	"	
HOVELL, JOHN S.	"	18	Oct. 16, "	"	
HOPKINS, BRYAN	"	31	" 9, "	"	
HERRICK, BENJAMIN F.	"	25	Jan. 5, 1864	Stockport.	Deserted. Apprehended and returned, May 23, 1864. Veteran. Recruit.
KAUFFMAN, MARTIN	"	18	Sept. 6, 1862	Brooklyn.	Absent. Deserted Sept. 1865. Deserted April 27, 1863. Returned July 5, 1865.
LANE, HENRY	"	21	Oct. 11, "	"	Re-

THE 159TH REGIMENT INFANTRY, N. Y. S. V.—COMPANY H.—Continued.

	Rank.	Age.	Joined. Date.	Joined. Place.	
Mustered Out with Regt.					
LYNCH, WILLIAM	Private.	18	Sept. 20, 1862.	Ghent.	Transferred from Co. G, Mar. 12, 1864. Detailed as Musician.
LUDLOW, DITMAS	"	44	" 10, "	Brooklyn.	Enrolled Corp. Reduced Dec. 26, 1862.
LUTZ, WILLIAM HENRY	"	18	" 4, "	"	
MILLER, PETER	"	21	" 20, "	"	
MARTIN, JOSEPH	"	26	" 20, "	"	
MURPHY, WILLIAM	"	27	" 23, "	New Lebn.	Transferred from Co. G, March 12, 1864.
MILLOTT, GEORGE	"	25	" 26, "	Brooklyn.	Absent. In confinement, sentence G. C. M. Deserted Aug. 20, 1863. Apprehended Feb. 21, 1864.
PETERSEN, NEIL	"	21	" 26, "		Recruit.
POWELL, CHARLES	"	19	Nov. 25, 1863.	3d District	
SMITH, LUCIUS R	"	18	Aug. 28, 1862.	Brooklyn.	Deserted Nov. 18, 1862. Apprehended and ret'd, July 15, 1863.
SIMONSON, WALTER	"	22	Sept. 24, "	"	
WARDROP, JOHN	"	35	" 18, "	"	
WENSTROM, CHARLES R	"	21	Oct. 31, "	"	Deserted Jan. 8, 1865. Apprehended and ret'd, April 16, 1865.
Discharged.					
PERRY, PERRY P	Corporal	18	Sept. 12, 1862.	Brooklyn.	Aug. 24, 1863. Disability. Enrolled Private. Promoted Dec. 26, 1862.
WORTMAN, WILLIAM H	Wagoner.	45	Oct. 1, "	Hudson.	June 7, 1864. Transferred from Co. G, Mar. 12, 1864.
ALBERTON, HENRY	Private.	44	" 1, "	Brooklyn.	Jan. 30, 1863. Disability.
HARRETT, THOMAS	"	35	" 3, "	"	Nov. 3, 1863. Disability. Trans. from Co. F, Mar. 10, 1863.
BENNETT, JAMES	"	34	Sept. 27, "	"	June 1, 1864. Disability.
BROWN, ALFRED	"		Nov. 11, 1863.	N. Orl's, La.	Aug. 12, 1864. Disability. Recruit.
BROWN, JAMES	"	44	Sept. 6, 1862.	Brooklyn.	Oct. 1, 1863. Disability.
FRENCH, STEPHEN M	"		Nov. 11, 1863.	N. Orl's, La.	Aug. 17, 1864. Expiration of service. Recruit.
HURLEY, DAVID	"	26	Sept. 25, 1862.	Brooklyn.	June 13, 1865. Enrolled Wagoner. Reduced June 21, 1863.
HERBERT, ROBERT	"	23	" 12, "	"	Mar. 27, 1865. Disability.
JACOBS, WILLIAM	"	32	" 13, "	"	June 7, 1865. Disability.
JENKINS, DAVIS	"	31	Oct. 21, "	"	Mar. 8, 1864. Disability.
LEMOND, AUGUSTUS G	"	18	Aug. 27, "	"	Feb. 17, 1865. Disability.
LEMOND, BENJAMIN	"	35	Sept. 4, "	"	June 10, 1865. Disability.

THE 159TH REGIMENT INFANTRY, N. Y. S. V.—COMPANY H.—Continued.

	Rank.	Age	Joined Date.	Joined Place.	
Discharged.					
McGreen, Edward	Private.	32	Oct. 21, 1862	Brooklyn.	Sept. 27, 1863. Disease. Enrolled 1st Sergt. Reduced Dec. 4, 1862.
Onderdonk, William H.	"	25	Sept. 16, "	"	Feb. 1, 1863.
Powell, Wickham	"	20	Nov. 23, 1863	2d District	Aug. 4, 1865. Recruit.
Roden, George	"	43	Sept. 29, 1862	Brooklyn.	Mar. 9, 1864. Disability.
Thomas, Joseph W.	"	24	Oct. 31, "	"	Dec. 15, 1863. Apprehended and returned.
Transferred.					
Smith, Herman	1st Sergt.	18	Sept. 3, 1862	Brooklyn.	Mar. 6, 1863, to N. C. S. Promoted Sergt.-Major. Enrolled Sergt. Promoted Dec. 4, 1862.
Price, Charles P.	Sergeant.	35	" 6, "	"	Jan. 27, 1863, to Co. K. Promoted 2d Lieut. Enrolled Corp. Promoted Jan. 21, 1863.
Martin, Henry	"	21	" 11, "	"	May 1, 1864, to Navy. Enrolled Private. Promoted Corp. Nov. 1, 1862. Promoted May 6, 1864.
Vandewater, Benjamin	Corporal	41	Oct. 1, "	Fishkill.	June 18, 1864, to V. R. C. Transf'd from Co. G, Mar. 12, 1864
Frier, William H.	Private.	21	Aug. 27, "	Brooklyn.	June 5, 1865, to V. R. C. Wounded Opequan, Va., Sept. 19, 1864
Moore, Alfred H. S.	"	24	Sept. 5, "	"	Nov. 2, 1862, to N. C. S. Promoted Hospital Steward.
Murtha, Michael	"	18	" 15, "	"	April 28, 1864, to V. R. C. Promoted Corp.
Pittinger, Edward	"	10	" 10, "	"	Sept. 11, 1863, to V. R. C. Reduced Jan. 21, 1863. Nov. 4, 1862.
Stickles, Cornelius	"	24	Oct. 7, "	Greenport.	April 10, 1864, to V. R. C. Transferred from Co. G, Mar. 12, 1864.
Died.					
Crowell, Thomas E.	Sergeant.	18	Oct. 16, 1862	Brooklyn.	May 27, 1863. In action, Port Hudson, La. Enrolled Corp. Promoted Jan. 21, 1863.
King, Edmund B.	"	18	Sept. 6, "	"	Nov. 5, 1863. Disease.
Darling, David W.	Corporal.	25	Aug. 28, "	"	June 14, 1863. Disease.
Neefus, John	"	18	Sept. 6, "	"	May 2, 1863. Of wounds in action, Irish Bend, La., April 14, 1863.
Uggla, William	"	38	" 10, "	"	May 27, 1863. In action, Port Hudson, La.

THE 159TH REGIMENT INFANTRY, N. Y. S. V.—COMPANY H.—Continued.

	Rank.	Age	Joined. Date.	Place.		
Died.						
ADAMS, WASHINGTON	Private.	44	Sept. 17, 1862.	Brooklyn.	Sept. 29, 1864.	Of wounds in action, Opequan, Va., Sept. 19, 1864.
CORSON, DANIEL	"	41	" 4, "	"	April 28, 1863.	Disease.
DALY, JOHN	"	19	" 15, "	"	May 27, 1863.	In action, Port Hudson, La.
DONOVAN, MATTHEW	"	23	Aug. 27, "	"	Jan. 29, 1864.	Disease.
LANDER, HENRY F.	"	18	Oct. 18, "	"	Sept. 19, 1864.	In action, Opequan, Va.
LOUGEA, JOHN L.	"	40	Aug. 30, "	"		Prisoner of war, Salisbury, N. C. Enr'd Corp.
MCCORMICK, JAMES	"	39	Sept. 11, "	"	May 27, 1863.	In action, Port Hudson, La.
ROSSITER, CHARLES	"	39	" 10, "	"	May 27, 1863.	In action, Port Hudson, La.
WALKER, JOHN	"	21	" 4, "	"	Nov. 27, 1862.	Disease.
WILSON, ANDREW	C'd Cook.	34	Nov. 28, 1863.	Thibo'x, La.	Nov. 4, 1864.	Disease. Recruit.
Deserted.						
ANDREWS, CHARLES	Sergeant.	25	Oct. 13, 1862.	Brooklyn.	Nov. 2, 1862.	
FARRELL, JAMES	Musician.	18	Sept. 5, "	"	Nov. 3, 1862.	
ARGENT, SAMUEL	Private.	39	" 26, "	"	Nov. 2, 1862.	
BURNS, DENNIS	"	39	Oct. 20, "	"	Nov. 1, 1862.	
CARROLL, JOHN	"	23	" 1, "	"	Nov. 2, 1862.	
DEVINE, THOMAS	"	23	Sept. 15, "	"	Nov. 10, 1862.	
EDWARDS, CHARLES	"	32	" 4, "	"	Nov. 3, 1862.	
FEENY, JAMES	"	25	" 29, "	"	Nov. 3, 1862.	
FITZSIMMONS, THOMAS	"	26	" 11, "	"	Nov. 12, 1862.	
FLANAGAN, EDWARD	"	29	" 22, "	"	Nov. 2, 1862.	
GRAY, WILLIAM	"	21	Oct. 9, "	"	Nov. 14, 1862.	
GREENFIELD, JOHN	"	21	Sept. 16, "	"	Nov. 15, 1862.	
HASKINS, MICHAEL	"	40	" 19, "	"	Nov. 14, 1862.	
KEEGAN, BERNARD	"	28	" 29, "	"	Nov. 17, 1862.	
KOLTSHORN, OSCAR	"	22	" 27, "	"	Nov. 20, 1862.	
LYNCH, JOHN	"	43	" 17, "	"	Nov. 19, 1862.	
MCDONALD, PATRICK	"	22	" 5, "	"	Mar. 1863.	
OLTHOFF, BARNEY	"	42	" 21, "	"		

THE 159TH REGIMENT INFANTRY, N. Y. S. V.—COMPANY H.—Continued.

	Rank	Age	Joined. Date.	Place.
Deserted.				
RILEY, SAMUEL	Private	41	Oct. 15, 1862	Brooklyn
STERLING, EDWARD A.	"	26	Sept. 20, "	"
SCOOT, PHILIP F.	"	24	" 4, "	"
SEYMOUR, HENRY	"	38	Oct. 14, "	"
WASSER, GILBERT	"	28	" 3, "	"
WELLAND, PETER	"	42	" 4, "	"
WELLS, WILLIAM	"	37	Sept. 11, "	"
WOLLER, FREDERICK R.	"	30	" 27, "	"

	Officers	Men
Original Strength	3	82
Gain by Appointment	1	
Gain by Recruits		6
Total genuine members	4	88
Promoted from Officers other Companies	1	
Transfers from other Companies		9
Total borne on Rolls	5	97

	Officers	Men
Brought forward	5	97
Discharged	1	19
Transferred	2	9
Died		15
Deserted, 32; returned, 6		26
Mustered Out on Rolls	3	69
Absent at Muster Out	2	28
		4
Present at Muster Out	2	24

THE 159TH REGIMENT INFANTRY, N. Y. S. V.—COMPANY I.

	Rank.	Age.	Joined. Date.	Place.	
Mustered Out with Regt.					
EDWARD TYNAN	1st Lieut.	22	Sept. 6, 1864.	Albany.	Appointed from civil life, Aug. 13, 1864. Commissioned Capt.
Discharged.					
EDWARD WARDLE	Captain.	26	Oct. 15, 1862.	Hudson.	Jan. 26, 1863. Dishonorably dismissed, sentence G. C. M.
JOSEPH G. MCNUTT	"	"	May 1, 1864.	Morganza, La.	Aug. 20, 1865. Appointed from civil life. Commissioned Major.
JOHN W. SHIELDS	1st Lieut.	28	Oct. 15, 1862.	Po'keepsie.	Dec. 7, 1863. Cashiered, sentence G. C. M.
WILLIAM PRINCE	"	"	Dec. 26, 1863.	Albany.	Sept. 13, 1864. Appointed. Never served with Regiment.
JACOB FINGAR	"	33	Oct. 10, 1862.	Hudson.	Jan. 26, 1863.
LAMBERT DINGMAN	2d Lieut.	23	Sept. 4, "	Kinderhook.	Feb. 3, 1864. Enrolled Sergt. Co. G. Prom. Jan. 27, 1863.
Transferred.					
CHARLES C. BAKER	Captain.	21	Sept. 1, 1862.	Brooklyn.	Feb. 10, 1864. Promoted Major 39th N. Y. S. V. Promoted from 1st Lieut. Co. II, Jan. 26, 1863.
Mustered Out with Regt.					
COVENTRY, CORNELIUS V.	1st Sergt.	39	Sept. 5, 1862.	Hudson.	Promoted Sept. 28, 1865. Promoted Sergt.
SCUTT, GROSVENOR	Sergeant.	24	Oct. 3, "	Gallatin.	Enrolled Private. Promoted.
BRAZIER, JAMES, SR.	Corporal.	41	" 3, "	Po'keepsie.	Enrolled Private. Promoted.
OSCHEITZ, WILLIAM	"	45	" 30, "	"	Absent. Sick in hospital. Enrolled Private. Promoted.
BUTLER, MICHAEL	Private.	18	" 2, "	"	
BOGARDUS, FREDERICK	"	21	" 18, "	"	Wounded Port Hudson, June 14, 1863.
BRAZIER, JAMES, JR.	"	18	" 3, "	"	Absent. In confinement. Deserted and apprehended.
COON, PHILIP H.	"	21	Sept. 27, "	Gallatin.	
COON, ALFRED R.	"	21	" 22, "	"	
COON, ALVARUS	"	16	" 27, "	"	
CAHALES, MARTIN	"	21	Oct. 4, "	Livingston.	
CLEMINSHIRE, JOHN E.	"	21	" 15, "	Po'keepsie.	
CORY, EUGENE A.	"	19	Dec. 9, 1863.	Brooklyn.	Veteran recruit.
DENNIS, HENRY	"	23	Sept. 16, 1862.	Gallatin.	
DEVLIN, JOHN	"	18	" 17, "	Kinderhook.	Wounded Irish Bend, La., April 14, 1863. Transferred from Co. G, March 12, 1864.
EDSON, ALMOND	"	29	Oct. 17, "	Po'keepsie.	

THE 159TH REGIMENT INFANTRY, N. Y. S. V.—COMPANY I.—Continued.

	Rank.	Age.	Joined.		
			Date.	Place.	
Mustered Out with Regt.					
FELLER, CHARLES	Private.	21	Oct. 30, 1862.	Clermont.	Recruit.
FOSTER, WILLIAM	"	24	" 18, "	Hudson.	Transferred from Co. G, Mar. 12, 1864.
FROST, CHARLES	"	19	Nov. 20, 1863.	Brooklyn.	
FARRINGTON, WILLIAM	"	32	Oct. 30, 1862.	Fishkill.	
HOWELL, JAMES	"	28	" 15, "	Po'keepsie.	
HOUCK, WALTER C	"	45	" 4, "	Gallatin.	Absent. In hospital. Wounded, Opequan, Va., Sept. 19, 1864.
KILMER, STEPHEN	"	42	" 1, "	Hudson.	Absent. Sick in hospital.
LAWRENCE, DAVID W	"	19	" 6, "	Gallatin.	Enrolled Private. Promoted 1st Sergt. Reduced Sept. 28, 1865.
LEE, JAMES R., Jr	"	19	" 9, "	Po'keepsie.	Absent. In confinement, sentence G. C. M.
ROACH, WILLIAM	"	21	" 8, "	Hudson.	Enrolled Corporal.
SCHOFIELD, GEORGE W	"		" 21, "	Po'keepsie.	
SHAW, WILLIAM H	"	42	Sept. 18, "	Hudson.	Absent. Sick in hospital.
TIFFANY, JOHN	"	17	Oct. 22, "	Po'keepsie.	
VEIGLE, GOTTFRIED F	"	40	Sept. 29, "		Enrolled Sergeant.
WILMEN, RICHARD	"	18	Oct. 3, "	Gallatin.	Deserted, apprehended and returned.
WAGONER, NORMAN	"	21	" 2, "	Livingston.	Wounded, Opequan, Va., Sept. 19, 1864.
WAGONER, WILLIAM H	"	38	Sept. 30, "	Claverack.	
WHITE, WASHINGTON I	"	20	Jan. 1, 1864.	Thibodeaux, La.	
HAYES, WILLIAM	C'd Cook.				Recruit.
Discharged.					
DUFFY, EDWARD	Sergeant.	32	Oct. 6, 1862.	Hudson.	May 23, 1864. Promoted 1st Lieut. Co. A. Transferred from Co. G, March 12, 1864.
BROWN, ELEAZOR PARMLY	"	19	Nov. 20, 1863.	Brooklyn.	June 22, 1865. Promoted 1st Lieut. Co. D. Recruit. Enrolled Private. Promoted.
DENNIS, JAMES	Corporal.	21	Sept. 30, 1862.	Hudson.	Aug. 22, 1863.
REED, JOSEPH O	"	22	Oct. 4, "	"	May 17, 1865. Disability from wounds in action, Halltown, Va., Aug. 24, 1864.
CLARK, CHARLES	Musician.	17	Sept. 15, "	Po'keepsie.	Mar. 22, 1863. Disability.
LEE, JORDAN N	"	18	Oct. 6, "	Hudson.	Jan. 26, 1865. Disability.
RACE, JOHN	Wagoner	45	" 18, "	"	Jan. 21, 1865. Disability.

XLIV

THE 159TH REGIMENT INFANTRY, N. Y. S. V.—COMPANY I.—Continued.

	Rank.	Age.	Joined. Date.	Place.		
Discharged.						
CAMPBELL, JOHN S.	Private.	45	Oct. 7, 1862.	Hudson.		
COON, PETER W.	"	47	" 25, "	Livingston.		
DECKER, JOSHUA	"	36	Sept. 26, "	"	Nov. 23, 1863.	
GARRETTSON, PETER S.	"	24	April 10, 1865.	New-York.	June 18, 1863.	Disability.
GRIFFIS, GEORGE	"	31	Mar. 14, "	Fishkill.	May 9, 1865.	Recruit.
HOSE, CHARLES H.	"	21	Feb. 23, "	Brooklyn.	May 9, 1865.	Recruit.
HYLER, WILLIAM H	"	19	April 10, "	New-York.	May 9, 1865.	Recruit.
KIRCHNER, GEORGE N.	"	45	Oct. 18, 1862.	Po'keepsie.	May 9, 1865.	Recruit.
LAWRENCE, JOHN M.	"	23	" 4, "	Gallatin.	June 7, 1863.	Disability. Enr'd Corp. Red'd Dec. 22, 1862.
LEE, JAMES R., Sr.	"	42	" 6, "	Po'keepsic.	Mar. 26, 1864.	Disability.
OSBORN, ARCHIBALD	"	44	Sept. 29, "	Pleasant V'y	June 27, 1863.	Writ Habeas Corpus.
ROTH, GUSTAVE	"	18	Feb. 16, 1865.	Hudson.	Dec. 3, 1862.	
SMITH, CARLISTON T.	"	45	Oct. 10, 1862.	"	May 9, 1865.	Recruit.
SNYDER, PETER H.	"	37	" 1. "	Gallatin.	May 30, 1865.	
SCOTT, THOMAS	"	21	" 3. "	"	Mar. 31, 1865.	Disability.
STARR, GEORGE	"	30	Dec. 14, 1863.	Brooklyn.	June 28, 1865.	Prisoner of war, Opequan, Va., Sept. 19, 1864.
TIFFANY, JAMES I.	"	44	Jan. 24, 1864.	Po'keepsie.	May 17, 1865.	Disability. Recruit.
TROY, DAVID	"	19	April 11, 1865.	New-York.	May 9, 1865.	Recruit.
VAIL, EDWARD	"	44	Oct. 8, 1862.	Pleasant V'y	May 9, 1865.	Disability.
VERMILYEA, HENRY F.	"	21	April 10, 1865.	New-York.	May 9, 1865.	Recruit.
Transferred.						
COON, JACOB	Private.	36	Oct. 14, 1862.	Livingston.	Mar. 23, 1863.	to V. R. C.
COSGROVE, EDWARD	"	40	Sept. 29, "	"	June 24, 1864.	to V. R. C.
SIMMONS, DAVID	"	44	" 30, "	Clinton.	June 24, 1864.	to V. R. C.
Died.						
BAKER, MARK	1st Sergt.	19	Oct. 13, 1862.	Po'keepsie.	April 14, 1863.	In action, Irish Bend, La.
KLINE, PLEASANT	Corporal.	18	Sept. 9, "	Taghkanic.	Sept. 28, 1863.	Disease.
LYNCH, JOHN	"	20	" 20, "	Ghent.		Transferred from Co. G, Mar. 12, 1864.
ALGER, CHARLES	Private.	36	" 9, "	Hudson.	Sept. 7, 1865.	Alcoholism.

XLV

THE 159TH REGIMENT INFANTRY, N. Y. S. V.—COMPANY I.—Continued.

	Rank.	Age	Joined. Date.	Joined. Place.		
Died.						
BOURER, THEODORE	Private.	23	Sept. 4, 1862.	Taghkanic.	April 14, 1863.	In action, Irish Bend, La.
BUGLE, HENRY	"	39	" 24, "	Livingston.	June 13, 1863.	
CAREY, DANIEL	"	44	" 8, "	Po'keepsie.	Sept. 25, 1863.	
CONROY, HENRY A	"	30	" 30, "	Gallatin.	July 15, 1863.	
COON, WILLIAM	"	17	" 27, "	"	May 25, 1863.	In action, Port Hudson, La.
COON, JOHN W	"	27	Oct. "	Livingston.	Aug. 3, 1865.	Gunshot wound, accident.
DUTCHER, CHARLES	"	44	" 7, "	Po'keepsie.	Mar. 8, 1863.	
HOUGHTALING, PHILIP	"	32	" 11, "	"	June 8, 1863.	
HAWS, WILLIAM H	"	42	Sept. 4, "	Hudson.	April 14, 1863.	In action, Irish Bend, La.
JACKSON, COLLINS	"	35	" 4, "	Po'keepsie.	Aug. 3, 1863.	
KELLERHOUSE, JEREMIAH	"	41	" 26, "	Livingston.	Sept. 18, 1863.	
KELLERHOUSE, WILLIAM	"	37	" 4, "	Gallatin.	May 31, 1863.	
KIPP, PHILIP H	"	44	Oct. 9, "	"	May 29, 1863.	
KNICKERBOCKER, WILLIAM	"	18	Sept. 23, "	Taghkanic.	Aug. 29, 1863.	Chronic rheumatism.
KILMER, MILTON	"	21	Oct. 10, "	Livingston.	Aug. 7, 1863.	
McCANLEY, JAMES	"	19	" 29, "	Stockport.	Mar. 6, 1863.	Disease.
McDARLEY, PETER	"	28	" 1, "	Gallatin.	Nov. 26, 1863.	
MOON, WILLIAM	"	45	" 4, "	Milan.	Aug. 21, 1864.	Disease.
MORTON, JAMES	"	18	Aug. 29, 1864.	Troy.	Jan. 3, 1865.	Prisoner of war, Salisbury, N. C. Recruit.
PALMER, ABRAM F	"	18	Oct. 4, 1862.	Livingston.	Mar. 22, 1863.	Typhoid fever.
PALMATER, OLIVER	"	19	" 8, "	Po'keepsie.	Aug. 4, 1863.	
PROPER, PETER	"	25	Sept. 23, "	Taghkanic.		
TESEL, RICHARD	"	31	Oct. 17, "	Po'keepsie.	July 1864.	Typhoid fever.
TERRY, JOHN	"	18	" 8, "	"	Mar. 10, 1863.	Disease.
VAN HOESEN, THOMAS	"	44	Sept. 23, "	Hudson.	April 27, 1863.	Drowned from transport.
WHALEN, MARTIN	"	30	Oct. 13, "	Po'keepsie.	Mar. 25, 1864.	Disease.
WORDEN, JOHN B	"	44	" 20, "	"	May 15, 1863.	
Deserted.						
HANEY, JOHN K	1st Sergt.	25	Oct. 7, 1862.	Po'keepsie.	April 1863.	
BROWN, WILLIAM	Sergeant.	33	" 4, "	"	Nov. 2, 1862.	

THE 159TH REGIMENT INFANTRY, N. Y. S. V.—COMPANY I.—Continued.

	Rank.	Age	Joined.		Deserted.
			Date.	Place.	
Deserted.					
KEEGAN, JOHN	Sergeant.	30	Oct. 12, 1862.	Po'keepsie.	Nov. 2, 1862.
COOK, JOHN	Corporal.	33	Sept. 29, "	Gallatin.	June 14, 1863. In action, Port Hudson, La.
BEST, STEPHEN F.	Private.	44	" 4, "	Hudson.	Nov. 10, 1862.
CLARK, PETER	"	30	" 12, "	Pleasant V'y	Nov. 2, 1862.
DENNIS, WILLIAM B.	"	44	Oct. 1, "	Clinton.	Nov. 10, 1862.
DONNELY, JOHN	"	28	" 16, "	Po'keepsie.	Nov. 10, 1862.
INGALLS, HENRY	"	22	Sept. 27, "	Gallatin.	Nov. 3, 1862.
KILMER, JACOB	"	36	" 6, "	Claverack.	Aug. 18, 1863.
MAYLEY, GEORGE	"	44	" 29, "	Gallatin.	July 1863.
MCAVOY, JAMES	"	25	Oct. 21, "	Po'keepsie.	Nov. 2, 1862.
MILLER, SAMUEL J.	"	21	" 28, "	Livingston.	Nov. 2, 1862.
SMITH, HENRY	"	23	" 8, "	Po'keepsie.	Nov. 15, 1862.
WINTERS, WILLIAM	"	28	" 8, "		Nov. 20, 1862.

	Officers.	Men.
Original Strength	3	93
Gains by Appointment	3	
Gains by Recruits		14
Total genuine members	6	107
Promoted from Officers other Companies	1	
Promoted from ranks other Companies	1	
Transferred from other Companies		4
Total borne on Rolls	8	111

	Officers.	Men.
Brought forward	8	111
Discharged	6	27
Transferred	1	3
Died		31
Deserted, 17; returned, 2		15
Mustered Out on Rolls	7	76
Absent at Muster Out	1	35
		6
Present at Muster Out	1	29

XLVII

THE 159TH REGIMENT INFANTRY, N. Y. S. V.—COMPANY K.

	Rank.	Age	Date.	Joined. Place.	
Discharged:					
JOE B. RAMSDEN	Captain.	26	Sept. 18, 1862.	Brooklyn.	July 30, 1863.
EDWARD SHERER	1st Lieut.	19	" 1, "	"	Nov. 3, 1862.
ALFRED H. BRUCE	"	23	" 15, "	Kinderhook.	May 17, 1865. Enrolled 1st Sergt. Co. G. Promoted Sergt.-Major, Jan. 14, 1863. Promoted 2d Lieut. Co. F, Mar. 6, 1863. Promoted April 30, 1863.
CHARLES H. BRUNDAGE	2d Lieut.		Dec. 18, 1863.	New Orleans, La.	April 9, 1864. Cashiered by sentence G. C. M. Promoted from Private 7th N. Y. H. A.
Died:					
DUNCAN RICHMOND	Captain.		Nov. 3, 1862.	Brooklyn.	Oct. 19, 1864. In action, Cedar Creek, Va. Appointed 2d Lt. Promoted 1st Lt. Co. H, Jan. 26, 1863. Prom. Feb. 20, 1864.
WILLIAM R. PLUNKETT	1st Lieut.	37	Sept. 27, "	"	April 17, 1863. Of wounds in action, Irish Bend, La., April 14, 1863. Enrolled 2d Lieut. Promoted Nov. 3, 1862.
CHARLES P. PRICE	2d Lieut.	35	" 6, "	"	April 18, 1863. Of wounds in action, Irish Bend, La., April 14, 1863. Enrolled Corp. Co. H. Promoted Sergt. Jan. 21, 1863. Promoted Jan. 27, 1863.
Mustered Out with Regt.					
MILLS, JAMES M	1st Sergt.	19	Aug. 21, 1862.	Brooklyn.	Enrolled Private. Promoted Corp. Feb. 1, 1863; Sergt. Dec. 31, 1863; 1st Sergt. Sept. 1, 1864. Reduced Aug. 16, 1865.
PELLETREAU, JOHN	Sergeant.	25	" 23, "	"	Enrolled Private. Promoted Sept. 9, 1865.
VAN ALSTINE, GEORGE H.	"	25	Sept. 19, "	Kinderhook.	Enrolled Private. Promoted Corp. May 1, 1864; Sergt. June 25, 1864.
TASSER, WILLIAM D.	Corporal.	36	Oct. 24, "	"	Enrolled Corp. Promoted Sept. 19, 1864. Transferred from Co. G. Mar. 12, 1864.
NEVALS, AUSTIN	"	22	" 7, "	Ghent.	Enrolled Private. Promoted Sept. 19, 1864. Transferred from Co. G. Mar. 12, 1864.
MYERS, GEORGE	Musician.	15	" 8, "	Brooklyn.	Enrolled Private. Promoted Sept. 19, 1864. Transferred from Co. G. Mar. 12, 1864.
HORAN, JOSEPH	"	17	" 6, "	"	
BRUSH, JOHN	Private.	30	Aug. 30, "	"	
BENDER, SALES	"	37	Sept. 30, "	"	

THE 159TH REGIMENT INFANTRY, N. Y. S. V.—COMPANY K.—Continued.

	Rank.	Age.	Joined. Date.	Place.	
Mustered Out with Regt.					
Brophy, Edward	Private.	18	Sept. 14, 1862.	Kinderhook.	Transferred from Co. G. March 12, 1864.
Corcoran, Joseph	"	40	Aug. 30.	Brooklyn.	
Davis, James	"	25	" 29.	"	
Denn, Peter	"	18	Oct. 4.	"	
Dolan, Timothy	"	20	Jan. 25, 1864.	Po'keepsie.	Absent. Pris'r of war, Opequan, Va., Sept. 19, 1864. Recruit.
Feeney, John	"	18	Aug. 28, 1862.	Brooklyn.	
Hahn, Henry	"	33	" 25.	"	
Hoffman, George A	"	26	Sept. 25.	Claverack.	Absent. Sick in hospital. Trans. from Co. G, Mar. 12, 1864.
Johnson, Edward A	"	32	" 13.	Brooklyn.	
Kelly, James	"	21	Aug. 23.	"	
Kewas, John M	"	31	Sept. 27.	"	
Kane, John	"	37	Dec. 31, 1863.	12th District.	Recruit.
Lafferty, Daniel	"	25	Aug. 28, 1862.	Brooklyn.	
Leonard, James S	"	21	" 20.	"	
McDivitt, John H	"	33	" 30.	"	
Mills, William	"	22	" 22.	"	
McCormick, Thomas	"	28	Sept. 23.	Hudson.	Absent. Sick in hospital. Trans. from Co. G, Mar. 12, 1864.
Myers, Cornelius	"	35	" 15.	Brooklyn.	Enrolled 1st Sergt. Reduced to Sergt. March 23, 1863. Reduced Aug. 16, 1865.
Stout, John	"	42	Oct. 30.	"	Transferred from Co. G. March 12, 1864.
Stickles, Henry S	"	36	Sept. 29.	Kinderhook.	Transferred from Co. G. March 12, 1864.
Shea, Thomas	"	24	Oct. 13.	Fishkill.	Absent. Detached. Transferred from Co. G. March 12, 1864.
Suydam, Clark B	"	18	Sept. 30.	Kingston.	Recruit.
Schrader, John	C'd Cook.	34	Feb. 7, 1865.	Thib'x, La.	Recruit.
Leonard, Daniel	"		Jan. 13, 1864.		Recruit.
Kelly, William	"		" 13.		Recruit.
Discharged.					
Day, John	1st Sergt.	23	Aug. 23, 1862.	Brooklyn.	Sept. 1, 1864, for promotion. Prom. 1st Lt. Co. B. Enr'd Corp.
Matthews, Richard	Sergeant.	29	" 20.	"	Nov. 24, 1863. Disability.
Vanderzaw, Francis I	Corporal.	22	" 21.	"	May 21, 1864. Commissioned 1st Lieut. 56th N. Y. S. V.

THE 159TH REGIMENT INFANTRY, N. Y. S. V.—COMPANY K.—Continued.

	Rank.	Age	Date	Place.	
Discharged.					
COUGHLIN, JOHN	Private.	30	Aug. 30, 1862.	Brooklyn.	Disability.
CLOSE, JAMES	"	43	" 26, "	"	Deserted, apprehended and ret'd, July 20, 1863.
CRUGER, EUGENE V	"	23	" 21, "	"	
GREEN, MICHAEL	"	29	Oct. 28, "	"	
GARDNER, RICHARD	"	45	Nov. 14, 1863.	Thib'x, La.	Expiration of service. Recruit.
GARRISON, JAMES M	"	40	" 14, "	"	Expiration of service. Recruit.
HYDE, DANIEL	"	28	Aug. 26, 1862.	Brooklyn.	Disability.
KELLY, PATRICK	"	28	" 28, "	"	Disability.
MATTHEWS, WILLIAM	"	39	" 20, "	"	Disability.
MAGUIRE, THOMAS	"	21	" 28, "	"	Disability.
POWERS, ALDEN	"	44	Sept. 27, "	"	
ROONEY, JAMES P	"	23	Aug. 23, "	"	
SIMONTON, GEORGE W	"	30	" 20, "	"	Disability.
VAN HOESEN, FRANCIS	"	28	Sept. 22, "	Ghent.	Transferred from Co. G, March 12, 1864.
YOUNG, FREDERICK	"	36	Aug. 25, "	Brooklyn.	Disability.
Transferred.					
BERGEN, THOMAS	1st Sergt.	29	Aug. 28, 1862.	Brooklyn.	July 22, 1863, to N. C. S. Promoted Commissary Sergt.
ASHTON, SAMUEL	Private.	21	" 28, "	"	May 1, 1864, to Navy.
MAHON, FRANCIS	"	28	Sept. 12, "	"	Deserted, apprehended, and was reported to Co. A as held for that Co. in Fort Columbus, New-York harbor.
Died.					
VAN MATER, JOHN	Corporal.	23	Aug. 28, 1862.	Brooklyn.	Mar. 29, 1863. In action, Irish Bend, La. Deserted Nov., 1862.
ASHELL, ANDREW	"	22	Sept. 18, "	"	April 14, 1863. Apprehended Feb. 18, 1863.
BRIDGES, EDWARD F	Private.	21	Sept. 28, "	"	May 27, 1863. In action, Port Hudson, La.
CARR, GEORGE	"	"	Nov. 14, 1863.	Thib'x, La.	April 14, 1863. In action, Irish Bend, La.
CONKLIN, PETER K	"	35	" "	"	July 21, 1864. Disease. Recruit.
DOLAN, BERNARD	"	28	Oct. 20, 1862.	Ghent.	Jan. 15, 1865. Prisoner of war, Salisbury, N. C. Transferred from Co. G, March 12, 1864.
DRAKE, ROBERT W	"	43	Aug. 25, "	Brooklyn.	April 1863. Pleurisy.

THE 159TH REGIMENT INFANTRY, N. Y. S. V.—COMPANY K.—Continued.

	Rank.	Age.	Joined.		
			Date.	Place.	
Died.					
GOSHIA, ANDREW	Private.		Sept. 30, 1862.	Chatham.	Jan. 21, 1865. Prisoner of war, Salisbury, N. C. Transferred from Co. G, March 12, 1864.
MILLER, DAVID	"	41	Aug. 26, "	Brooklyn.	April 14, 1863. In action, Irish Bend, La.
TRUMVILL, ALBERT C.	"	25	" 25, "	"	June 24, 1863. Of wounds in action, Port Hudson, La., May 27, 1863
Deserted.					
SMITH, WALTER	Sergeant.	26	Oct. 31, 1862.	Brooklyn.	Nov. 20, 1862.
PAINE, GEORGE C.	"	30	Aug. 22, "	"	Dec. 2, 1862.
ROBERTS, LOUIS	Corporal.	24	" 23, "	"	Nov. 22, 1862.
PATTERSON, ALEX. R.	"	37	" 26, "	"	Nov. 22, 1862.
BAILEY, JOSEPH A.	Private.	28	Sept. 12, "	"	Dec. 3, 1862.
BAKER, EDWARD D.	"	26	" 15, "	"	Nov. 5, 1862.
BEVAN, WILLIAM	"	18	Oct. 4, "	"	Nov. 5, 1862.
CONDON, MICHAEL	"	23	Aug. 25, "	"	Nov. 5, 1862.
COLYER, JOSEPH	"	21	Sept. 22, "	"	Nov. 5, 1862.
CARSON, HENRY	"	21	" 20, "	"	Nov. 5, 1862.
DONELLY, THOMAS	"	21	" 20, "	"	Nov. 2, 1862.
EMMONS, JOHN	"	30	Aug. 25, "	"	Aug. 27, 1863. In action, Port Hudson, La.
GARHOLT, AUGUSTUS	"	43	" 26, "	"	June 14, 1863.
GANLEY, JOHN	"	39	" 29, "	"	Nov. 22, 1862.
HAWKER, WILLIAM	"	20	" 30, "	"	Nov. 1, 1862.
HARDING, JAMES	"	28	" 25, "	"	Nov. 2, 1862.
HART, SHERMAN	"	40	" 27, "	Hudson.	Aug. 10, 1865. Trans. from Co. G, Mar. 12, 1864. Deserted Mar. 24, 1864. Returned July 7, 1864.
HAVERTY, PATRICK	"	33	Oct. 16, "		
JONES, THOMAS	"	21	" 27, "	Brooklyn.	Nov. 2, 1862.
KING, PATRICK	"	22	Aug. 26, "	"	Nov. 5, 1862.
KELLY, JOHN P.	"	19	Sept. 25, "	"	Nov. 10, 1862.
KELLY, JOHN, Jr.	"	37	" 30, "	"	Nov. 10, 1862.
LYNCH, THOMAS B.	"	21	Aug. 27, "	"	Nov. 20, 1862.
MAHON, FRANCIS	"	28	Sept. 12, "	"	Nov. 5, 1862. Apprehended and reported to Co. A.

THE 159TH REGIMENT INFANTRY, N. Y. S. V.—COMPANY K.—Continued.

	Rank.	Age	Joined.		Place.
			Date.		
Deserted.					
MILLER, WILLIAM	Private.	21	Aug. 20, 1862.		Brooklyn.
MALLON, PATRICK	"	31	" 30,	1862.	"
MILLER, THOMAS	"	23	" 26,	1862.	"
McMAHON, MICHAEL	"	35	Sept. 19,	1862.	"
McNULTY, JAMES	"	26	" 23,	1862.	"
McPARLAND, PATRICK	"	34	Oct. 28,	1862.	"
MORRISON, JAMES	"	22	Aug. 30,	1862.	"
MYLET, JAMES	"		Oct. 1,	1863.	Baton Rouge, La.
QUINN, PETER	"	27	Aug. 29,	1862.	"
TOWNSEND, SAMUEL	"	21	" 23,	1862.	"
WALLACE, RICHARD	"	26	Sept. 15,	1862.	"

	Officers.	Men.
Original Strength	3	78
Gain by Appointment	2	
Gain by Recruits		8
Total genuine members	5	86
Promoted from Officers other Companies	1	
Promoted from ranks other Companies	1	
Transfers from other Companies		13
Total borne on Rolls	7	99

	Officers.	Men.
Brought forward	7	99
Discharged	4	18
Transferred		3
Died	3	10
Deserted, 37; returned, 3		34
Mustered Out on Rolls	7	65
Absent at Muster Out		34
		4
Present at Muster Out		30

THE 159TH REGIMENT INFANTRY, N. Y. S. V.

Recruits unassigned to Companies not accounted for at Muster Out.

	Rank.	Age.	Joined.		Place.
			Date.		
BATCH, JOHN B.	Private.	39	Dec. 8, 1863.		Brooklyn.
BEZE, JOSEPH	"	22	" 16, "		"
BLACK, LEWIS	"	30	Jan. 18, 1864.		Copake.
COLLETT, GEORGE F.	"	33	Dec. 10, 1863.		5th dist. N. Y.
GOLL, PETER	"	21	" 1, "		Brooklyn.
HACKER, HIRAM	"	21	" 22, "		Claverack.
LARIES, ALFRED	"	35	Nov. 19, "		Brooklyn.
LINCH, THOMAS	"	20	Dec. 1, "		"
MASTEN, PIERRE	"	22	" 10, "		9th dist. N. Y.
MARSELLE, ALFRED	"	34	Nov. 23, "		Brooklyn.
MUNSER, LEWIS	"	27	Dec. 1, "		"
MONFORT, CHARLES	"	26	" 7, "		"
PARRAIN, LEWIS	"	29	" 1, "		"
ROBBERTS, JOSEPH	"	34	Nov. 19, "		"
ROACIE, JOSEPH	"	25	" 24, "		"
SULLIVAN, HARRY B.	"	21	Dec. 1, "		"

Reported as being sent to the Regiment, but no record is shown of their joining.

Total, 16.

Deserters reported as apprehended, but never returned and not shown on Rolls.

COHEN, H ....Reported from New-York, June 14, 1864, as arrested and delivered to A. A. P. M. Gen'l, N. Y. City.
JOHNSON, WILLIAM ......Reported Dec. 22, 1863, and August 17, 1864, as in Camp Distribution, Alexandria, Va.

www.ingramcontent.com/pod-product-compliance
Lightning Source LLC
Chambersburg PA
CBHW020826230426
43666CB00007B/1111